The Soviets, the Munich Crisis, and the Coming of World War II

The Munich crisis is everywhere acknowledged as the prelude to World War II. If Hitler had been stopped at Munich, then World War II as we know it could not have happened. The subject has been thoroughly studied in British, French, and German documents, and consequently we know that the weakness in the Western position at Munich consisted in the Anglo–French opinion that the Soviet commitment to its allies – France and Czechoslovakia – was utterly unreliable. What has never been seriously studied in the Western literature is the whole spectrum of East European documentation. This book targets precisely this dimension of the problem. The Romanians were at one time prepared to admit the transfer of the Red Army across their territory. The Red Army, mobilized on a massive scale, was informed that its destination was Czechoslovakia. The Polish consul in Moldavia reported the entrance of the Red Army into the country. In the meantime, Moscow focused especially on the Polish rail network. All of these findings are new, and they contribute to a considerable shift in the conventional wisdom on the subject.

Hugh Ragsdale is a former Fulbright scholar and American Council of Learned Societies fellow. He resides in Charlottesville, VA.

The Soviets, the Munich Crisis, and the Coming of World War II

HUGH RAGSDALE

CAMBRIDGE
UNIVERSITY PRESS

PUBLISHED BY THE PRESS SYNDICATE OF THE UNIVERSITY OF CAMBRIDGE
The Pitt Building, Trumpington Street, Cambridge, United Kingdom

CAMBRIDGE UNIVERSITY PRESS
The Edinburgh Building, Cambridge CB2 2RU, UK
40 West 20th Street, New York, NY 10011-4211, USA
477 Williamstown Road, Port Melbourne, VIC 3207, Australia
Ruiz de Alarcón 13, 28014 Madrid, Spain
Dock House, The Waterfront, Cape Town 8001, South Africa

http://www.cambridge.org

First published 2004

Printed in the United States of America

Typeface Bembo 11/12 pt.   *System* LATEX 2ε   [TB]

A catalog record for this book is available from the British Library.

Library of Congress Cataloging in Publication Data
Ragsdale, Hugh.
The Soviets, the Munich Crisis, and the coming of
World War II / Hugh Ragsdale.
p.   cm.
Includes bibliographical references and index.
ISBN 0-521-83030-3
1. World War, 1939–1945 – Diplomatic history – Soviet Union.
2. Munich Four-Power Agreement (1938)   3. World War, 1939–1945 – Diplomatic
history – Germany.   4. World War, 1939–1945 – Causes.   I. Title.
D727.R335   2003
940.53′112 – dc21   2003043598

ISBN 0 521 83030 3 hardback

To the peoples of Europe,
especially those of Czechoslovakia,
whom short-sightedness,
folly, and pusillanimity
delivered to
a tragedy from which
they were powerless to save themselves

and

Прекрасной даме
for whose people
the deal done at Munich
led to an unimaginable catastrophe

Contents

List of Maps

Acknowledgments

I am much indebted, for their cordial reception and unstinting assistance in the Romanian Military Archive, to Colonel Alexandru Oşca (Director), Lieutenant Colonel Eftimie Ardeleanu, and Ms. Alina Keszler; to Larry Watts, who introduced me at the military archive and gave seasoned advice about archival research in Bucharest more generally; to Dr. Dumitru Preda, Director of the Romanian Archive of Foreign Affairs, who kindly introduced me to work in the documents there, and to Ms. Daniela Bleoanca and Ms. Irina Ionescu for their generous and expert assistance in the reading room; to Ms. Laura Cosovanu and Ms. Blanka Pasternak for similar generous assistance in the Hoover Institution Archive; to Professor Dov B. Lungu of the University of Toronto and Professor Viorica Moisuc of the University of Constanţa for a variety of good advice and general orientation in a subject in which they were more at home than I was; to Ms. Aura Ponta for checking my translations from Romanian; and to Ms. Gabriella Merryman for checking my translation from Italian; to the American Philosophical Society and the International Research Exchanges Board for financial support of this research in Moscow and Prague; to Josef Anderle for advice on Czech literature and sources and for introducing me to the specialists in the subject in Prague; to Gerhard Weinberg for the advice to look by preference at the military perspective and facts of the matter; to Robert C. Tucker for constant interest and encouragement; to Milan Hauner for a variety of advice, for bringing Polish and German materials to my attention, and for checking my translations from Polish; to Bruce Menning for orientation and assistance in the Rossiiskii gosudarstvennyi voennyi arkhiv and for informed discussion of military esoterica; to Cynthia Roberts for advice and support and elucidation of particular issues; to Tanya Gizdavcic of the Slavic and Baltic Division of New York Public Library for all kinds of indispensable assistance with bibliography; and to Don Fry for an expert reading of the manuscript as literature.

Obviously, no one shares responsibility for the views presented here, which are entirely my own.

List of Abbreviations

DBFP	*Documents on British Foreign Policy*
DGFP	*Documents on German Foreign Policy*
DDF	*Documents diplomatiques français*
DVP SSSR	*Dokumenty vneshnei politiki SSSR*
RGVA	Rossiiskii gosudarstvennyi voennyi arkhiv
RMAE	Romania. Ministerul Afacerilor externe
AMR	Arhivele militare române
SS	Schutzstaffel – literally, bodyguard, Hitler's military elite corps
SA	Sturmabteilung – literally, Storm Troopers
GPU	Gosudarstvennoe politicheshoe upravlenie, Soviet security police

Foreword

A Capsule History of Munich in Contemporary Quotations

Appeasement (a definition): "a clever plan of selling off your friends in order to buy off your enemies."

— *Manchester Guardian*, 25 February 1939

We shall never be great statesmen unless we have a nucleus of... eighty to one hundred million colonizing Germans!... Part of this nucleus is Austria.... But Bohemia and Moravia also belong to it, as well as the western regions of Poland.... The Czechs and the Bohemians we shall transplant to Siberia or the Volhynian regions.... The Czechs must get out of Central Europe. As long as they remain, they will always be a center of Hussite–Bolshevik disintegration. Only when we are able and willing to achieve this shall I be prepared... to take the deaths of two or three million Germans on my conscience.

Adolf Hitler
— H. Rauschning, *Voice of Destruction*, 37–8

To celebrate my fiftieth birthday, please invite a series of foreign guests, among them as many cowardly civilians and democrats as possible, whom I will present a parade of the most modern of armies.

Hitler to Ribbentrop, 20 April 1939
— Erich Kordt, *Wahn und Wirklichkeit*, 153

Had a French premier said in 1933 (and if I had been French premier, I would have said it): the man who wrote the book *Mein Kampf*... has become Reich

chancellor. The man cannot be tolerated in our neighborhood. Either he
goes or we march. That would have been entirely logical.

> Joseph Goebbels, press conference, April 1940
> – H.-U. Thamer, *Verführung und Gewalt*, 310

French military attaché, Colonel Delmas, to Romanian chief of staff, 28
September 1938, the day before the Munich meeting: "Do you not think
that it is time to arrest the expansion of Germany?"
    General Ionescu: "In my opinion, it is the last chance. If we let it pass, we
can no longer contain Germany or, in any event, it will require enormous
sacrifices, while today the victory seems certain."

> – DDF, 2nd series, 11: 685 (No. 457)

I do wish it might be possible to get at any rate *The Times*, Camrose, Beaverbrook Press etc. to write up Hitler as the apostle of peace. It will be terribly
short sighted if this is not done.

> Henderson, British minister, Berlin, September 1938
> – DBFP, 3rd series, 2: 257 (No. 793)

Never – even in the darkest period of Habsburg subjection – were Bohemia's
natural frontiers erased from the map, until in our own day two panic-stricken
statesmen from the West tried to purchase from triumphant gangsters a peace
that was no peace.

> R. W. Seton-Watson, 1943
> – *History of the Czechs and Slovaks*, 20

I am not sure now [that] I am proud of what I wrote to Hitler in urging
that he sit down around a table and make peace [at Munich]. That may have
saved many, many lives now, but that may ultimately result in the loss of
many times that number of lives later.

> FDR, November 1939
> – Henry Morgenthau, *Diaries*, 2: 48–9

Stalin said . . . that the only way to meet the present situation was by some
scheme of pacts. Germany must be made to realize that if she attacked any

other nation she would have Europe against her. As an illustration he said: "We are six of us in this room; if Maisky chooses to go for any one of us, then we must all fall on Maisky." He chuckled at the idea, Maisky grinned somewhat nervously. Stalin continued that only by this means would peace be preserved.

Josef Stalin, March 1935
– Anthony Eden, *Facing the Dictators*, 173

The Soviet government maintains the principles that it has not ceased to defend in the course of these last years, the necessity for the peaceful powers to form a front for peace, to organize themselves to bar the route to the aggressors. The Muscovite Cassandra continues to preach the urgency of action, for which there is not, according to it, a moment to lose; but seeing that no one is listening and feeling that it is mistrusted, its voice grows little by little more distant, its accents more embittered.

French Chargé Levi in Moscow, April 1938
– DDF, 2nd series, 9: 225–7 (No. 115)

It is not out of the question, if Russia is separated from the Western Powers, that we will see Hitler collaborating with the Soviets. In that case the countries situated between Germany and Russia, namely Poland, Czechoslovakia, and Romania, will be absolutely at the disposal of [these] two Great Powers.

Edvard Beneš to a Romanian diplomat, April 1938
– RMAE, Fond 71/Romînia, Vol. 101, p. 204

Appeasement (a reminder): "a clever plan of selling off your friends in order to buy off your enemies."

– *Manchester Guardian*, 25 February 1939

Preface: A Test Case of Collective Security

The Munich crisis remains among the most dramatic and tragic military–diplomatic crises of the twentieth century. Hitler used the plausible claim of self-determination of peoples to demand and achieve annexation – without war – of the 3.5 million Sudeten Germans in Czechoslovakia, a state of approximately 12 million people, chiefly Slavs. He thereby took possession of the fortified mountain frontier along the border of Germany and Czechoslovakia and rendered indefensible the previously most immediate – and most formidable – barrier to his planned takeover of Eastern Europe. Czechoslovakia and its allies, France and the Soviet Union, could muster a combined military force six or seven times larger than that of Germany at the time, yet Hitler's *public* demands were met without a fight. If the fight had occurred in September 1938, given both the odds against a German victory and the prospect of an effective conspiracy against Hitler inside the German high command – some of his generals planned to attack *him* if war broke out *at that time* – World War II as we know it simply could not have happened. The Czech army begged to fight, but Czech President Edvard Beneš capitulated. Forsaken by his French allies, he was afraid that the Soviets would not assist him without French support, that the Czechoslovak Republic would be left to face the Wehrmacht alone against hopeless odds.

Books about Munich are by no means rare. Most of ours in English emphasize the diplomacy of the problem and rely principally on the sources from Western and Central Europe, the published British, French, and German diplomatic documents.[1] These sources are, of course, indispensable,

---

[1] *Documents on British Foreign Policy, 1919–1939* (hereafter DBFP), 2nd series: 1929–1938, 21 vols. (London: H. M. Stationery Office, 1946–1984); 3rd series: 1938–1939, 9 vols. (London: H. M. Stationery Office, 1949–1961); *Akten zur deutschen auswärtigen Politik, 1918–1945*, Series D: 1937–1945 [1941], 7 vols. (Baden-Baden: Imprimerie nationale, 1950–1986); *Documents on German Foreign Policy, 1918–1945* (hereafter DGFP), Series D: 1937–1945 [1941], 13 vols. (Washington, DC: U.S. Government Printing Office, 1949–1964); *Documents diplomatiques français, 1932–1939* (hereafter DDF), 2nd series, 1936–1939, 19 vols. (Paris: Imprimerie nationale, 1963–1986).

and they will be taken carefully into account here. The purpose of this book, however, is to look for new perspectives, to explore elements of the problem that have been relatively neglected, to emphasize the role of East European countries – and documents – in search of new information, to render somewhat more comprehensible the mysterious surrender of a potentially overwhelming coalition of powers in the face of Hitler's more and more obvious plans of imperial conquest.

If the East European diplomatic documents have not received the attention they are due, the military dimension of the problem has been especially neglected. Was it not Stalin who said that honest diplomacy is like iron wood or dry water? Then perhaps his curious intentions may become more apparent by an examination of his presumably more honest military activities, and they will be closely followed here. This mix of sources and perspectives is used to focus most specifically on two particular closely related problems: (1) to illuminate Soviet policy objectives at Munich and thereby (2) to clarify the question of Moscow's preference for collective security or the alliance with Hitler.

The preponderant consensus of the many Western studies based predominantly on Western sources is extremely skeptical about the genuineness of repeated Soviet advocacy of collective security and its corollary, assurances of Soviet assistance to Czechoslovakia. Only a representative sample need be mentioned here: John Lukacs, *The Great Powers and Eastern Europe* (1953)[2]; Keith Eubank, *Munich* (1963); Telford Taylor, *Munich: The Price of Peace* (1979); and Gerhard Weinberg, *The Foreign Policy of Hitler's Germany*, Vol. 2, *Starting World War II* (1980). Perhaps the two most prominent works representing the other side of the issue are Jonathan Haslam, *The Soviet Union and the Search for Collective Security in Europe, 1933–1939* (1984) and Geoffrey Roberts, *The Soviet Union and the Origins of the Second World War: Russo–German Relations and the Road to War, 1933–1941* (1995).[3]

This issue has traditionally been obscured by a variety of conditions. Before 1989, East European historical scholarship, especially in nearly contemporary questions clearly remembered and bitterly contested among different camps of protagonists, was naturally regarded in the West with some suspicion. Moreover, until the collapse of the Berlin Wall, work in East European archival materials was severely restricted. In addition, most Western historians did not use East European languages and hence East

---

[2] See especially Appendix to Part II: "Munich in Retrospect," 166–89.
[3] The most convenient introduction to the controversy is in two authoritative articles of Teddy J. Uldricks, "Soviet Security Policy in the 1930s," in Gabriel Gorodetsky, ed., *Soviet Foreign Policy 1917–1991: A Retrospective* (Portland, OR: Frank Cass, 1994), 65–74; idem, "Debating the Role of Russia in the Origins of the Second World War," in Gordon Martel, ed., *The Origins of the Second World War Reconsidered*, 2nd ed. (New York: Routledge, 1999), 135–54.

European literature and source materials. Among those who did, as Milan Hauner has pointed out, most concentrated on diplomatic documents and ignored the evidence of military developments.[4] Although the Soviets themselves published a remarkably large quantity of their own documents, most of them, although widely available – some in English – have been little used.[5] Thus most of our conceptions about the East European dimensions of this crisis rest on a very insecure documentary foundation, and a probing examination of the East European sources both refutes and confirms these conceptions and misconceptions in a variety of informative ways.

More recently, the works of several prominent émigré historians have turned our attention to both published and unpublished documents from Czechoslovak sources: Jiri Hochman, *The Soviet Union and the Failure of Collective Security, 1934–1938* (1984); Igor Lukes, *Czechoslovakia Between Stalin and Hitler: The Diplomacy of Edvard Beneš in the 1930s* (1996); and Ivan Pfaff, *Die Sowjetunion und die Verteidigung der Tschechoslowakei, 1934–1938* (1996). The conclusions of these works are remarkably consonant with those of their West European predecessors, and this fact raises a curious point, for Soviet, Polish, and Romanian sources actually provide a substantial amount of contrary evidence.[6]

My intention from the outset of this research was to emphasize the Eastern European perspective, as I expected that it was in Eastern Europe that I would find pertinent new evidence; that expectation turned out to

---

[4] "A lot of the literature on the subject of Munich suffers until our own day a fundamental disproportion between excessive concentration on the diplomatic negotiations on the one hand and disparagement of the factors of military strategy on the other." Milan Hauner, "Září 1938: kapitulovat či bojovat?," *Svědectví* 13 (1975): 151–68.

[5] *Dokumenty po istorii Miunkhenskogo sgovora, 1937–1939,* ed. V. F. Mal'tsev (Moscow: Politizdat, 1979); and its Czech edition, *Dokumenty k historii mnichovského diktátu, 1937–1939,* eds. Hana Tichá et al. (Prague: Svoboda, 1979); *New Documents on the History of Munich,* ed. V. F. Klochko (Prague: Orbis, 1958); *Dokumenty i materialy po istorii sovetsko–chekhoslovatskikh otnoshenii,* 5 vols. (Moscow: Nauka, 1973–1988); and its Czech edition, *Dokumenty a materialy k dějinam československo-sovetských vztahů,* eds. Čestmír Amort et al., 5 vols. (Prague: Academia, 1975–1984); *Dokumenty i materialy po istorii sovetsko–pol'skikh otnoshenii,* ed. I. A. Khrenov, 12 vols. (Moscow: USSR Academy of Sciences, 1963–1986); and its Polish edition, *Dokumenty i materialy do historii stosunków polsko–radzieckich,* eds. N. Gasiorowska-Grabowska et al., 12 vols. (Warsaw: Polish Academy of Sciences, 1963–1986). In English is Oleg Rzheshevskii, *Europe 1939: Was War Inevitable?* (Moscow: Progress Publishers, 1989), very tendentious but containing some authentic facts often overlooked on Soviet military preparations, pp. 103–7. J. Hochman, *The Soviet Union and the Failure of Collective Security,* misses the capital collection of documents, *Dokumenty i materialy po istorii sovetsko–chekhoslovatskikh otnoshenii;* and I. Lukes, *Czechoslovakia Between Stalin and Hitler,* and I. Pfaff, *Die Sowjetunion und die Verteidigung der Tschechoslowakei,* miss the important military documents from the same collection as well.

[6] There are useful reappraisals by various authors in Maya Latynski, ed., *Reappraising the Munich Pact: Continental Perspectives* (Baltimore and Washington, DC: Johns Hopkins and Wilson Center Presses, 1992).

be correct. I have found nevertheless that here East and West are, contrary to Kipling's conception, inextricably interlinked and fused. If much of the story from Western Europe is familiar, it still forms an essential part of the whole, as it provides an indispensable element of context without which the Eastern part of the story lacks the full dimension of authenticity – and credibility. The policy of both Prague and Moscow depended heavily on initiatives taken first in Paris and later in London.

Relatively early in the process of this research, I discovered a series of surprising facts. In the Moscow archives, I found that the Red Army mobilized before Munich on a rather massive scale. I found in addition that the mobilized troops of the Red Army were informed that they must be *prepared to defend Czechoslovakia*. In the Bucharest archives, I found, contrary to all conventional wisdom, that the Romanian General Staff gave its *approval* to the transit of the Red Army across Romania to assist Czechoslovakia. In Polish documentary publications, I found that the Polish consul in Kishinev reported the transit through Bessarabia of significant quantities of Soviet military matériel on its way to Czechoslovakia. These findings were more than promising enough to motivate further research, and it is the body of that research that comprises the story told here.

– Hugh Ragsdale, Charlottesville, Virginia

Introduction: The Nature of the Problem

In retrospect, it is all too easy to see the common interests of the nations of Europe to band together to stop the onward march of ugly Nazism. At the time, it was obviously easier for these nations to see instead their own immediate individual interests, and they lost sight of their permanent common interests until too late.

Not only did the legacy of World War I naturally divide the victors from the vanquished; it also left the victors divided among themselves. In the idiom of Winston Churchill, Britain was a sea animal, and France was in 1918 primarily and unavoidably a land animal. From the date of the armistice, their interests diverged. That document stipulated the surrender of the German navy, the German colonies, and a large part of the German merchant marine; in other words, of all the instruments of German *Weltpolitik* of primary concern to the maritime interests of Great Britain. Although it also stipulated general German disarmament, it did not give the French anything comparable to God's own gift to the British, that great moat of the high seas, the English Channel, between London and the continent. So the French reached for substitutes. They proposed breaking up Southwestern Germany into separate states, but the British and the Americans refused, as it would violate the sacred principle of self-determination. The French then demanded an Anglo–American alliance to guarantee the security of their German frontier. Woodrow Wilson and David Lloyd George consented, but the U.S. Congress refused, after which His Majesty's Government also declined. For all of its suffering at the heart of the alliance against Germany during the war, France felt deceived and abandoned. If German disarmament brought the French short-term security, the long term was far from sure. As Premier Georges Clemenceau said to Lloyd George at one of their early postwar meetings, "I have to tell you that from the very day of the armistice I found you the enemy to France." Lloyd George's response was a memorable example of callous facetiousness, as sad as it was true: "Well, *was it not always our traditional policy?*"[1]

The postwar security policy of the two wartime allies soon reflected their divergent geostrategic needs. In Britain, J. M. Keynes published his hugely successful criticism of Versailles, "the peace of God," as he called it, "for it surely passeth all understanding." The burden of Keynes's case was that the peace was unrealistically severe, unjust, and, in its reparations provisions, unworkable – never mind that the peace the Germans imposed on the defeated Russians, or would have imposed on the Anglo–French given a different outcome of the war, was substantially more draconian than the terms they got.[2] In any event, a revisionist spirit ensued, and pacificism mushroomed in Britain both among historians and among the public more generally: "Ashamed of what they had done, they looked for scapegoats and for amendment. The scapegoat was France; the amendment was appeasement."[3] As a Foreign Office paper later characterized postwar British policy, "From the earliest years following the war, it was our policy to eliminate those parts of the Peace Settlement which, as practical people, we knew to be untenable and indefensible."[4] The problem with this policy was that, given the privileged advantages that seagoing Britain had derived from the armistice and its callous disregard of French land-based security needs in the peace, the British conception entailed sacrifices of others for the benefit of Britain. Therefore, although the British revisionist spirit was resented on the continent, Britain in turn blamed German ill temper on the strategic intransigence of the increasingly abandoned and exposed French – as in the Ruhr invasion of 1923, for example. When French Foreign Minister Louis Barthou informed London in 1934 that France could not accept adjustments in the disarmament clauses of Versailles in favor of German rearmament, he added that he would gladly change his mind at any time if offered a British alliance in defense of the treaty. London had become de facto the champion of German rights, and for a time it led Hitler himself to ponder the prospect of a British alliance.

Hitler's sometime fondness for Britain made little impression on the qualified and professional British ambassadors in Berlin in the early and middle 1930s. Sir Horace Rumbold characterized Nazism without illusions from the early days of its triumph. "I have the impression that the persons

---

[1] Georges Clemenceau, *Grandeur and Misery of Victory*, trans. F. M. Atkinson (New York: Harcourt, Brace, 1930), 121 (emphasis in original).

[2] Fritz Fischer, *Germany's Aims in the First World War* (London: Chatto and Windus, 1967).

[3] Martin Gilbert and Richard Gott, *The Appeasers* (Boston: Houghton Mifflin, 1963), 3.

[4] Keith Middlemas, *Diplomacy of Illusion: The British Government and Germany, 1937–1939* (Aldershot, England: Gregg Revivals, 1991), 11.

directing the policy of the Hitler Government are not normal. Many of us, indeed, have a feeling that we are living in a country where fantastic hooligans and eccentrics have got the upper hand." His successor, Sir Eric Phipps, described Hitler as "a fanatic who would be satisfied with nothing less than the dominance of Europe." He would not make war before 1938, Phipps predicted, but "war is the purpose here."[5]

The wisdom of these seasoned sentiments was scarcely shared in the Foreign Office itself in London – with the consistent and well-known exception of Sir Robert Vansittart. In the mid-1930s the word *appeasement* was not yet in bad odor. Sir Anthony Eden, who would later resign as foreign secretary in protest against the policy, told the House of Commons in 1936 that "it is the appeasement of Europe as a whole that we have constantly before us."[6] Prime Minister Neville Chamberlain was not ashamed at an Imperial Conference in 1937 to name the proper subjects of appeasement: the German areas of Austria, Czechoslovakia, Poland, and Lithuania.[7] It was ironically enough to Soviet Ambassador Ivan Maisky that Chamberlain made his pathetic remark, "If only we could sit down at a table with the Germans and run through all their complaints and claims with a pencil, this would greatly relieve all tensions."[8] In November 1937, in the absence of the foreign secretary, Sir Anthony Eden, and without his prior knowledge of the arrangements, Chamberlain sent Lord Halifax on a visit to Hitler, to sit down with pencil and paper and listen to German complaints. Halifax left a record in his own words of what he suggested to Hitler: "I said that there were no doubt . . . questions arising out of the Versailles settlement which seemed to us capable of causing trouble if they were unwisely handled, e.g., Danzig, Austria, Czechoslovakia. On all these matters we were not necessarily concerned to stand for the status quo as today, but we were concerned to avoid such treatment of them as would be likely to cause trouble. If reasonable settlements could be reached with

---

[5] Gilbert and Gott, *The Appeasers*, 17, 36, 38. Unfortunately, Sir Eric did not uphold on his next post, Paris, the better standard of diplomatic representation and reporting that he had exhibited in Berlin, and he was followed in Berlin by an ambassador generally regarded as a disastrously uncritical partisan of appeasement, Sir Nevile Henderson. John Herman, *The Paris Embassy of Sir Eric Phipps: Anglo–French Relations and the Foreign Office, 1937–1939* (Portland, OR: Sussex Academic, 1998); Peter Neville, *Appeasing Hitler: The Diplomacy of Sir Nevile Henderson, 1937–1939* (New York: Macmillan, 2000); Felix Gilbert, "Two British Ambassadors: Perth and Henderson," in Gordon A. Craig and Felix Gilbert, eds., *The Diplomats, 1919–1939*, 2 vols. (New York: Atheneum, 1963), 2: 537–54.

[6] Telford Taylor, *Munich: The Price of Peace* (New York: Vintage Books, 1980), 249.

[7] R. A. C. Parker, *Chamberlain and Appeasement: British Policy and the Coming of the Second World War* (New York: St. Martin's, 1993), 78.

[8] Middlemas, *Diplomacy of Illusion*, 53.

the free assent and goodwill of those primarily concerned we certainly had no desire to block."[9] It was not until 1939 that the *Manchester Guardian* had the nerve to define appeasement as "a clever plan of selling off your friends in order to buy off your enemies."[10]

In Moscow, it seems to have been widely assumed that Chamberlain and company were trying through appeasement in the East to divert Hitler's aggression in that direction.[11] I know of no documentation of such a strategy, but there is an intriguing and little publicized suggestion of Prime Minister Stanley Baldwin to a Parliamentary delegation in July 1936: "We all know the German desire, and he has come out with it in his book, to move east, and if he should move East [sic] I should not break my heart. . . . If there is any fighting in Europe to be done, I should like to see the Bolshies and the Nazis doing it."[12]

The fatal flaw in the outlook of the British Cabinet that faced the Munich crisis was what we might define as projection, the attribution to very different personalities of a character like their own, that of a British gentleman. Surely Hitler was amenable to reason, was he not? Halifax wondered aloud why, if Hitler could get most of what he wanted without war, he should risk war for the marginal remainder. Chamberlain confided to his intimates that Britain should say to Germany, "Give us satisfactory assurances that you won't use force to deal with the Austrians and the Czechoslovakians and we will give you similar assurances that we won't use force to prevent the changes you want, if you can get them by peaceful means."[13] Of course, such an outlook was a fundamental misunderstanding of the mentality of Hitler. As Sir Horace Rumbold had vainly warned the Foreign Office in 1934, "the persons directing the policy of the Hitler Government are not normal."

The French approached their strategic security quite differently. First, they exerted themselves in the 1920s – when Germany was defeated, disarmed, and weak and they themselves were proportionately strong – to enforce the terms of the treaty punctiliously, literally with a vengeance, as was apparent in their invasion of the Ruhr valley in 1923 when Germany had defaulted on reparations. Second, they sought, as they had traditionally done since at least the seventeenth century, allies on the far frontier of

---

[9] Account by Lord Halifax of his visit to Germany, 17–21 November 1937; DBFP, 2nd series, 19: 540–54, quote on 545 (No. 336).

[10] Frank McDonough, *Neville Chamberlain, Appeasement and the British Road to War* (New York: Manchester University Press, 1998), 2.

[11] See, e.g., Gabriel Godetsky, *Grand Delusion: Stalin and the German Invasion of Russia* (New Haven, CT: Yale University Press, 1999).

[12] Michael Jabara Carley, *1939: The Alliance That Never Was and the Coming of World War II* (Chicago: Ivan Dee, 1999), 33.

[13] Middlemas, *Diplomacy of Illusion*, 225–6, 137–8.

Germany in Eastern Europe. In the wake of the revolutionary maelstrom of that quarter of the continent in 1917–1918, they looked to alliances with the successor states of the Austrian, German, and Russian Empires. Thus the French allied in 1921 with Poland and in 1924 with Czechoslovakia. Third, beginning in 1929–1930, they built the Maginot Line.

The Maginot Line was never the ridiculous misconception that the fate of France in 1940 sometimes made it appear to be. Both to spare expenses and to avoid fencing the Belgians out of the French defensive perimeter, it covered the German frontier and stopped short of the Belgian border. It did not fall; it was avoided by the Germans, who detoured around it.[14] The misconception here was the failure to form a mechanized corps capable of mobile offensive operations beyond the Maginot Line. The French strategic conception was schizoid, self-contradictory: on the one hand, to stand behind the defenses of the Maginot Line and, on the other, to presume to defend allies on Germany's faraway Eastern frontier. The Maginot Line was not portable, of course, and it was useful to France's Eastern allies only insofar as it enabled the French to enhance the efficiency of their frontier defense such as to liberate and multiply mobile forces for an invasion of Germany. The Maginot Line actually incorporated this strategic conception. Not a perfectly continuous line of fortifications, it left an open front around the Saar River valley between the Région fortifiée de Metz and the Région fortifiée de la Lauter (Lauter River at Lauterbourg north of Strasbourg). Here was the staging area for a French offensive into the Rhineland (it was also mined for flooding in the event of a German attack) as was, also, the whole of Belgium. The French, however, never did create the counterparts of Hitler's Panzer divisions to pose an offensive threat to Germany. And so, as Jean-Baptiste Duroselle put it, "One may not have at the same time little allies far away and a purely defensive army."[15]

Finally, when the effort grew too great, the conception too confused, and the nation too bewildered, the French governments, twenty-four of them in the 1930s, concluded that only the support of perfidious Albion could save them. It was a crisis of confidence and a counsel of despair, and at that point, French foreign policy became so dependent on London as to forsake its solemn treaty obligations in Eastern Europe. What had happened to *la grande nation*?

---

[14] Martin S. Alexander, "In Defence of the Maginot Line: Security Policy, Domestic Politics and the Economic Depression in France," in Robert Boyce, ed., *French Foreign and Defence Policy, 1918–1940: The Decline and Fall of a Great Power* (London: Routledge, 1998), 164–94; J. E. and H. W. Kaufman, *The Maginot Line: None Shall Pass* (Westport, CT: Praeger, 1997).

[15] Jean-Baptiste Duroselle, "Introduction," in *Munich 1938: mythes et réalités* (Paris: Institut national d'études slaves, 1979), 38.

The answer is largely the story of the psychological impact of the war –
and the dread of another like it. The 1920s were *l'après-guerre*; the 1930s
were *l'avant-guerre*; the entire period was *l'entre-deux-guerres*. At Verdun,
1,000 men had died per square kilometer. Patriotism was suspect. Pacificism was irrepressible. Among the schoolteachers, a quarter of whom
had served in the trenches, it was epidemic. The birthrate was low, nearly
a quarter of married couples remaining childless. And, of course, there
was alcoholism. Twice as many French as German draftees were rejected
on grounds of health. These were "the hollow years," "*la décadence.*" In
1939, enlisted men on their way to the front routinely refused to salute
officers, and the General Staff, having no radio, communicated by carrier
pigeons.[16] The seeds of what Marc Bloch called the "strange defeat" were
sown long before 1940.[17]

In Southeastern Europe, Danubian and Balkan Europe, the victors –
or, rather, the beneficiaries of the victory – did not conduct their foreign policies initially at such cross purposes as did Britain and France.
Among the chief of these beneficiaries were the nations newly independent of the Austro–Hungarian Empire: Czechoslovakia, where Bohemia,
Moravia, and Slovakia came together to form a new country; Yugoslavia,
where Slovenia and Croatia were freed to join Serbia and Montenegro
in what eventually became the Kingdom of Yugoslavia[18]; and Romania,
which realized large gains in all directions, Transylvania at the expense of
Hungary, Dobrudja at the expense of Bulgaria, Bessarabia from the fall-
out of the Russian Empire, and Bukovina from Austrian Galicia. Austria
and Hungary were, of course, ravished by the defeat and decomposition
of the Habsburg Empire, the formerly most ethnically ramshackle state
of Europe. The most natural inclination of the ethnic nature of Austria
was to move in the direction of Germany. The Hungarians, shorn by the
Treaty of Trianon, an adjunct of the Treaty of Versailles, of all ethnically
non-Hungarian territory and substantial Hungarian components in Slovakia and Romania as well, lost approximately 60 percent of their former
dominion.

The three powers either arising out of the ruins of Austria–Hungary
or growing substantial at the expense of it naturally banded together to
forestall any reactionary revival of it. In 1920–1921, Czechoslovakia, Romania, and Yugoslavia formed the Little Entente. The three bilateral treaties
among them were dedicated to the maintenance of Trianon and stipulated

---

[16] Eugen Weber, *The Hollow Years: France in the 1930s* (New York: Norton, 1994).

[17] Marc Bloch, *Strange Defeat*, trans. Gerard Hopkins (New York: Octagon, 1968). For a persuasive
update, see Eugenia C. Kiesling, *Arming Against Hitler: France and the Limits of Military Planning*
(Lawrence, KS: University Press of Kansas, 1996).

[18] Formally, until 1929, the Kingdom of the Serbs, Croats, and Slovenes.

that an attack on anyone of them by Hungary would bring the assistance of the other two.[19] The aspiration of these three little states was to be together what individually they could not be, a major power factor in Europe for the protection of their own interests. Unfortunately, as Alfred Cobban has observed, "the combination of any number of weak states does not make one strong one."[20] Similarly, Dov Lungu characterizes the Little Entente as "a strong alliance against the weak and a weak alliance against the strong."[21] Its fate depended, as did that of so much of the continent, on France and Germany. France had a formal political alliance with Czechoslovakia and a moral alliance in the form of treaties of friendship with Romania and Yugoslavia (1926 and 1927, respectively).[22] Throughout the 1920s, so long as Germany was weak, such arrangements sufficed.

Before the revival of German power, the international politics of Eastern Europe were at least superficially stable, but they were infested with problems that the rise of Germany would empower and aggravate. The outcome of the war naturally divided the nations of the continent into victors and vanquished, or status quo and revisionist powers, those perceiving themselves as the justly liberated and those perceiving themselves as the unjustly ravished. Among the latter, there was no more passionately revisionist power in Europe than Hungary. The Treaty of Trianon had forced Hungary to surrender more than half its – largely non-Hungarian – population, the most severe sacrifice required of any nation in Europe, and it left in Romanian Transylvania the largest expatriate population – Hungarian – among all the powers, large and small. As the great student of Hungarian foreign policy of the time, Magda Ádám, has put the matter, "In the period between the wars, the foreign policy of Hungary was entirely dedicated to the recovery of the territories lost as a consequence of the First World War."[23]

There were for a long time, however, insuperable obstacles to this aspiration, especially the size and the power of Hungary relative to those of the three powers of the Little Entente. Hungary had a population of approximately 8 million, but Trianon reduced its army to 35,000 men, and the combined populations of the Little Entente were over five times

[19] *Survey of International Affairs, 1920–1923* (London: Oxford University Press, 1927), 505–8.

[20] Alfred Cobban, *The Nation-State and National Self-Determination* (London: Collins/Fontana, 1969), 300.

[21] Dov B. Lungu, *Romania and the Great Powers, 1933–1940* (Durham, NC: Duke University Press, 1989), 33.

[22] Two of the members of the Little Entente, Romania and Yugoslavia, joined in 1934 with Greece and Turkey to form the Balkan Entente, the substance of which was a mutual guarantee of the Balkan frontiers of the member states, especially against Bulgaria.

[23] Magda Ádám, "Documents relatifs à la politique étrangère de la Hongrie dans la période de la crise tchécoslovaque (1936–1939)," *Acta historica Academiae scientiarum Hungaricae* 10 (1964), 89.

as large, its armed forces fifteen times as large.[24] In the 1920s, Hungary was relatively isolated. Moreover, its government looked for support at that time to London. The authoritarian chief executive of Hungary between the wars – he was designated to be the Habsburg *regent* of a kingless kingdom – was the former commander-in-chief of the Austro-Hungarian navy, Admiral Miklós Horthy. Horthy never lost the respect that his training had taught him for the British navy, and he was convinced that Britain would triumph over Germany in the next war as it had in the last. The British navy, however, was a poor instrument of territorial irredenta in the landlocked conditions of Hungarian geography. Horthy had a pathological hatred of Czechs and of President Edvard Beneš in particular, whom he considered challenging to a duel. He discussed with the Germans in 1936 the liquidation of Czechoslovakia as a "cancerous ulcer of Europe."[25]

Still, Hungary was not entirely isolated in East Central Europe, as it shared a variety of interests – and values – with one of the beneficiaries of Versailles, Poland. Both societies were rather strongly aristocratic and looked without favor on the radical democracy and conspicuous socialism of republican Czechoslovakia and especially on the legal status of the Communist Party there. If Hungary had territorial claims in Slovakia, Poland had designs on the Czech enclave of Teschen, occupied by the Czechs in 1919. In the midst of the Polish–Soviet War of 1920–1921, Czechoslovakia refused to permit the transit across its territory of French arms aid to Poland. Both Poland and Hungary resented the asylum commonly granted in Czechoslovakia to political refugees from across their frontiers. The prominence and the sometimes tutorial tone of Czechoslovak Foreign Minister, later President, Beneš were not to their liking either.[26]

Poland had been before the partitions the largest state in Europe west of Russia. Shared at the end of the eighteenth century among Prussia, Russia, and Austria, it emerged after the Napoleonic Wars largely in the possession of the same three powers with elements of autonomy – temporarily – in the Russian Empire of Alexander I. Born again in 1919 under the leadership of Józef Piłsudski (d. 1935), it still faced its most bedeviling traditional problem, its situation between the larger and stronger powers of the Germans in the west and the Russians in the east.

---

[24] Hugh Seton-Watson, *Eastern Europe Between the Wars, 1918–1941*, 3rd ed. (New York: Harper & Row, 1962), Appendix; Joseph Rothschild, *East Central Europe Between the Two World Wars* (Seattle, WA: University of Washington Press, 1974), 157.

[25] Henryk Batowski, *Rok 1938: dwie agresje hitlerowskie* (Poznań: Wydawn. Poznańskie, 1985), 437.

[26] Henryk Batowski, "La politique polonaise et la Tchécoslovaquie," in *Munich 1938: mythes et réalités*, 51–55; Jürgen Pagel, *Polen und die Sowjetunion 1938–1939: Die polnisch–sowjetischen Beziehungen in den Krisen der europäischen Politik am Vorabend des Zweiten Weltkrieges* (Stuttgart: Franz Steiner Verlag, 1992), 99–100.

Piłsudski devised Polish foreign policy between the wars to be independent of either strong neighbor. The Polish foreign minister, Colonel Józef Beck, made a nonaggression pact with the Soviet Union in 1932 and another with Germany in 1934. Between the Germans and the Russians, however, he preferred the former. Beck was a man of strong views, and his sentiments in East European politics were well known. He often said that two states among the progeny of Versailles were artificial and destined to disappear: Austria would naturally join Germany, and multiethnic Czechoslovakia would naturally dissolve into its constituent parts. In fact, he was willing to cooperate with the Hungarians and the Germans in partitioning it: the Sudetens for Germany, Slovakia for Hungary, and Teschen for Poland.[27]

Beck had a special dread of the Russians, and he did not think that his allies in Paris had the resolve to face up to the challenges posed for them by Germany. He told them accusingly, "You will yield again and again."[28] Beck was obviously not entirely wrong about France, but he was in a position to strengthen the French alliance system by working *with*, not *against*, Czechoslovakia, and he adamantly refused. As the influence of the Nazis loomed ever more imminent on the scene, Beck looked on Hitler as the most likely instrument to deliver to Poland the spoils of Czechoslovakia. Hence he wished to protect Hitler against the Jews and the Communists.[29] His pro-German, even pro-Nazi, sentiments were not shared by the Polish public at large, but Beck cared nothing for public opinion.[30] To make matters worse, there was personal antagonism between Beck and Beneš. When the premier of France, the ally of both of them, brought to Beck Beneš's question what Poland would do if Germany attacked Czechoslovakia, Beck responded, "Tell M. Beneš that I refuse to answer the question. That is the categorical and official attitude of the Polish government." Here was one designated victim of Hitler undermining another, a potential ally against him. Telford Taylor characterized Polish policy appropriately: "Brave, benighted, quixotic Poland – anti-Russian, anti-German, and anti-Semitic; born of Versailles but in league with [its enemies]; culturally Francophile, friendless among the great powers other than France, yet scornful of her

---

[27] Anna Cienciala, *Poland and the Western Powers, 1938–1939: A Study in the Interdependence of Eastern and Western Europe* (Toronto: University of Toronto Press, 1968); idem, "The View from Warsaw," in Maya Latynski, ed., *Reappraising the Munich Pact: Continental Perspectives* (Washington, DC, and Baltimore: Wilson Center Press and Johns Hopkins University Press, 1992); idem, "The Munich Crisis of 1938: Plans and Strategy in Warsaw in the Context of the Western Appeasement of Germany," in Igor Lukes and Eric Goldstein, eds., *The Munich Crisis, 1938: Prelude to World War II* (Portland, OR: Frank Cass, 1999), 48–81.

[28] Taylor, *Munich*, 188.

[29] Pagel, *Polen und die Sowjetunion, 1938–1939*, 91–2.

[30] Batowski, "La politique polonaise et la Tchécoslovaquie," 51.

own protector, spurning her neighbors with whom she might have made common cause against the German peril – was off and running on the road to suicide."[31] Beck's real aim was not the acquisition of Teschen, which was merely a pretext. His real aim was, like Hitler's, the destruction of Czechoslovakia, but beyond that goal, he aspired to the building of a "third Europe," a bloc of states independent of either the victors or the vanquished of Versailles, including in particular Poland, Romania, Hungary, Yugoslavia, and Italy.[32]

The triumph of Hitler in January 1933 changed, of course, all security perspectives, and the forces of collective security began at once to gird themselves for the challenge. Only seventeen days after Hitler became chancellor of Germany, the powers of the Little Entente convened to coordinate more closely their commercial relations, banking, railroad and air traffic, and the post. More important, this Organization Pact – sometimes called the Reorganization Pact – stipulated three meetings per year of their foreign ministers to assess and manage their foreign policy.[33]

In 1933, Germany dropped out of the League of Nations, and, in September 1934, the Soviet Union, formerly hostile to it, did a reappraisal of the European situation and joined the League. The Soviets by this time had had nearly a decade and a half to recover from World War I and their own civil war, had implemented a dramatic economic resurgence in the Five-Year Plan, and had reemerged as a more important factor in international affairs. In May 1935, the French and the Soviets signed a treaty of alliance. Two weeks later, Czechoslovakia and the Soviet Union signed a nearly identical one. The Franco–Soviet Treaty stipulated their mutual military assistance in the event that either power were attacked by another European power. The Czechoslovak–Soviet Pact contained an additional provision stipulating Soviet aid to Czechoslovakia only following that of France.[34]

In spite of such instruments of collective security as these, the will of the powers dedicated to maintaining peace proved unequal to that of the aggressors. Three events of the middle 1930s turned the tide in favor of the challengers.[35]

---

[31]   Taylor, *Munich*, 189, 191–2.

[32]   Batowski, *Rok 1938: dwie agresje hitlerowskie*, 433.

[33]   Vladimir Streinu [Nicolae Iordache], *La Petite Entente et l'Europe* (Geneva: Institut universitaire de hautes études internationales, 1977), 162–7.

[34]   Sir John W. Wheeler-Bennett, Text of the treaties of 2 and 16 May 1935 in *Documents on International Affairs, 1935*, 2 vols. (London: Royal Institute of International Affairs and Oxford University Press, 1936), 1: 116–19 and 138–9.

[35]   Of course, a fourth event, the Spanish Civil War, was by no means without influence on the road to war, illustrating clearly as it did the daring ambitions of the Axis powers and the supine pusillanimity of the victors of Versailles. But it is a story dreary, depressing, and familiar and of less immediate impact in the evolution of affairs in Eastern Europe than the three items described here.

First was the assassination in Marseille in October 1934 of King Alexander of Yugoslavia and French Foreign Minister Louis Barthou, a tragic setback for the cause of collective security. Barthou was probably the last best hope for a dynamic and courageous French foreign policy. The perpetrators of the deed were Croat dissidents of the Ustaše terrorist organization operating with the support and protection of Italy and Hungary. When Yugoslavia turned to the League of Nations to bring charges against these two nations, the British and the French refused to support the move. They were afraid of driving Italy into the arms of Germany. The Yugoslav government, obviously frustrated, was forced to consider a rapprochement with Italy in order to gain some control of the Ustaše.[36] The Little Entente as a whole could not have missed the political lesson of these developments.

Second was the Italo–Ethiopian crisis. Although Italy was one of the victors of World War I, it did not believe itself adequately rewarded at the peace conference. Mussolini aspired to annexations at the expense of Austria, Albania, and Yugoslavia and to compensations in colonial areas. He evinced a kind of volatile grand ambition to match the egotism of his adolescent posturing. In the 1920s and early 1930s, he was unable seriously to disturb the peace, but the rise of Germany brought to the balance of power – for a time – a kind of malleable, pliable equilibrium that had not been seen since the end of the war. In these circumstances, there was room for the maneuvering of such an ambitious state and presumptive great power as Italy, and Mussolini was inspired to embark on the conquest of the old Italian colonial goal of Ethiopia. It was a galling violation of all that the League of Nations stood for. The League declared Italy an aggressor, and Great Britain led the movement there to organize under Article 16 an economic embargo against Italy. The French, afraid again of driving Italy into the German camp, consented to cooperate with Britain and the League only with great reluctance and bad grace. The Little Entente powers, still in the embrace of collective security, gave full support at the cost of considerable economic sacrifice, especially in Yugoslavia. When the League considered adding oil and coal to the list of embargoed items, a move that would have crippled the Italian military effort in Ethiopia, Romanian Foreign Minister Nicolae Titulescu promised full compliance – Romania supplied 60 percent of Italy's oil.[37] France, however, refused to cooperate, Britain lost its nerve, and the embargo never happened. The Italians then consummated their conquest. Haile Selassie, the dispossessed emperor of Ethiopia, appeared before the League to deliver a prophetic lecture. "Us today, you tomorrow," he said as he finished. The League leaders, the

[36] Jacob B. Hoptner, *Yugoslavia in Crisis, 1934–1941* (New York: Columbia University Press, 1962).
[37] Lungu, *Romania and the Great Powers, 1933–1940*, 68–9.

victors of Versailles, were forsaking their own cause, abandoning the small powers who looked to them for sustenance.

The lessons of Ethiopia were admirably summed up in Robert L. Rothstein's study of the alliance problems of small powers: "The implications of the Ethiopian episode were not lost on the . . . European Small Powers. A collective security system in which the support of the Great Powers was grudging and inconsistent, and in which the Small Powers were urged to accept burdensome duties which could only be justified if Great Power support was assured, was worse than no system at all. Allegiance to the ideals of collective security was safe under two conditions: if no threat serious enough to activate the system arose, or if the system met its first challenges successfully enough to warrant continued support. After 1936 neither condition held, and the European Small Powers desperately sought to dilute whatever commitments they still maintained toward the security provisions of the Covenant."[38]

The third and last such turning point, the most dramatic and important test of collective security before the Munich crisis, was the remilitarization of the Rhineland on 7 March 1936. It was in some respects decisive, because it largely ruined respect for France in the eyes of its allies and its enemies alike, and it thereby destabilized the very foundation of the status quo and undermined the collective nature of security.

The Treaty of Versailles had stipulated in Articles 42 and 43 that Germany was forbidden to maintain any military establishment whatever, however transiently (i.e., the staging of maneuvers), on the left bank of the Rhine or within fifty kilometers of the right bank. The purpose of this provision was to enable the armed forces of the victors, especially those of the neighboring powers of France and Belgium, to advance into Germany unopposed in order to enforce the implementation of terms of the peace treaty that the Germans could hardly be expected to welcome. The demilitarization of the Rhineland was regarded by the Germans – along with reparations, unilateral disarmament, and the loss of East Prussia – with great distaste as elements of the "*Diktat*," the dictated nature of the peace treaty in spite of Wilson's promise of "open covenants openly arrived at." Germany reacted to these terms with great bitterness, which climaxed in the default of reparations, whereupon the French and the Belgians took advantage of the demilitarized Rhineland to occupy the Ruhr River Valley in 1923 in order to extract the defaulted increment. This crisis so alarmed the powers, including even the remote and isolationist Americans, as to prompt an effort to resolve the conflict and to ameliorate its bitterness. The result was the Locarno Conference (1925), the series of treaties that it produced, and the Era of Good Feeling that followed.

[38]   Robert L. Rothstein, *Alliances and Small Powers* (New York: Columbia University Press, 1968), 43.

The West European arrangements of Locarno were in part a reiteration of Articles 42 and 43 of Versailles, but the Germans found in them one distinct difference important to their sense of self-esteem: Locarno was, unlike the *Diktat* of 1919, at least in superficial appearance, a voluntary pact of equals. At Locarno, moreover, Germany, France, and Belgium accepted their common national boundaries, and Britain and Italy guaranteed them. If Germany violated the demilitarized nature of the Rhineland, it was to be brought to the attention of the League Council, which would then recommend to the other signatories of Locarno whatever appropriate military action they were all obliged to take.[39]

Hitler knew how eager the apprehensive supporters of collective security were for reassurance, and he found promises to be cheap and useful. In 1934 and 1935, he issued public statements guaranteeing his respect for Locarno and its provisions for the Rhineland.[40] When the Franco–Soviet Pact was signed, however, he argued that its provisions were incompatible with the League Covenant and therefore with the Treaty of Locarno. In other words, the violation of the Covenant and Locarno released Germany, he argued, from the obligations undertaken under Locarno. If so, Germany was clearly, by implication, free to remilitarize the Rhineland.

There was a superficial plausibility in his argument. The League Covenant entitled member nations to go to war only with the blessing of a unanimous vote of the League Council, not including the votes of Council members party to the dispute under consideration (Article 15, paragraph 6). The Franco–Soviet Pact, on the other hand, called on France and the Soviet Union to go to war either with the sanction of this qualified unanimity of the League Council or without it.[41] The significance of this point is summarized ably by James Emmerson, who has studied the matter at length[42]:

> The merit of the Franco–Soviet pact was claimed to be that it closed 'the gap in the Covenant' which released members from all obligations if the League council did not reach a unanimous decision. Germany contended that Moscow and Paris had arrogated to themselves the right to render assistance, even if the League council could not agree or voted that an act of aggression had not been committed. This meant, in German eyes, that

---

[39] The treaty articles pertaining to this situation, i.e., those of Versailles, of the League Covenant, of Locarno, as well as the subsequent Soviet alliance of 1935 are all assembled conveniently in the appendix of James T. Emmerson, *The Rhineland Crisis, 7 March 1936: A Study in Multilateral Diplomacy* (Ames, IA: Iowa State University Press/London School of Economics, 1977), 251–4.

[40] Ibid., 30.

[41] "Franco–Soviet Treaty of Mutual Assistance, 2 May 1935," *Documents on International Affairs, 1935*, 116–19.

[42] Emmerson, *The Rhineland Crisis*, 254.

'in certain circumstances', Paris would act as though the Locarno pact and League covenant were void. As a result, according to the German memorandum of 7 March [1936], the Rhine pact [Locarno] had 'lost its significance and practically ceased to be'.

In fact, the German argument seems specious on two grounds. Most generally, Hitler was attempting here to interpret, and to hold other powers to the terms of, a Covenant that he had rejected when, in 1933, he abandoned the League. More particularly, the League Covenant plainly specified in Article 15, paragraph 7, that "if the Council fails to reach a report which is unanimously agreed to by the members thereof, other than the Representatives of one or more of the parties to the dispute, the Members of the League reserve to themselves the right to take such action as they shall consider necessary for the maintenance of right and justice."

In any event – we do not expect to find Hitler on the side of the angels – on 7 March 1936, he marched in a *new* contingent of troops and *announced* a remilitarized Rhineland. Substantial numbers of troops had already been there in violation of Versailles. The French diplomats had warned of the imminence of this development for some time. French General Staff intelligence had reported for months the renovation of prewar barracks, of military roads and airfields, and the construction of earthwork defenses.[43] German troop strength, counting all categories and including even paramilitary personnel (e.g., police) in the area, was estimated at approximately twenty-one or twenty-two divisions or perhaps as many as 295,000 men.[44] The chief of the French General Staff, General Maurice Gamelin, had warned that Germany would seize the Rhineland in order "to neutralize the French army by constructing on its western frontiers a fortified barrier comparable to our own. . . . Hence, free from any fear of an offensive from us, Germany would be completely at liberty to settle the fate

---

[43] Stephen A. Schuker, "France and the Remilitarization of the Rhineland, 1936," *French Historical Studies* 14 (1986): 308–9; Taylor, *Munich*, 128–9; for Gamelin's account, Maurice Gustave Gamelin, *Servir*, 2 vols. (Paris: Plon, 1946–1947), 2: *Le prologue du drame (1930-août 1939)*, 193–217.

[44] Schuker, "France and the Remilitarization of the Rhineland," 308; Jean-Baptiste Duroselle, *La décadence, 1932–1939* (Paris: Imprimerie nationale, 1985), 168; Martin S. Alexander, *The Republic in Danger: General Maurice Gamelin and the Politics of French Defence, 1933–1940* (Cambridge, England: Cambridge University Press, 1992), 259; Pierre Le Goyet, *Le mystère Gamelin* (Paris: Presses de la Cité, 1976), 125. Schuker finds the German force to be perhaps too formidable for the French to overcome without a really major effort. Le Goyet disagrees, arguing that nearly 90 percent of it consisted of Landespolizei, Arbeitsdienst, corps national automobil, SS, and SA, only 30,000 men being genuine Wehrmacht. We know now that, contrary to reports that the German army would have retreated at the first sign of resistance, Hitler had given orders that, if the French marched in, the German forces were to engage in a spirited fighting retreat. He was not bluffing. Gerhard Weinberg, *The Foreign Policy of Hitler's Germany*, 2: *Starting World War II* (Chicago: University of Chicago Press, 1980), 252.

of the Little Entente powers."[45] This example is precisely what the Little Entente powers apprehended. At the same time, General Gamelin reported that Hitler could mobilize 120 divisions, whereas in fact he had scarcely a third that number. French intelligence on Hitler's intentions was quite good, but before Munich it vastly overestimated German military strength. On top of the exaggerations of German power, Gamelin himself often misrepresented the information in his possession, apparently to persuade the French government that any strategy other than a purely defensive one was out of the question.[46]

The French did what Hitler expected that they would: They consulted with their allies, turned to the League, and consulted with the Locarno signatories. The Czechoslovaks said that they would respond precisely as the French did, however the French did.[47] The Poles were cagier. As Colonel Beck said to the French ambassador, "This time it is serious." Yet while assuring the French of his loyalty, Beck checked the terms of the alliance and found that they did not cover a contingency short of a German invasion of France, and he assured the Germans at the same time that he was loyal to his treaty of nonaggression with them. There was no explicit conflict between his French and his German démarches, of course, only a conflict of spirit, and Beck lost nothing save honor.[48] When the French turned to the League and their Locarno allies, they found as little enthusiasm for a strong response as they themselves had. There was no appetite in the peace camp for war, and so the ugly deed was allowed to stand. The Treaty of Locarno did not entitle France and Belgium to go to war with Germany for violation of the Rhineland; rather, such entitlement depended solely on a German attack on the territory of France or Belgium. French strategic posture, along with French prestige, however, had deteriorated disastrously, and everyone knew it.

The French response – or lack of response – struck the allies of the Little Entente a devastating blow. The consequences were incalculable, but they were suggested by the various observations made in the different capitals of Central and Eastern Europe at the time. The tone was set by the premier of Yugoslavia, Milan Stojadinović. As he told the French minister, "We are now obliged to reckon with the German danger, which you allowed to emerge and spread." The Greek minister in Paris said

[45] Robert J. Young, *In Command of France: French Foreign Policy and Military Planning, 1933–1940* (Cambridge, MA: Harvard University Press, 1978), 119.

[46] Peter Jackson, *France and the Nazi Menace: Intelligence and Policy Making, 1933–1939* (New York: Oxford University Press, 2000), 170–2 and passim.

[47] Le Goyet, *Le mystère Gamelin*, 128.

[48] Noël to Flandin, 7 March 1936; DDF, 2nd series, 1: 415–16 (No. 303); Emmerson, *The Rhineland Crisis*, 158–9; Piotr Wandycz, *The Twilight of French Eastern Alliances, 1926–1936* (Princeton, NJ: Princeton University Press, 1988), 431–45; Taylor, *Munich*, 190.

that a country whose policy was like that of France in the Rhineland crisis "could not pretend to the name of a great power." The capital question was posed by Romanian Foreign Minister Nicolae Titulescu to Léon Blum: "If on 7 March you could not defend yourself, how will you defend us against the aggressor?" The Czechoslovaks were altogether demoralized. The Czechoslovak delegate at the League declared collective security dead: "No one cares about Czechoslovakia, which is nonetheless the cornerstone of order and the status quo in Central Europe." Even Pope Pius XI condemned French passivity: "If you had immediately advanced 200,000 men into the zone reoccupied by the Germans, you would have rendered an immense service to the whole world."[49]

The French fully realized the momentous consequences.[50] Gamelin stated flatly at a General Staff meeting of April 1936 that when the Germans fortified the Rhineland, the French army would be unable to penetrate into Germany; hence the Wehrmacht could turn against Poland and Czechoslovakia with impunity.[51] As Raymond Aron put it, it was a turning point.[52]

The Germans realized it, too. On his way from his former post in Moscow to his new post in Paris in May 1936, American Ambassador William Bullitt stopped in Berlin for conversations with his counterparts there. Foreign Minister Constantin von Neurath told him that Germany would do nothing active in foreign affairs until "the Rhineland had been digested" and properly fortified, that thereafter it would be a different question.[53] A Polish diplomat told him that Hitler's next step would be to encircle Austria – an Austrian official agreed, "Next time it will be our turn"[54] – and that "shortly thereafter Beneš would appear in Berlin on his knees."[55] The Austrian official was right, and the observation of the Polish diplomat is the substance of this book.

[49] Duroselle, *La décadence*, 179; Anthony Adamthwaite, *France and the Coming of the Second World War, 1936–1939* (London: Frank Cass, 1977), 41; Nicole Jordan, *The Popular Front and Central Europe: The Dilemmas of French Impotence, 1918–1940* (Cambridge, England: Cambridge University Press, 1992), 91; Thomas L. Sakmyster, *Hungary, the Great Powers, and the Danubian Crisis, 1936–1939* (Athens, GA: University of Georgia Press, 1980), 61.

[50] Weinberg, *Foreign Policy of Hitler's Germany*, 2: 253. See also DDF, 2nd series, 1 (Nos. 156, 256, 270).

[51] Réunion des chefs d'État-major général, 30 April 1936; DDF, 2nd series, 2: 217–18 (No. 138). Sakmyster, *Hungary, the Great Powers, and the Danubian Crisis*, 60.

[52] *Munich 1938: mythes et réalités*, 191.

[53] Orville H. Bullitt, ed., *For the President, Personal and Secret: Correspondence Between Franklin D. Roosevelt and William C. Bullitt* (Boston: Houghton Mifflin, 1972), 159.

[54] Taylor, *Munich*, 145.

[55] Bullitt to Secretary of State, 7 March 1936; *Foreign Relations of the United States: Diplomatic Papers 1936*, 5 vols. (Washington, DC: Government Printing Office, 1953–1954), 1: 213.

In November 1937, Hitler addressed his military leaders and laid out explicitly his plans of expansion. His views on Czechoslovakia came into especially sharp focus. He believed that Great Britain and Paris had already given up the idea of defending Czechoslovakia, that Germany was effectively poised to destroy it along with Austria. The incorporation of Czechoslovakia and Austria into the Reich would enable Germany to engage in the forcible deportation of 3 million persons from the two states, to increase the food supply at the disposal of Germany sufficiently to feed 5 or 6 million persons, and to raise an additional armed force of perhaps twelve divisions.[56]

A few days later, he received Neville Chamberlain's emissary, Lord Halifax, who confessed London's willingness to consider the revision of East European borders, including those of Czechoslovakia. At this point, Hitler obviously advanced his timetable.

In March 1938, he annexed Austria. Naturally, this step worried those powers of Eastern Europe that had profited by the collapse of Austria–Hungary in 1918. As the French military attaché reported from Vienna at the time, "the prestige of France in Central Europe, already seriously damaged by the events of 7 March 1936" – the Rhineland – "comes out of the Austrian affair, however much it might have been foreseen and inevitable,

---

[56] Niederschrift über die Besprechung in der Reichskanzlei am 5.ll.1937 von 16.15 Uhr bis 20.30 Uhr; Friedrich Hossbach, *Zwischen Wehrmacht und Hitler*, 2nd ed. (Göttingen, Germany: Vandenhoeck und Ruprecht, 1965), 181–9, especially 186–7. A. J. P. Taylor, *The Origins of the Second World War* (New York: Atheneum, 1966) once argued that the Hossbach memorandum was controversial, perhaps unreliable. Recent authoritative histories rely on it without reservations: Weinberg, *The Foreign Policy of Hitler's Germany*, Taylor, *Munich*; Ian Kershaw, *Hitler, 1936–45: Nemesis* (New York: Norton, 2000). Taylor's views of the matter have now been subjected to a detailed and devastating review in Gordon Martel, ed., *The Origins of the Second World War Reconsidered: A. J. P. Taylor and the Historians*, 2nd ed. (New York: Routledge, 1999), especially an article devoted precisely to Taylor on Hossbach, Richard Overy, "Misjudging Hitler: A. J. P. Taylor and the Third Reich," pp. 103–4: "Taylor had little respect [for] the so-called Hossbach memorandum.... Taylor was skeptical of its provenance and authenticity, and of the views it purported to express, partly, no doubt, on grounds of scholarship, but partly because the document – taken at face value – made it hard for him to argue that Hitler was at heart a moderate revisionist with no discernible program. *The authenticity and accuracy of Hossbach's account should no longer be in doubt.*" (Emphasis here is mine.) See the same decisive judgment in Jonathan Wright and Paul Stafford, "Hitler, Britain and the Hossbach Memorandum," *Militärgeschichtliche Mitteilungen* 42 (1987): 77–123, especially, 78–84, subtitled "The Authenticity of the Hossbach Memorandum"; and Bernd-Jürgen Wendt, *Grossdeutschland: Aussenpolitik und Kriegsvorbereitung des Hitler-Regimes* (Munich: Deutscher Taschenbuch Verlag, 1987), Chapter 1, "Der 5. November 1937: Ein 'Schicksalstag' der deutschen Geschichte?" pp. 11–37. His conclusion (was 5 November 1937, the day of the memorandum, fateful?): absolutely. In other words, there is now a formidable and authoritative historiographic tradition of the authenticity of Hossbach.

completely destroyed, even among those professing to be our most loyal friends."[57] Everyone understood clearly what the next step in Hitler's imperial plan would be.

The issue that gave Hitler an ostensibly respectable entrée into Czechoslovak politics was the presence there of the German minority known as the Sudetens. There were German minorities all over Europe, the legacy of the medieval German *Drang nach Osten*, a movement partly reflecting Catholic conversion crusades, especially the Teutonic Knights in East Prussia and farther north along the Baltic littoral, partly petty political imperialisms of both feudal and manorial colonization, and sometimes the commercial aggrandizement of the Hanseatic League. There were a million Germans in Poland, half a million in Hungary, half a million in Yugoslavia, nearly three quarters of a million in Romania, and over 3 million in Czechoslovakia. They had long been valued for the skills and capital that they brought and resented for their economic and technical superiority and the attitudes of cultural superiority that naturally accompanied them. Of course, they had occasioned more than a little trouble after their settlement – in the wars of religion of the Reformation era, the Thirty Years' War in particular, as well as in World War I. In World War II they more or less consciously designed and inflicted the trouble, as a consequence of which, in great part, they were subsequently driven out of most of the area in one of the largest instances of forced migration of modern times.

It was the thirteenth-century kings of Bohemia who facilitated the settlement of large numbers of Germans, especially merchants and mining engineers, inside the Sudeten Mountains (Erzgebirge and Riesengebirge) that form the present boundary between the Czech Republic and the Bundesrepublik. These communities governed themselves in some respects as independent city–states under the merchant law known as the Magdeburg Recht. During what was perhaps the most brilliant period of Czech history, Prague was the de facto capital of the German (Holy Roman) Empire under Emperor Charles IV (1346–1378), host of Cola di Rienzi and Petrarch, founder of Charles University and the spa at Carlsbad, and builder of the Charles Bridge and St. Vitus Cathedral.

Perhaps the harmony of German–Czech relations never recovered entirely from the religious dissent, proto-Protestantism, of John Hus (d. 1415) and the Hussite Wars that followed. The Thirty Years' War (1618–1648) was a continuation of the same struggle. It was in particular the loss of the Battle of the White Mountain (1620) in the suburbs of Prague that turned the tide in the conflict entirely in favor of the Germans, and the Imperial forces of the Counter-Reformation set out thereupon to deprive

---

[57] Lt.-Col. Salland, 21 March 1938; DDF, 2nd series, 9: 15–19 (No. 10).

the heretical Czech nation of its cultural roots and heritage. For two centuries, Czech virtually ceased to be a written language. By the middle of the nineteenth century, nationalistically minded lexicographers were giving it rebirth.

In the meantime, the politics of the Austrian Empire – successor to the defunct (1803) German Empire – ran a somewhat retarded course characteristic of the pan-European model of politics of the period. Awkwardly and by fits and starts, from the revolutions of 1848 to 1914, the Habsburgs introduced first cautious liberal constitutionalism and restricted electoral franchise and eventually universal manhood suffrage, and the Czechs acquired during the last generation of the Empire the right to use their own language in the administration of their own country. Yet the modern furies of rabid nationalism ran their natural course, too, and a variety of the multiple national units of this polyglot empire were only awaiting their opportunity to tear it apart.

And so, surprisingly suddenly, in 1918, when the loss of the war dissolved the Empire and conferred independence on the Czechs and Slovaks, the Germans east of the Sudeten mountains ceased to be the *Herrenvolk* and became a mere minority in a state of people whom they were accustomed to regard as inferior. When the new state of Czechoslovakia was formed, the Sudeten Germans were bent on joining the residual new Austrian Republic, but the Congress of Versailles decided otherwise. In the meantime, a provisional constitution was drawn up by a Czechoslovak committee and subsequently approved by a Czechslovak National Assembly. The Czechoslovak constitution was written, then, without regard to the views of the Germans, who were still clamoring for citizenship in the Austrian Republic. The constitution stipulated a parliamentary system in a bicameral legislature elected by proportional representation and a unitary state, not a federal organization; hence the more than 3 million Germans lacked, as did the other minorities – the Slovaks (2 million), the Magyars (745,000), the Ruthenians (460,000), and the Poles (76,000) – any mode of political expression independent of the Slavic majority of Czechs (6.8 million).[58]

If it was the interwar experience, and that of Munich in particular, that would make minority problems and ethnic conflict notorious in Eastern Europe, these matters were by no means obscure in 1919–1920, and the fathers of the new Czechoslovak state, the charismatic Tomáš Masaryk and his young assistant, Edvard Beneš, were fully sensitive to them. It was obvious to them at the time that the minority whose allegiance to its traditionally powerful big brothers next door might make it really

[58] Statistics from Seton-Watson, *Eastern Europe Between the Wars, 1918–1941*, appendix. Compare Rothschild, *East Central Europe Between the Two World Wars*, 89.

dangerous was the German one. Germany could likely not be forever so subdued as it was in 1919. Masaryk and Beneš, then, set out to win over the Germans, and the pattern of relations between Prague and the Sudetens ran a course almost precisely parallel to that of the relations of Berlin with Paris and London, an awkward period of adjustment down to the mid-1920s, a period of reconciliation and good feeling through the latter part of the 1920s, and, beginning with the great depression of 1929, a period of growing dissent and increasingly ugly demands for political revisions.

What was the basis for Sudeten discontent? Apart from the lack of a federal division of power, for which the Sudetens themselves were partly responsible, there was in the early years very little dissatisfaction, as the period of ethnic and political comity from 1925 to 1929 illustrated. The Sudetens were entitled to the use of German in government business in any region where two thirds of the population was German or to bilingual proceedings almost anywhere. They received more than their numerically proportionate share of the state educational budget. They did not receive their numerically proportional share of state civil service posts, because they made relatively little use of the Czech language, which was the official language of the state adjusted by the exceptions cited. When the depression struck, the tourist industry and the consumer-goods industry characteristic of the Western Sudeten regions of the country were especially hard hit, and the division of relief funds reflected a perfectly fair distribution under the administration of the minister of health, Dr. Ludwig Czech, who was, in spite of his name, a Sudeten German Social Democrat. Government construction contracts, on the other hand, tended to go to the larger Czech firms from Prague, as they were powerful enough to submit lower bids, and when those firms arrived for jobs in Sudeten areas, they naturally brought their own central Bohemian/Czech labor with them.

There were naturally complaints about these issues. Yet the Germans re-mained remarkably loyal to the basically Czech government. There were two German ministers in the government in the latter part of the 1920s, the only government on the continent at the time having minority rep-resentation! In the three elections of 1920, 1925, and 1929, 24 percent of the House of Deputies was elected by German parties, and 74–83 percent of the German votes were for parties loyal to the state. The electoral expe-rience of the republic demonstrates clearly that it was not the depression that generated the fatal discontent. Rather it was the propaganda and sub-versive agitation of Hitler in the context of the superior performance of the German economy across the frontier.[59]

[59] In the presentation of issues so controversial as these, viewpoint is important. I have drawn chiefly on Radomír Luža, *The Transfer of the Sudeten Germans: A Study of Czech–German Relations, 1933–1962*

The Sudeten Germans were, according to *Mein Kampf,* a principal objective of Hitler. Perhaps more significantly, given the manner in which he ignored Mussolini's Carinthian Germans in Northern Italy, the Sudetens presented him a fortunate instrument, a lever that he could use ostensibly in the name of the hallowed axiom of self-determination of nations. What we know of Hitler's published objectives and what we can observe of his pursuit of them suggest that the Sudeten Germans provided him the pretext that he needed to destroy Czechoslovakia. Hitler's primary early objective was the destruction of France, without which he did not feel safe to make his big move in the East. Yet he could not confidently attack France while leaving a viable Czechoslovak or Polish ally of France in his rear.

In fact, there scarcely was a Sudeten German issue before Hitler's becoming chancellor of Germany. There had long been a genuinely Czech and respectable party in Czechoslovakia known as the National Socialist Party. It was a Czech nationalist variant of social democracy without the internationalist impulse. It had nothing in common with the Nazi Party, the National Socialist German Workers' Party, which did, however, extend across the Czech border and assert itself in the wake of Hitler's triumph in Berlin, whereupon it was banned as a subversive organization.

In its place arose what was effectively a front organization for the Nazis, the Sudeten German Party, headed by Konrad Henlein. He declared that his party was not part of the German Nazis but was a loyal opposition, standing without reservation for a democratic republican form of Czechoslovak government. In fact, he got funds, advice, and instructions from Berlin, on which he was dependent. He was on standing orders to make "demands . . . that are not acceptable to the Czech Government"; "always to negotiate and not to let the link be broken, on the other hand, always to demand more than could be granted by the other side."[60] Whether it was precisely what he intended, he unavoidably became Hitler's proxy in Czechoslovakia, the instrument of a design larger than himself. Yet, always the British gentleman in London, Henlein invariably made a good impression there.

(New York: New York University Press, 1964) and J.W. Bruegel, *Czechoslovakia Before Munich: The German Minority Problem and British Appeasement Policy* (Cambridge, England: Cambridge University Press, 1973). Radomír Luža was a former Czech citizen whose father, General Vojtěch Luža, perished in the resistance during the war. Radomír was himself active in the resistance as well. J. W. Bruegel, on the other hand, was a Sudeten German and member of the Social Democratic party. Both books are sober and unpolemical. See also Victor S. Mamatey and Radomír Luža, eds., *A History of the Czechoslovak Republic, 1918–1948* (Princeton, NJ: Princeton University Press, 1973) and Robert W. Seton-Watson, *A History of the Czechs and Slovaks* (Hamden, CT: Archon Books, 1965).

[60] Report on Henlein's conversation with Hitler, 28 March 1938; DGFP, Series D, 2: 197–9 (No. 107); Secret instructions from German Foreign Office, 18 August 1938; ibid.: 587 (No. 369).

In Prague, at the center of the diplomatic maelstrom that this concatenation of developments was about to unleash, was President Edvard Beneš. Beneš had come of age politically during World War I as the protégé of the renowned Czechoslovak statesman, subsequently president of Czechoslovakia, Tomáš Masaryk. Together they were credited with achieving independence from Austria–Hungary and the formation of the new state. The confidence of Masaryk had given Beneš confidence, a great deal of it, and under Masaryk's wing, Beneš had served as foreign minister of the republic from 1919 to 1935. When Masaryk surrendered to old age and resigned the presidency in 1935, he designated, virtually ordained, Beneš as his successor, and Beneš was duly elected. Beneš's strong suit, however, remained foreign policy, and that is precisely the area in which he was about to be tested.

Beneš was a good deal of a lone wolf. In unusual circumstances, he became an indispensable lieutenant to the enormously prestigious Masaryk. In his early thirties he was the chief delegate of Czechoslovakia to the Paris Peace Conference. In fact, given his mastery of the arcana of Eastern Europe, its complex politics and ethnography, his knowledge of that troublesome area of the world extended his influence beyond strictly Czechoslovak questions. He assumed a stature to which few of the diplomats of that part of the world could presume.

Beneš remains a puzzling paradox of great gifts and common failures. We are now in possession of an authoritative biography drawn for the first time from the Beneš archive in Prague.[61] Physically modest, he was not modest intellectually, and his early successes nourished his vanity. Although he took a doctorate in philology from the distinguished Charles University, the oldest in Central Europe, he had, according to his biographers, a thin, nasal voice, and "never mastered the art of speaking in any language."[62] In fact, the German minister in Prague reported late in the 1930s that, although Beneš habitually spoke German with him, "he has only an imperfect command of it and frequently has to seek for the correct expression."[63] This was a remarkable shortcoming for an academic personality in Prague, where the intelligentsia had always been bilingual – Franz Kafka wrote in German.

Perhaps more remarkably, Beneš considered politics a "scientific pursuit," and he considered himself – ironically, given the outcome of his two great crises of 1938 and 1948, Munich and the communist coup of

[61] Zbyněk Zeman with Antonín Klimek, *The Life of Edvard Beneš, 1884–1948* (Oxford, England: Clarendon, 1997).

[62] Ibid., 12.

[63] Eisenlohr to foreign ministry, 11 November 1937; DGFP, Series D, 2: 38 (No. 18).

February 1948 – an infallible practitioner of politics.[64] "I have never failed in my life and never will," he was heard to boast. He had "an almost mystical *faith in his mission* derived from his conviction that he would certainly escape from any danger, including a hail of bullets in the front line." He did not delegate responsibility. "Beneš found it hard to tolerate rivals and competition in his proximity; and he did not like men who worked with him to express opinions different from his own." He bore grudges and did not forgive.[65] His talents were undeniable, yet few statesmen endured more shattering failures to render politics scientific. He proceeded with consummate self-assurance in the face of, into the maw of, disaster. As the crisis began to break, he spoke reassuringly to the nation by radio. "I have made plans for all eventualities," he said, "I see things clearly, and I have my plan."[66] Unfortunately, his were not the only plans, nor the most cunning nor powerful. More unfortunately, he was deserted by friends and allies who had committed themselves to him by treaty, allies who shared his interests, although they did not recognize it in time.

In foreign policy, Beneš was oriented toward Western Europe – Prague is west of Vienna. As he told the *London Times*, "We are a Western country, bound to the evolution of Western Europe."[67] The same point was made by Czechoslovak Foreign Minister Kamil Krofta, who spoke of "the desire to draw as close as possible to the culture and civilization of the West."[68] More particularly, Beneš was a Francophile. Yet he was acutely attuned to German sensibilities. He did not support the Franco–Belgian invasion of the Ruhr in 1923. He supported close relations between France and Britain, because he thought that Britain would restrain the more aggressive impulses of France in enforcing the letter of the law of the Versailles settlement. He had sponsored and facilitated German entry into the League of Nations in 1926. As he told Anthony Eden in March 1935, "I bear the burden of German proximity, but I bear it in the interest of all. That is why I always advise Paris to come to terms with Germany."[69]

Germany's minister in Prague, Ernst Eisenlohr, was a seasoned diplomat who, unlike many of Hitler's state servants, represented the reality of Czechoslovakia to his masters in Berlin in a thoroughly professional

---

[64] This was the first observation that Dr. Klimek made to me in our meeting at the Historical Institute of the Czech Armed Forces in Prague in June 1996.

[65] Zeman with Klimek, *Life of Edvard Beneš*, 2, 20, 47, 55, 60, 107.

[66] Hubert Ripka, *Munich: Before and After* (New York: Fertig, 1969), 111–12.

[67] Interview, 5 March 1938; *Documents on International Affairs, 1938*, 2: 118.

[68] Eisenlohr to foreign ministry, 21 December 1937; DGFP, Series D, 2: 81 (No. 38). Krofta spoke at a banquet in honor of visiting French Foreign Minister Yvon Delbos.

[69] Bruegel, *Czechoslovakia Before Munich: The German Minority Problem and British Appeasement Policy*, 175.

fashion. Soon after Eisenlohr took up his post in Prague (February 1936), Beneš invited him for a talk. In fact, as Eisenlohr reported, Beneš himself talked for the better part of three hours as if he were delivering a university lecture. As Eisenlohr explained, Beneš had necessarily based his foreign policy on the League and therefore on Britain and France, not on France alone, as was widely believed in Germany. He found in British policy the necessary corrective of excessively aggressive French enforcement of the peace. He had constantly urged more moderation on the French. He had had misgivings about the award of the Sudeten territories to Czechoslovakia in 1919. He had always urged German–French détente. He had tried in discussions with German Foreign Minister Gustav Stresemann (1923–1929) to establish more harmonious relations with Germany. He had repeatedly received friendly responses in private but never in public. The pact with Russia was based on fear of Germany. He was determined to fight communism in Czechoslovakia. He could have had a military convention with the Soviet Union but had refused, and he adamantly denied the perpetual German rumor that there were Soviet airfields in Czechoslovakia. Eisenlohr consistently reported that Beneš would make all necessary and reasonable concessions to the grievances of the Sudeten Germans for the sake of relations with Germany and political harmony inside Czechoslovakia.[70]

Eisenlohr did his job conscientiously and reported Beneš's intentions to Berlin persistently. He believed that Beneš's professions of good will toward Germany were genuine "for the simple reason that a politician of his experience must long since have realized that the most important condition for the maintenance of the State which he helped to create must be a permanent good relationship to the German people outside and inside the borders of the Czechoslovak State. For this reason I am also inclined to assume that he really wishes to improve the position of the German minority." He believed that he could not afford, however, to dispense with the French and Soviet alliances, "as he would otherwise be facing us alone and would have to become our vassal." Any pressure from Germany on the issue of Sudeten rights would unite the Czech people in suspicion of German intentions. A relaxation of relations between Germans and Czechs inside Czechoslovakia was possible only if Czechs developed "the confidence that we have no wish to touch the Czech nation and the Czechoslovak frontiers."[71] "[Beneš's] aim was to obtain for the Germans the status of full equality of rights and contentment within the State." He could not tolerate any interference from the Reich in a purely domestic question, but "he was always prepared to discuss minority question [sic]

---

[70] Eisenlohr to foreign ministry, 23 February 1936; DGFP, Series C, 4: 1177–83 (No. 580).
[71] Ibid., 11 November 1937; ibid., Series D, 2: 36–44 (No. 18).

with us in a friendly fashion."[72] Hitler, however, was cynically indifferent to such sweetly reasonable sentiments as these. He was determined to destroy Czechoslovakia.

As the conflict approached, Beneš looked to three sources of support, the French, the Soviets, and his nearby allies in the Little Entente. As German revisionism advanced, as the French moved more clearly into the camp of British appeasement, and as Soviet support of Czechoslovakia depended on the prior initiative of the French, Beneš's Little Entente allies, Romania and Yugoslavia, looked on nervously.

In the face of this new German *Drang nach Osten*, if the small states of the Little Entente could not count on the support of the French, then they had to consider making some kind of accommodation with the Axis powers. Yugoslav Premier Milan Stojadinović had specifically warned French Premier Léon Blum accordingly. After Ethiopia and the Rhineland, the Little Entente powers unavoidably began to make such policy adjustments. In March 1937, Stojadinović negotiated and signed with Italian Foreign Minister Galeazzo Ciano a treaty of friendship. They agreed to refrain from hostile acts against each other, to consult on matters of mutual interest in international affairs, to settle all disputes between them by peaceful means, "not to tolerate in their respective territories, or aid in any way, activities directed against the territorial integrity or the existing order of the other Contracting Party," and to make serious efforts to expand trade between them.[73]

An equally important element of the Little Entente's adjustment to German aspirations in Danubian Europe was a more flexible attitude toward the grievances of Hungary. Hungarian revisionism had to be accommodated somehow if it were not to serve as a cat's paw of Axis ambitions. Hungary was as intent as Italy and Germany on splitting the Little Entente, and it naturally sought the support of its two bigger co-conspirators to do so. There were, however, considerable differences of opinion on how to proceed. Hitler, focused on Prague, advised Budapest to seek rapport with Yugoslavia and Romania and territorial compensation from Czechoslovakia. Italy, in contrast, had long advised a pro-Romanian, anti-Yugoslav policy – before, of course, the treaty of March 1937. The Hungarians themselves preferred compromise with Yugoslavia, where their losses of 1919 had been relatively small, and pursuit of their much larger territorial claims against Romania.[74] In any event, it was largely the turning point of

[72] Ibid., 18 December 1937; ibid., 75–6 (No. 34).

[73] The Italo–Yugoslav Political Agreement of March 25, 1937; Hoptner, *Yugoslavia in Crisis*, 301–3.

[74] Magda Ádám, "La Hongrie et les accords de Munich (1938)," in *Munich 1938: mythes et réalités*, 43; idem, *Richtung, Selbstvernichtung: Die Kleine Entente, 1920–1938*, trans. Brigitte Engel (Budapest: Corvina, 1988), 111–12.

the Rhineland crisis that opened up sufficient doubts about the wisdom of the past policy on the part of the Little Entente powers and gave the Hungarians their opportunity.

A Hungarian delegation attended the Little Entente foreign ministers' meeting at Sinaia, Romania, in August 1937. It proposed to issue a declaration of nonaggression against the member states in exchange for the concession of equality in armaments, and it demanded improved conditions among Hungarian minorities in the three countries. The Yugoslavs were ready to negotiate, the Romanians deferred, and the Czechoslovaks demanded reciprocity. Negotiations were soon deadlocked. In April 1938, Hungarian Foreign Minister Kálmán Kánya went to Belgrade and offered to sign a treaty guaranteeing recognition of the Trianon frontier between Hungary and Yugoslavia in exchange for a declaration of Yugoslav neutrality. Stojadinović promised neutrality but refused to issue a declaration. At the Bled (Yugoslavia) meeting of Little Entente foreign ministers in August 1938, formal agreement was reached conceding Hungarian rights of arms equality in exchange for a declaration of nonaggression; but the disputes over the treatment of Hungarian minorities continued, because Budapest demanded considerably more of the Czechoslovaks than of the others, and Beneš refused to grant more than his allies had.[75]

By this time, Yugoslavia had moved far from the spirit of the Little Entente. In fact, Stojadinović had told his new friends in Italy that, if Hungary stayed out of the Munich conflict, he was indifferent to the outcome of it. Romania, however, at the heart of this story, remained loyal to Czechoslovakia and therefore a potential conduit of Soviet troops to assist Hitler's targeted victim, a subject that will be explored at length in subsequent chapters, as Romania's role in the crisis has been too little appreciated in the literature. Thus Soviet–Romanian relations must be examined with some care. Romanian policy naturally depended in great part on the support that it could expect from the great powers. And therefore we must first have a look at relations among the three potential great-power constituents of collective security: Moscow, Paris, and London.

---

[75] Ádám, "Documents relatifs a la politique étrangère de la Hongrie dans la période de la crise tchécoslovaque," 93–96; idem, *Richtung, Selbstvernichtung: Die Kleine Entente*, 129; Sakmyster, *Hungary, the Great Powers, and the Danubian Crisis*, 174.

PART ONE

Background of the Munich Crisis

Chapter 1

The Shaky Foundations of Collective Security: Moscow, Paris, London

On 11 March 1938, Hitler sent to Vienna the ultimatum precipitating the *Anschluss*. On the 12th, the German army marched in. On the 13th, the annexation of Austria to Germany was proclaimed.

Naturally, this development posed the question, as everyone understood, of the fate of the Sudetenland. In a move typical of Hitler's foreign policy – dishonest, deceptive, yet for a long time credible to the credulous – Field Marshal Göring contacted the Czechoslovak minister in Berlin and "gave [Vojtěch] Mastný his word of honor that the entry of German troops into Austria had been 'nothing more than a family affair' and that Germany was disposed to maintain her former policy of mutual improvement of relations with Czechoslovakia," as a proof of which, Prague was informed, the German army had been given strict orders not to approach closer than fifteen kilometers to the Czechoslovak frontier.[1] The Hungarian ambassador in Berlin, Döme Sztójay, witnessed Göring repeat the statement to Mastný three times. In private, on the other hand, in the absence of Mastný, when Sztójay raised the question of Czechoslovakia, Göring revealed a different plan: "At the present time, it is a question of arranging the affair of Austria, and subsequently the turn of Czechoslovakia will certainly come." He emphasized that "the preparations were not yet sufficiently advanced to be able to unleash an attack that would require considerable forces."[2] Göring's statement of reassurance, however, was given wide circulation by both the Germans and the Czechoslovaks.[3] Not everyone was reassured, and nervous diplomatic adjustments began at once.

---

[1] Eisenlohr (Prague) to Foreign Ministry, 12 March 1938; DGFP, Series D, 2: 157 (No. 72); same to same, 13 March 1938; ibid., 158–60 (No. 74).

[2] Sztójay to ministry, 12 March 1938; Magda Ádám, "Documents relatifs à la politique étrangère de la Hongrie dans la période de la crise tchécoslovaque (1936–1939)," *Acta historica Academiae scientiarum Hungaricae* 10 (1964), 103–4.

[3] Krofta to legations, 12 March 1938; V. F. Klochko, ed., *New Documents on the History of Munich* (Prague: Orbis, 1958), 17–18 (No. 1).

Anschluss was, of course, a direct challenge to collective security, the most material support of which was the Franco–Soviet Pact. In Moscow, however, the *Anschluss*, and especially the lack of response to it, looked very much like *déjà vu*. Already on the remilitarization of the Rhineland in March 1936, Foreign Commissar Maksim Litvinov spoke his mind about Anglo–French apathy to U.S. Ambassador William Bullitt. Litvinov, Bullitt wrote, displayed almost violent rage. Bullitt asked him whether he would not welcome the German–Lithuanian nonaggression pact that Hitler had typically offered in the aftermath in order to calm the alarm of Europe. It would mount a barrier, Bullitt observed, to a German attack on the USSR. Litvinov "replied that the promise of a dog, liar, and blackguard like Hitler was worthless to Lithuania or any other country. Litvinov said that he was disgusted by the proposal of Hitler to reenter the League of Nations" – another gossamer bait that Hitler had dangled – "and even more disgusted by the fact that the British would welcome the reentry of Germany." It would mean, Litvinov said, "the death of the League. The League has no meaning at all unless it stands for collective security. . . . It is impossible to imagine the League functioning in the direction of collective security if Germany is a member of the League."[4] Bullitt asked Litivinov "if he hoped that France would march troops into the Rhineland." Litvinov replied – and here is a surprise for much of the traditional historiography – "that *he did not as that would mean immediate war*." He thought, on the other hand, "that there was no chance whatsoever that French troops would enter the Rhineland."[5]

About the same time, Soviet Ambassador Ivan Maiskii shared with his French colleague Charles Corbin in London a note that he had addressed to the Foreign Office. It cited the familiar list of German treaty violations and suggested that German aggression could only be curtailed by a resolute opposition rather than by acquiescing in the deeds and proposals of the Reich. "The government of the USSR is ready to take part in any action against Germany that is decided by the League of Nations," but it was opposed to any negotiation with Germany.[6]

As Paris and London reacted to this idea with their usual nonchalance, Maiskii sketched in a speech to a Socialist and Trades Union meeting the threatening implications of ignoring Soviet proposals of collective security. Try to imagine the world, he suggested, without the Russian Revolution: "Tsarist Russia would by now be either crushed by other aggressive Powers

---

[4] Bullitt to Secretary of State, 7 March 1936; *Foreign Relations of the United States: Diplomatic Papers, 1936*, 5 vols. (Washington, DC: Government Printing Office, 1953), 1: 212–13. Of course, the question of German reentry into the League was soon forgotten.

[5] Ibid. (emphasis mine).

[6] Corbin to Quai d'Orsay, 10 March 1936; DDF, 2nd series, 1: 486 (No. 366).

and made their vassal, or she would have joined the Fascist League of aggressors." In either event, there would be "a tremendous bloc of aggressive States, stretching from the Far East to the North Sea, and Western Mediterranean, having at its disposal unlimited resources in men, materials and technique, ensuring its absolute invincibility in any struggle with the rest of the world. The Western democracies would be in mortal peril." Not even the intervention of the United States would essentially redress the correlation of forces. "Let them ponder on this, those who, while protesting their interest in the cause of progress and democracy, are apt to cast a stone against the real or imaginary shortcomings of the U.S.S.R. The mere existence of the Soviet Union greatly assists all forces of progress and peace and puts a check on all forces of reaction and war."[7]

About the same time, Litvinov himself was making the same point in a different manner. In December 1937 he granted an interview to the correspondent of the French newspaper, *Le Temps*, who made notes for French Ambassador Robert Coulondre. Litvinov expressed himself *"avec sévérité"* on the policy of France in general and on its attitude toward the USSR in particular.

M. Luciani asked what Litvinov's own reaction was to the unsatisfactory state of Soviet relations with France:

Litvinov: "Other arrangements (*combinaisons*) are possible."
Luciani:　"With Germany?"
Litvinov: "Why not?"
Luciani:　"But is a German–Soviet rapprochement possible?"
Litvinov: "Perfectly. In acceding to power, Hitler renewed the treaty of
　　　　　 1926 with us. He wanted to remain on good terms with us. He
　　　　　 changed his attitude when he realized that we were opposed
　　　　　 to German expansion in Central Europe, that we wanted to
　　　　　 maintain the territorial status quo, that by our policy of collective
　　　　　 security we formed an obstacle to his projects."

Litvinov added that the security of France depended on defending the system of Versailles, for which Moscow, not represented there, was not responsible.[8]

Ambassador Coulondre took Litvinov's threat seriously. He observed that the Soviet government "could be led eventually to envisage a rapprochement with Germany. Presuming to consider an entente with the Reich as easy from the moment when the USSR ceased to defend the maintenance of the status quo in Europe, he added that such a thing could

[7]　Max Beloff, *The Foreign Policy of Soviet Russia, 1929–1941*, 2 vols. (New York: Oxford University Press, 1947–1949), 2: 108 (24 November 1937).
[8]　Note de M. Luciani, 25 December 1937; DDF, 2nd series, 7: 787–8 (No. 390, annexe).

be arranged without the formalities of treaties. . . . It is improbable, given the seriousness of the subject, even while speaking unofficially to a journalist, that M. Litvinov would have dared upon such a point without having been authorized in advance from on high, and his declaration appears to me as a sort of warning that the Soviet government wished to give us in a roundabout way." Taking full account of all the ulterior motivations that might be imagined – the fear of being left out of a general European diplomatic settlement, the fear that the imperial ambitions of the Reich threaten the Soviet Union itself, or the mortal danger that a war would pose to the Soviet Union in its present internal crisis – we can recognize, Coulondre wrote, that "if they are abandoned by us, the Soviets would consent to serious sacrifices in order to obtain from Germany at least a truce that would assure them the several years of respite that they need." Coulondre was convinced that Moscow sought above all to avoid diplomatic isolation in Europe. "In order to define our eventual attitude toward the Soviets, we must take into account that if the USSR is not with us, it will be against us."[9]

Coulondre repeated the warning insistently through the following spring. "If the Western powers should permit the strangulation of Czechoslovakia, the Soviet government would then break with [collective security] and turn to Germany, leaving it a free hand in Europe." The Soviets' fear of isolation might suffice to make them consent to a German alliance. They might be willing to sacrifice even the Comintern, and for Hitler such a sacrifice might suffice to prompt the reorientation of his Soviet policy.[10]

If Soviet isolation were to be avoided, then France would be obliged to offer Moscow something more tangible than the mutual-assistance pact of 1935. In any event, once Hitler focused the attention of the continent on his next quarry, it would have been logical for the French and the Soviets to make contingency plans. Moscow had long proposed to engage in General Staff talks to form a military convention, as the French and the Imperial Russians had done in 1894. The Soviets were obviously more eager for the idea than the French. The French evidently understood their mutual-defense pact with Moscow to form an obstacle to a Nazi–Bolshevik understanding, and apparently that was all that they sought from the pact. They were, then, satisfied with their relations with Moscow.[11]

---

[9] Coulondre to Delbos, 28 December 1937; ibid., 785–6 (No. 390).
[10] Coulondre to Bonnet, 31 May 1938; ibid., 9: 965–76 (No. 492).
[11] Robert J. Young, *In Command of France: French Foreign Policy and Military Planning, 1933–1940* (Cambridge, MA: Harvard University Press, 1978), 93; Martin S. Alexander, *The Republic in Danger: General Maurice Gamelin and the Politics of French Defence, 1933–1940* (Cambridge, England: Cambridge University Press, 1992), 292.

From the early fall of 1936, on the other hand, the Soviet ambassador in Paris, V. P. Potemkin, began to complain with some regularity of the deference that France exhibited to London and its indifference to relations with Moscow.[12] Édouard Daladier was serving at the time as minister of defense – at the time of Munich, he would be both defense minister and premier – and he, like others in the French government, was afraid that military talks with Moscow would offend the British.

The French military was actuated by the same fear. In September 1936, General Victor-Henri Schweisguth, deputy chief of staff, observed and reported on the annual Soviet military maneuvers.[13] He and his Soviet host, Commissar of Defense Marshal Kliment Voroshilov, traded assessments of the probable intentions of Hitler. Schweisguth suggested that Hitler looked on the USSR as the source of all the evils of Europe, that he accused Czechoslovakia of being complicit with Moscow in them, and that he was possibly contemplating taking possession of Bohemian airfields in order to preempt what he perceived as a planned Soviet aerial bombardment of Germany. Voroshilov disagreed. He thought that all of Hitler's railing against the Soviets was but a mask to disguise his real intention of destroying France. Obviously, each of them was trying to enhance the value of the alliance of his own country in the eyes of the other.

Voroshilov insisted that Hitler intended to attack France first in order to rid himself of danger from that quarter. He thought that Hitler would be sufficiently rearmed to take the initiative in two years. This same line of argument – France as Hitler's preeminent target – was pursued by officials of the foreign commissariat as well. They regretted the lack of French response in the Rhineland in March 1936; they believed that Hitler would have withdrawn. "Only one attitude is possible vis-à-vis Germany: to oppose to it the greatest firmness; to reinforce the bloc of nations loyal to the [League] pact; not to separate the East and the West in the organization of collective security." These officials insisted that Hitler would attack first in the west, and Soviet Chief of Staff Marshall Mikhail Tukhachevskii had himself spoken to Colonel Paul de Villelume, a General Staff liaison officer at the French Foreign Ministry, "with a certain insistence on the interest that the two general staffs shared in exchanging information."

Finally, Schweisguth observed that Moscow seemed to want ever-closer cooperation with France, perhaps a military convention. Yet, on the other hand, it also preferred to see France become the first target of Hitler's attack, which would leave it in the position of the United States in 1918, that

---

[12] Potemkin to Commissariat of Foreign Affairs, 17 September 1936; DVP SSSR, 19: 428–9 (No. 269).
[13] Schweisguth report, 5 October 1936; DDF, 2nd series, 3: 511–14 (No. 343).

is, in a position to serve as the arbiter of the continent on which the other powers would be exhausted by a long struggle.

Daladier took careful note of Schweisguth's report before forwarding it to Minister of Foreign Affairs Yvon Delbos, accompanied by his own remarks. The suggestion of General Staff talks "follows similar initiatives that have been repeated for more than a year." Daladier thought that it would be better to precede such talks by an agreement between the French and the Czechoslovak General Staffs to which the Soviets might then be invited to accede. Any such talks would, however, animate the German fear of encirclement and perhaps render the situation more dangerous than it already was.[14]

In the early spring of 1937, Moscow posted a new military attaché to Paris, obviously with instructions to return to the subject of General Staff talks. General A. S. Semenov held a series of talks from January through March with Schweisguth and Villelume as well as with the principal political figures in French government.[15] In January, he spoke with Premier Camille Chautemps, who observed that it was a risky business to proceed with military talks until they were better prepared for war, which news of such talks might make more likely.[16] In the middle of February, Potemkin was talking to Premier Léon Blum, and General Semenov was discussing the project with the army chief of staff, General Louis Colson.[17] Potemkin said that Soviet military aid to France could be extended in two variants. If Poland and Romania "fulfill[ed] their duty" and provided the necessary means of transport for passage of Soviet troops across their territories, either on their own initiative or in consequence of a decision of the League of Nations, "in this case, the USSR will itself lend its assistance with all [branches of] its forces and to the indispensable extent [dans la mesure indispensable] that must be defined by a special agreement between the interested states." On the other hand, "if, for incomprehensible reasons, Poland and Romania oppose the extension of Soviet assistance to France and Czechoslovakia and do not consent to permit passage of Soviet troops over their territory, in this case the assistance of the USSR will necessarily be limited." Moscow would in these circumstances send land forces to France by sea – "Potemkin personally insisted on this

[14] Daladier to Delbos, 13 October 1936; ibid., 510–11 (No. 343).

[15] Alexander, Republic in Danger, 299–302; Nicole Jordan, The Popular Front and Central Europe: The Dilemmas of French Impotence, 1918–1940 (New York: Cambridge University Press, 1992), 262–77; Michael J. Carley, 1939: The Alliance That Never Was and the Coming of World War II (Chicago: Ivan R. Dee, 1999), 24–6; Telford Taylor, Munich: The Price of Peace (New York: Vintage, 1980), 512–15.

[16] Potemkin's notes on conversation, 19 January 1937; DVP SSSR, 20: 43–6 (No. 20).

[17] Potemkin to Commissariat of Foreign Affairs, 17 February 1937; ibid., 88–9 (No. 50).

point" – and air forces to Czechoslovakia and France. "The scope of this aid should be defined by a special accord among the interested states." In either case, the USSR could furnish fuel oil/heating oil [*mazout*], lubricants [*des huiles*], manganese, foodstuffs, armaments, [including] motors, assault tanks, planes, etc."[18]

In the same conversation, Potemkin pointedly asked what kind of assistance France could offer the Soviet Union, and he wanted it spelled out precisely. At the end of the interview, General P.-H. Gerodias raised the curious question why the Soviets could not envisage passage of their troops through Lithuania. Potemkin said that the Soviet General Staff envisaged passage over states friendly to France, that if other avenues were available, it was up to France, in agreement with the USSR, "to prepare them." Here is a vitally important point, and it will reappear, as we shall see, in the relations of both these powers with Romania.

At a subsequent meeting in March, an occasion witnessed by General Schweisguth, Potemkin read to Blum a very cordial personal letter from Stalin on the need for a military alliance. One historian of the scene says that Blum was "impressed"; another, that he was "shaken."[19]

The French military exhibited no enthusiasm for the Soviet overtures. In fact, the military chiefs engaged in deliberate stalling tactics. As Gamelin wrote to Schweisguth, "We need to drag things out .... we should not hurry but avoid giving to the Russians the impression that we were playing them along, which could lead them into a political volte-face [i.e., with Germany] .... gain time, without rebuffing the Russians and without proceeding to staff talks."[20] In the meantime, Semenov left for consultations in Moscow, promising to return in a matter of weeks. In fact, he never returned. An embassy colleague told the French that he had undergone a "serious operation"[21] – undoubtedly a ballistic operation. By this time, Potemkin had gone to Moscow to assume the position of deputy commissar of foreign affairs, and he complained to the new Soviet ambassador in Paris, Iakov Surits, in May that the staff talks were still not proceeding.[22]

By this time, the French General Staff was committing to paper its deliberations on the proposal.[23] It observed that the Franco–Soviet Pact was directed expressly against Germany. Drawn up within the framework of the League Covenant, it came into play under particular conditions: a

[18] Blum's notes, 17 February 1937; DDF, 2nd series, 4: 787–8 (No. 457).
[19] Carley, *1939: The Alliance That Never Was*, 26; and Jordan, *The Popular Front and Central Europe*, 262, respectively, both using the Schweisguth papers in the Archives nationales.
[20] Carley, *1939: The Alliance That Never Was*, 25, referring to Schweisguth papers.
[21] Taylor, *Munich*, 513.
[22] Potemkin to Surits, 4 May 1937; DVP SSSR, 20: 227–8 (No. 137).
[23] Note de l'État-major de l'Armée: réflexions sur les conséquences possibles d'un contact militaire franco-soviétique, May 1937; DDF, 2nd series, 5: 825–8 (No. 480).

unanimous recommendation of the League Council, the decision of the
two countries alone in default of a unanimous League decision, or the
recognition of German aggression by the signatories of Locarno. In view of
the fact that League unanimity was impractical and that the remilitarization
of the Rhineland had rendered Locarno superfluous, the activation of the
Franco–Soviet Pact at that point depended on Moscow and Paris alone.

The conclusion of the pact, the General Staff document noted, had provoked unfavorable reactions in Germany, Poland, and Romania. Poland
had made it plain that it would never grant passage to Soviet troops and
announced that close French relations with the Soviet Union were incompatible with such relations with Poland. Nicolae Titulescu of Romania had attempted a rapprochement with Moscow, but it encountered
strong opposition. Among members of the Little Entente, both Romania
and Yugoslavia, unlike Czechoslovakia, worried about Soviet designs in
Southeastern Europe.

Any Franco–Soviet military convention would necessarily stipulate Soviet movement across either Poland or Romania or both. "It seems
very difficult, in these conditions, to open military negotiations with the
USSR without indicating their scope to the general staffs of Warsaw and
Bucharest, without which, rightly or wrongly, they will continue to suspect that the invasion of their countries has been studied and prepared in
spite of them." Moreover, Yugoslavia could not be brushed aside. Both
Poland and the Little Entente, then, would have to be informed.

Thus it was a question of drawing up a balance sheet of advantages
and disadvantages of the diverse reactions of different countries to such a
convention.

Advantages: It would place the power of Russia more securely in the
French camp. It would strengthen the security of Poland and Romania
against Germany *on the condition that* they accept Soviet assistance, which
was improbable for Poland and doubtful for Romania.

Disadvantages: It would provoke a vehement reaction, at least in Germany. It would risk the disruption of the Franco–Polish alliance and the
formation of a German–Polish alliance. It would risk the breakup of the
Little Entente and the consolidation of a Polish–Romanian bloc capable
of neutralizing the USSR and leaving France alone to face Germany. It
would offend English opinion (the French documents habitually designate
the British as English – Norman Davies would not). The gravest dangers
for France would be the provocation of a German declaration of war and
the abandonment of France by Britain.

Conclusion: French security rested above all on a close understanding
with England. In the event of conflict, English strength was worth more
to France than Russian strength, as the experience of the last war demonstrated. A closer Russian alliance was desirable if the English would tolerate

it, as Russian power was more substantial than that of the Little Entente. Therefore any military convention with the USSR must follow an understanding on the question with England and be preceded by a Soviet pact of assistance with Poland and the Little Entente, which in present circumstances seemed impossible. Such a convention might well drive Poland into the embrace of Germany. Yet without it, there was the prospect of driving the Soviets and Germany together.

However severely we may judge the inadequacies of French defense policy and diplomacy in the period, we must admit that the logic of this document is formidable and impeccable. In short, here was a nearly intractable dilemma.

If a choice of alternatives at some early date in May 1937 thus appeared difficult, help soon came from Moscow. On 26 May, Tukhachevskii was arrested, and that fact precipitated a decision in Paris. Gamelin observed that the Soviet Union "is annihilating itself . . . . we must not breathe a word of Russian passage across [Poland and Romania]; those people have placed themselves outside humanity."[24] The advocates of the alliance were seriously embarrassed. As Schweisguth put it, "If we had listened to them, we would have had an accord now, which would have been signed [by] Toukhatchevsky."[25]

At this point, early in June the French General Staff repeated – and *revised* – the assessment of a prospective Soviet military convention that it had drawn up just a month previously. This new assessment came to more unambiguous conclusions than the preceding one, and, in particular, it took into account, as the previous one had not, the internal situation of the Soviet Union, which had become so spectacular in the intervening few weeks. It began by largely repeating the analysis of the previous assessment, including a nearly identical list of advantages and disadvantages. The risk of German–Polish rapprochement was this time assessed as especially serious, as it would lead to a bloc of 100 million people, and the Polish army, equipped and supplied by the arsenals of Germany, would be able to hold the Soviet army in check, which would, in turn, relieve pressure on Germany's Eastern frontier such that it could direct its whole force against France. It would also supply Germany with the agricultural resources to enable it to endure a long war. Thus a Franco–Soviet rapprochement might well yield "a null or even negative result."

Now for the first time, it observed that "the internal situation of Soviet Russia, and especially the complete instability of the military high command, considerably diminish the authority of the Soviet officers who would at present be designated to establish liaison with the representatives

[24] Pierre le Goyet, *Le mystère Gamelin* (Paris: Presses de la Cité, 1975), 205–6.
[25] Jordan, *The Popular Front and Central Europe*, 279.

of the French General Staff," and it mentioned in particular the disgrace of Tukhachevskii and his entourage. Especially troubling was the unforeseeable nature of such events. Hence talks with the Soviet high command must be postponed at least until the present purge passed: "It seems then that before engaging in military conversations, it would be prudent to wait for the appearance of a certain internal pacification in the USSR."[26] Here, then, was the end of the affair of General Staff talks. The French ambassador in Moscow, Robert Coulondre, continued to lobby for them, but the French military was not listening.[27] The Soviet army requested an invitation to observe French army maneuvers in September 1937, but the request was rejected.[28]

Soviet Foreign Commissar Maksim Litvinov was soon to observe to American Ambassador Joseph Davies that "France has no confidence in the Soviet Union and the Soviet Union has no confidence in France."[29] Stalin himself later explained matters to Charles de Gaulle in similar terms: "When we concluded the Franco–Soviet pact, we did not sufficiently understand. Later, we understood that Laval and his colleagues did not trust us as allies. In signing the pact with us, they wanted to entangle us and to prevent us from forming an alliance with Germany. We Russians also did not completely trust the French, and this mutual distrust spoiled the pact."[30]

The two basic axioms of French foreign and defense policy in the 1930s were that France could not survive another war of attrition on her own soil and that France lacked the financial, economic, and demographic resources to confront Germany alone.[31] Having abandoned the idea of a close reliance on the Soviets, the French then turned inevitably to Britain. And there the French found their support virtually as frail as the Soviets found that of the French.

In fact, the French response to *Anschluss* largely validated Moscow's judgment of French policy. On the day afterward, 14 March, the French minister of foreign affairs, Joseph Paul-Boncour, asked the British government

[26] Note de l'État-major de l'Armée sur l'éventualité d'un contact militaire franco–soviétique, 9 June 1937; DDF, 2nd series, 6:50–2 (No. 35).

[27] Robert Coulondre, *De Staline à Hitler: souvenirs de deux ambassades 1936–1939* (Paris: Hachette, 1950), 140, 142–6, 153.

[28] Anthony Adamthwaite, *France and the Coming of the Second World War* (London: Frank Cass, 1977), 73.

[29] Diary entry, 18 March 1938; Joseph Davies, *Mission to Moscow* (New York: Simon & Schuster, 1941), 290.

[30] *Sovetsko-frantsuzskie otnosheniia vo vremia Velikoi Otechestvennoi voiny, 1941–1945: dokumenty i materialy*, 2 vols. (Moscow: Gospolitizdat, 1983), 2: 165 (No. 88).

[31] Henry Dutailly, *Les problèmes de l'armée de terre française (1935–1939)* (Paris: Imprimerie nationale, 1988), 18–19.

to declare publicly that, if Germany attacked Czechoslovakia and France went to the defense of the victim, the British government would declare war in support of France. The British Cabinet predictably declined.[32] It was a decided British policy at the time to take a position of ambivalence and caution in respect to the Sudeten problem. The British government did not wish the French government to count *on* British support nor the German government to count *against* it.[33] This was the gist of Chamberlain's statement in the House of Commons on 24 March: "His Majesty's Government would not pretend... that, where peace and war are concerned, legal obligations are alone involved and that if war broke out it would be likely to be confined to those who have assumed such obligations.... This is especially true in the case of two countries with long associations of friendship like Great Britain and France."[34]

While French and British policy continued to be defined principally by somnolent, aimless drift, Hitler's own moves catalyzed the pace of developments and posed questions of urgent decisions. On 23 April, just over a month after Austria had been absorbed into Germany, the Sudeten German Party of Czechoslovakia opened its annual congress in Karlsbad. Konrad Henlein, the Party's Führer, in response to Hitler's private instructions to insist on concessions that were insatiable, impossible, demanded among other things the legal entitlement to carry on Nazi propaganda inside Czechoslovakia.[35] It soon became obvious that a Sudeten crisis was being brewed and seasoned as surely as the *Anschluss* had been.

As Göring's reassuring lie to the Czechs grew more and more obvious – *Anschluss* was a family affair and Germany had no designs on Czechoslovakia – and an atmosphere of danger, more serious this time, spread abroad, it was symptomatic of the moral crisis of Europe that the French ministers were repeatedly hastening to Britain, while the British ministers themselves scurried to Germany. The French were seeking support. The British were seeking relief.

Of course, personal factors played a role, in many respects a decisive role, in the development of the crisis. Neville Chamberlain has traditionally borne the bulk of the onus for the discredited policy of appeasement. The reputation of no one else has suffered so much from the failure of the policy. Yet he was not a narrow-minded ignoramus. Although he had no

[32] Phipps to Halifax, 15 March 1938; DBFP, 2nd series, 2: 50 (No. 81); Halifax to Phipps, 15 March 1938 and note, Ambassade de France à Londres (enclosure in No. 82), 13 March 1938; ibid., 50–1 (No. 82).

[33] Diary entry, 7 March 1938; Oliver Harvey, *Diplomatic Diaries, 1937–1940*, ed. John Harvey (London: Collins, 1970), 110.

[34] *Documents on International Affairs, 1938*, ed. Monica Curtis, 2 vols. (New York: Oxford University Press, 1943), 2: 120–3, quote on 122.

[35] *Documents on International Affairs, 1938*, 2: 136.

higher education, he was interested in music and art and went to concerts and exhibits regularly. He practiced gardening, was notorious for fishing, went on hunting parties, kept a bird house at home. He enjoyed historical biographies, for example, of Napoleon, of Pitt, of Canning. He was not gregarious, not a clubby type, and did not care for dinner gatherings, which interfered with his work in the evenings.

At the time of his coming to 10 Downing Street (May 1937), he manifestly represented the characteristic outlook of the British public on appeasement in general and policy toward Germany in particular. In the opinion of one close student of his policy, he came to power with his whole diplomatic game plan in mind and persuaded the cabinet to follow him.[36] That game plan was to appease until the British program of rearmament enabled him, by 1939 as he thought, to do otherwise, a policy sometimes called cunctation.[37] He was unusually self-confident, certain that he had more ability than the colleagues with whom he worked – as his letters to his sisters amply testify – and his natural authority led them to his own views with remarkable ease. Hence he naturally lacked the faculty of critical evaluation, especially of his own judgment. "It seemed impossible for him to think himself mistaken."[38]

Yet the onward march of Hitler's uncontested successes did gradually erode public respect for Chamberlain's foreign policy. By the time of Munich his government was no longer able to use the term "appeasement" in public in spite of its vigorous management of the press. As early as February 1938, at the time of Anthony Eden's resignation as foreign secretary, an apparently reliable poll showed that 58 percent of Britons did not approve of Chamberlain's foreign policy, that 71 percent thought Eden right to resign.[39] As he began to lose approval, Chamberlain reacted self-righteously. He described the Labor opposition as "a pack of wild beasts . . . I think what enables me to come through such an ordeal [of criticism in the Commons] successfully, is the fact that I am completely convinced that the course I am taking is right, and therefore [I] cannot be influenced by the attacks of my critics."[40]

To make matters worse, neither could he be influenced by the advice of his friends, which he avoided. In July 1937, U.S. President Roosevelt proposed to Chamberlain an Anglo–American consultation on international threats to the peace. Without consulting his foreign secretary, Chamberlain

---

[36] Keith Middlemas, *Diplomacy of Illusion: The British Government and Germany, 1937–1939* (Aldershot: Gregg Kevivals, 1991), 59.

[37] Robert A. C. Parker, *Chamberlain and Appeasement: British Policy and the Coming of the Second World War* (New York: St. Martin's, 1993), 101.

[38] Ibid., Chapter 1, "Personality and Policy," quotation on p. 11.

[39] Middlemas, *Diplomacy of Illusion*, 287.

[40] Ibid., 290.

abruptly refused – he did not like Americans: "We have the misfortune [here] to be dealing here with a nation of cads."[41] Churchill's reaction was appropriate: "To Britain [American support] was a matter almost of life and death. . . . That Mr. Chamberlain, with his limited outlook and inexperience of the European scene, should have possessed the self-sufficiency to wave away the proffered hand stretched out across the Atlantic leaves one . . . breathless with amazement."[42]

In November of 1937, Chamberlain decided to send an emissary, Lord Halifax, on a visit to Hitler for conversations that, in his opinion, might lead to a clearing of the air or to an improvement of Anglo–German relations designed to improve the prospect of peace. Again, he proceeded without reference to his foreign secretary or, in this case, the cabinet.[43] In May of 1938, Chamberlain proclaimed, again without consultation with his foreign secretary, that the form of Czechoslovakia would have to be adjusted.[44] As the Sudeten crisis heated up, Chamberlain was ill and away on vacation virtually the whole month of August. The cabinet met only once, on the 30th, for the first time in five weeks.[45]

In the meantime, Chamberlain relied on a select, curtailed inner cabinet of himself, Sir John Simon (Exchequer), Sir Samuel Hoare (Home Secretary), and Lord Halifax, who had by this time succeeded the dissident Anthony Eden at the Foreign Office. This group was convoked, consulted, cultivated, and managed with some regularity. Yet even these colleagues were bypassed on what was Chamberlain's most spectacular initiative in foreign affairs, his heralded trip to confront Hitler face-to-face at Berchtesgaden on 15 September – "Plan Z," as he called it. Chamberlain discussed it with Sir Horace Wilson before the end of August and informed the cabinet after he had telegraphed the idea to Hitler.[46] Before the second of his meetings with Hitler at Godesberg, Chamberlain was instructed by the cabinet to break off talks if Hitler introduced the subject of Polish and Hungarian claims on Czechoslovakia, but he violated the instructions.[47] Finally, in the opinion of Halifax's secretary, by the time of Munich, Chamberlain "has cut loose from his Cabinet. He has no proper

[41] Ibid., 143ff.; Parker, *Chamberlain and Appeasement*, 44.
[42] Winston S. Churchill, *The Second World War*, 6 vols. (New York: Bantam Books, 1961), 1: *The Gathering Storm*, 229.
[43] Frank McDonough, *Neville Chamberlain, Appeasement and the British Road to War* (Manchester, England: Manchester University Press, 1998), 51; Middlemas, *Diplomacy of Illusion*, 132ff.
[44] Middlemas, *Diplomacy of Illusion*, 230.
[45] McDonough, *Neville Chamberlain*, 63; Middlemas, *Diplomacy of Illusion*, 336.
[46] Ian Colvin, *The Chamberlain Cabinet: How the Meetings in 10 Downing Street, 1937–1939, Led to the Second World War* (New York: Taplinger, 1971), 153.
[47] Ibid., 161. Harvey, *Diplomatic Diaries*, 191.

official advisers and it has never entered his head to take Halifax with him [to Munich]."[48]

Across the channel, his beleaguered nominal counterpart was the Radical Socialist leader, Édouard Daladier, the executive chief of a formerly formidable country currently undergoing "*la décadence*," "the hollow years," the doldrums of the Third Republic. Reputed a dynamic and strong personality, the "bull of the Vaucluse" – his critics said that he had the horns of a snail – was about to have his mettle tested to the limit. Serving simultaneously as premier and minister of defense, he was not on good terms with his chief of the General Staff, General Maurice Gamelin, and he did not have full confidence in his foreign minister, the ill-reputed Georges Bonnet, who was perhaps in spirit Chamberlain's real counterpart in France.

In fact, Daladier was most unfortunate in the frail support that he found in Gamelin and Bonnet. At home, Gamelin was a dedicated pessimist, using the most unrealistically inflated figures of German military strength. He thought Germany might be able at the time of Munich to mobilize as many as 200 divisions, including 50 divisions facing the French frontier.[49] When summoned to the joint cabinet meetings in London, on the other hand, he gave an altogether confident performance. Although he wished to conceal from the British the weakness of the French air force, he asserted that the preponderance of force on the allied side would eventually prevail. Now he said – this time accurately – that the Germans had only eight divisions on the French frontier. The French army could be ready for the offensive against the German front in five days, he asserted. It would advance easily against the hastily improvised system of German fortifications, the Siegfried Line, then withdraw to the Maginot Line to wait for the Germans to break their strength against it. Why should they do that? he was asked. He had no clear answer, although he had eccentric ideas of driving through the Italian Alps to Vienna[50] – as Bonaparte had done in 1796–1797. At home, he was talking of attacking the Italians in Libya – as a way of defending Prague![51]

Georges Bonnet at the foreign ministry virtually conducted an independent foreign policy of his own. He was notoriously proappeasement.

---

[48] Ibid., Entry of 29 September 1938; 202.

[49] Williamson Murray, *The Change in the European Balance of Power, 1938–1939: The Path to Ruin* (Princeton, NJ: Princeton University Press, 1984), 218–19, 221; Pierre Le Goyet, *Munich, "un traquenard"?* (Paris: France-Empire, 1988), 116.

[50] Taylor, *Munich*, 859–60 (whose sources here are cabinet papers); Girard de Charbonnières, *La plus évitable de toutes les guerres* (Paris: Albatros, 1985), 167.

[51] Peter Jackson, *France and the Nazi Menace: Intelligence and Policy Making 1933–1939* (New York: Oxford University Press, 2000), 283–4.

As early as 20 July, quite without the authorization of the French Cabinet or consultation with Daladier, he undertook to warn Czechoslovak Ambassador Štefan Osuský that France would not honor its alliance: "The Czechoslovak government should have a clear understanding of our position: France will not go to war over the Sudeten affair. Of course, we will publicly affirm our solidarity as the Czechoslovak government desires – but this affirmation of solidarity should permit the Czechoslovak government to obtain a peaceful and honorable solution. In *no case* should the Czechoslovak government believe that if war breaks out will we be at its side, especially as in this affair our diplomatic isolation is almost total."

Bonnet's notes on his conversation with Osuský were found after the war with Daladier's comments scribbled on them. Daladier wrote that French foreign policy was formed by "the council of ministers and not by the decision of [single] minister [sic].... F[rance] will make war if aggression [sic] ...?"[52] In the meantime, while Bonnet assured the Germans that France *would* fight if Czechoslovakia were attacked,[53] he continued to assure the Czechoslovaks that it would not. On 16 September, he reiterated the warning to Osuský: "I repeated to him that it was out of the question that France would march in this affair if there were not a complete agreement on all points with Great Britain.... I begged M. Osuský to advise M. Beneš in Prague at once and to discontinue the illusions in which he has lived for so many months."[54] According to the most authoritative study of French policy in the Munich crisis, Bonnet had a "personal policy." He modified or suppressed despatches and telephoned instructions to ambassadors without always keeping an official ministerial record. In other words, he used his position to represent and misrepresent both official policy and the record of it.[55]

Daladier was honest and graft-free. A widower, he had long lived with his two sons and his sister. He had been in the trenches in World War I. He was a serious student of history. In the face of decision, he deliberated, reconsidered, and equivocated. He lacked the stature of Georges Clemenceau and Raymond Poincaré, "he worried ceaselessly as to what he was going to do, what he was doing, and what he had done." In the face of war, he was "possessed of an [executive] omnipotence quite out of tune

[52] Note of Bonnet, 20 July 1938; DDF, 2nd series, 10: 437–8 (No. 238). Duroselle, *La décadence, 1932–1939*, 334–5; idem, "Introduction," *Munich 1938: mythes et réalités*, 37.

[53] Welczek (ambassador) to Foreign Ministry, 2 September 1938; DGFP, Series D, 2: 682–4 (No. 422).

[54] Notes of Bonnet, 16 September 1938; DDF, 2nd series, 11: 267–8 (No. 177).

[55] Yvon Lacaze, "Daladier, Bonnet and the Decision-Making Process during the Munich Crisis, 1938," in Robert Boyce, ed., *French Foreign and Defence Policy* (London: Routledge, 1998), 224; also Lacaze, *La France et Munich: étude d'un processus décisionnel en matière de relations internationales* (Bern, Switzerland: Peter Lang, 1992), passim.

with his temperament.... He was sustained neither by an impelling force from within nor by any plan of action adopted once and for all. Conscious of his weakness, he feared that all could see it .... he had neither the true freedom which comes from a self-sufficient intellect nor that which springs from strength of character."[56] In the face of the crisis, he seemed capable of managing it. He told the British ambassador, Sir Eric Phipps, early in September that, if Germany attacked Czechoslovakia, "the French will march as one man." Meanwhile, Bonnet, according to Phipps, was desperate to avoid a fight.[57] Late in September, American Ambassador William Bullitt found the same attitude: "Just after seeing Bonnet this morning I saw Daladier. If Bonnet was devious and weak Daladier was sure of himself and strong."[58]

Yet Daladier was, beyond the borders of France, weak because France was weak. Hence he and France became the dependents of Britain, and the British knew it. As Robert Coulondre – French ambassador in Moscow 1936–1938, in Berlin 1938–1939 – observed, after the *Anschluss* Chamberlain and the British took every initiative without consulting the French.[59] When bilateral consultations were required, the French flew to London – repeatedly. Although the British Cabinet consulted the Germans before sending a mediator into the Sudeten conflict, it did not consult the French; nor did London share the news of this mission in Prague with Paris until it was nearly six weeks old.[60]

It was Daladier who first had the idea of what today would be called a summit meeting among the chiefs of Britain, France, and Germany. On 13 September, he telephoned Chamberlain to say that "it is necessary... to convene the political leaders of England, Germany, and France in order to discuss the possibilities of a peaceful settlement."[61] Chamberlain avoided him and responded the following day that he was considering "another possibility."[62] That possibility was Plan Z, the meeting at Berchtesgaden that *left Daladier out.*

[56] Pertinax (André Geraud), *The Gravediggers of France: Gamelin, Daladier, Reynaud, Pétain, and Laval: Military Defeat, Armistice, Counterrevolution* (Garden City, NY: Doubleday, 1944), 88, 102, passim.

[57] Élisabeth du Réau, *Édouard Daladier, 1884–1970* (Paris: Fayard, 1993), 254.

[58] Bullitt to Secretary of State, 26 September 1938; Orville H. Bullitt, ed., *For the President, Personal and Secret: Correspondence Between Franklin D. Roosevelt and William C. Bullitt*, intro. George F. Kennan (Boston: Houghton Mifflin, 1972), 290.

[59] Coulondre, *De Staline à Hitler: souvenirs de deux ambassades 1936–1939*, 134.

[60] Jean-Baptiste Duroselle, "Introduction," *Munich 1938: mythes et réalités*, 37–8; 38 idem, *La décadence, 1932–1939* (Paris: Imprimerie nationale, 1985), 340.

[61] Daladier to Chamberlain (telephone conversation), 13 September 1938; DDF, 2nd series, 11: 195 (No. 122).

[62] Halifax to Phipps, 14 September 1938; DBFP, 3rd series, 2: 318 (No. 866). Colvin, *The Chamberlain Cabinet*, 152.

The balance of deference between these two allies obviously did not favor France, and when the French were treated to a dismissively humiliating lack of consideration again and again, it naturally led to some bitterness, which Daladier later expressed to U.S. Ambassador Bullitt: "Daladier [said] that he considered Chamberlain a dessicated stick; the King a moron; and the Queen an excessively ambitious woman who would be ready to sacrifice every other country in the world in order that she might remain Queen Elizabeth of England. He added that he considered Eden a young idiot and did not know for discussion one single Englishman for whose intellectual equipment and character he had respect. He felt that England had become so feeble and senile that the British would give away every possession of their friends rather than stand up to Germany and Italy."[63] Of course, the British regard for their French allies was equally as contemptuous. As Halifax's private secretary put the matter, Georges Bonnet was "a public danger to his own country and to ours."[64] In the British Cabinet, it was commonly observed that the French had "no Government, no aeroplanes, and no guts."[65]

And yet, in the various meetings between them, suspicion was suppressed and civility prevailed. On 28–29 April, Daladier and company were in London for a meeting with the British Cabinet. Chamberlain commented on the military weakness of both France and Britain and observed that "if the German Government decided to take hostile steps against the Czechoslovak State, it would be impossible, in our present military situation, to prevent those steps from achieving immediate success." The present composition of the Czechoslovak state seemed sufficiently problematic, in any event, as to make its recomposition in present form of doubtful prudence even after a successful war. President Beneš must be persuaded to make all reasonable concessions.[66]

The French delegation brought to London quite a different perspective. Previous French foreign ministers, Yvon Delbos and Joseph Paul-Boncour, had warned London that Hitler's agenda included the incorporation of Austria and the destruction of Czechoslovakia. Delbos had insisted that, if Prague managed to satisfy Henlein, Hitler would find another prextext of dissatisfaction.[67] J. W. Bruegel suggests that if Delbos or Paul-Boncour

[63] Bullitt to Secretary of State, 6 February 1939; Bullitt, *For the President, Personal and Secret*, 310.

[64] John Harvey, ed., *The Diplomatic Diaries of Oliver Harvey, 1937–40* (London: Collins, 1970), 233.

[65] Colin Coote, *A Companion of Honour: The Story of Walter Elliot* (London: Collins, 1965), 162.

[66] Record of Anglo–French conversations, held at No. 10 Downing Street, 28–9 April 1938; DBFP, 3rd series, 1: No. 164, pp. 198–234 (here 214); DDF, 2nd series, 10 (No. 258). The substance of the texts is the same. Given the fact that the conversations took place in British circumstances, I have assumed superior authority in the English text.

[67] J. W. Bruegel, *Czechoslovakia Before Munich: The German Minority Problem and British Appeasement Policy* (Cambridge, England: Cambridge University Press, 1973), 165.

had been at the Quai d'Orsay in the summer of 1938, "there never would
have been the pilgrimage to Canossa renamed Munich."[68]

It was, however, Daladier and the dissonant Bonnet who were in
charge. Daladier took issue with Chamberlain. He said that in his opinion "Czechoslovakia had done more for the minorities than any other
European State.... Nowhere else had greater concessions been made to
minorities." Daladier was convinced that "Herr Henlein was not, in fact,
seeking any concessions and that his real object was the destruction of
the present Czechoslovak State." It was not on Prague, then, that pressure must be brought but on Germany. Daladier said that, had he been
in power at the time of the Rhineland reoccupation, he would have opposed it by force! After the Rhineland had been remilitarized, Austria had
been destroyed, and today it was a question of Czechoslovakia. Tomorrow
it would be Romania, "and when Germany had secured the petrol and
wheat resources of Roumania, she would then turn against the Western
Powers, and it would be our own blindness which would have provided
Germany with the very supplies she required for the long war which she
admitted she was not now in a position to wage."[69] Although "every effort should be made to avoid war...," he continued, "war could only be
avoided if Great Britain and France made their determination quite clear
to maintain the peace of Europe by respecting the liberties and the rights
of independent peoples. If we were to act accordingly... to save the independence of Czechoslovakia" after she had made reasonable concessions,
"then he felt an improvement would take place in the European situation.
Only then could we expect to see Yugoslavia,... Roumania and perhaps
even Poland, change their present attitude and give us their support in the
cause of peace. If, however, we were once again to capitulate when faced
by another threat, we should then have prepared the way for the very war
we wished to avoid."[70]

Daladier's observations were flawlessly prophetic, but they made little
impression in London, as Chamberlain was naturally of a different opinion.
To take the sort of strong stand that Daladier recommended, he said, was to
engage in "what the Americans in their card games called bluff," whereas
"for his part he doubted very much whether Herr Hitler really desired to
destroy the Czechoslovak State."[71]

Daladier reminded his British colleagues that it was Hitler who was
on the offensive, who was playing the game of bluff, whereas the French
were simply committed by duty and law to positions of a purely defensive

[68] Ibid., 167.
[69] DBFP, 3rd series, 1: 216–17.
[70] Ibid., 217–18.
[71] Ibid., 220–1.

character, to a treaty that threatened no one. "If we submitted on every occasion before violent measures and the use of force, the only result would be to precipitate renewed violence and ensure further success for the use of forceful methods." If Germany were allowed by Western passivity to master more and more the resources of Central and Eastern Europe, then "countries which were now hesitating would feel compelled to submit to the hegemony of Germany and then, as we had been warned in 'Mein Kampf', Germany would turn to the west," thus precipitating a catastrophe.[72] It was precisely what France's eastern allies were warning of.

No consensus was reached, of course, but we must credit Daladier's foresight as tantamount to the wisdom of hindsight. He was virtually reciting the prologue of World War II. Britain, of course, had no army. The French army had no offensive capacity. And the Red Army had no legitimate mode of access to Germany. Yet Hitler's bluff could be called, *as on the eve of Munich it was*, thus bringing him to the conference that bears the name.

Still, at the time of the Anglo–French meeting, there was little immediate cause for alarm, as Hitler was in no hurry. Just as he had needed time to digest the Rhineland, so did he need such time, as Göring had suggested to Hungarian Minister Sztójay, to digest Austria before "the time for Czechoslovakia will certainly come."

The Czechoslovak military was convinced that its preparations would enable it to give a good account of itself in a conflict with Germany so long as such a challenge found the Czech border fortifications *properly mobilized and manned*. The most important consideration here was not to be taken by surprise, not to face a German attack without full alert and mobilization. Hence, in the imagination of the Czech General Staff, the most favorable case that Hitler might devise for his planned offensive would be to disguise his own mobilization and preparation for attack in the form of conventional exercises for the training of troops. He had sprung the *Anschluss* in just such a fashion.

Municipal elections were scheduled in Czechoslovakia for Monday 22 May, and in the excited conditions of the spring of 1938, they naturally stimulated in the Sudeten provinces somewhat more passion, turbulence, and, most important, provocation than so ordinary an event would usually have done. In these circumstances came reports on 19 May of substantial German troop movements – ten divisions or so in the vicinity of Dresden – in the direction of the Czech frontier. The British and the French ambassadors in Berlin despatched the news immediately. The Czechoslovak General Staff called up reserves and manned the frontier in what amounted to a partial mobilization. The French and the Soviet Foreign Offices

---

[72] Ibid., 225–6.

announced that their respective countries would stand by their obligations to the Czechoslovaks. More dramatically, on 21 May and again the following day the British sent to Berlin a stern warning: "If... a conflict arises, the German Government must be well aware of the dangers which such a development would involve. France has obligations to Czechoslovakia and will be compelled to intervene in virtue of her obligations if there is a German aggression on Czechoslovakia.... In such circumstances His Majesty's Government could not guarantee that they would not be forced by circumstances to become involved also."[73]

The war scare was all a mistake somehow. No German attack was planned. The intelligence was false. How it occurred has never been clarified, although there are hypotheses.[74] It was nevertheless consequential. The Czechoslovaks were reassured – misled, perhaps, as it turned out – by the support of their allies and sympathizers, and the conclusion that the friends of collective security were eager to draw from this episode was that it was precisely the British warning that had stayed Hitler's hand. Of course, as this version of events began to fill the European press, it made the Führer furious. On May 30, Hitler signed a directive to his high command: "It is my unalterable decision to destroy Czechoslovakia by military action" not later than 1 October.[75]

From 30 May, Hitler, stirring up the Sudeten German Party by instructions and financial support, orchestrated a crescendo of terrible tension. It climaxed, not entirely according to his plans, in the last two weeks before 1 October. At the annual party conference in the Sudetenland on 24 April, Henlein announced the notorious Karlsbad program, a list of demands, one of which was the freedom to carry on Nazi propaganda inside Czechoslovakia. The British minister in Prague, Sir Basil Newton, was not optimistic about the prospects of a realistic compromise: "My intuitive impression [is] that the Sudeten German party might continue indefinitely to exact from the Czechoslovak Government the maximum concessions obtainable under whatever pressure could be applied, and that then, however favourable the position achieved might be, they would feel perfectly

---

[73] Halifax to Henderson (Berlin), 21 May 1938; ibid., No. 250, pp. 331–2; Henderson to Halifax, 21 May 1938; ibid., No. 254, pp. 334–5.

[74] See, e.g., Igor Lukes, "Did Stalin Desire a War in 1938? A New Look at the May and September Crises," *Diplomacy and Statecraft* 2 (1991): 3–53; idem, *Czechoslovakia Between Stalin and Hitler: The Diplomacy of Edvard Beneš in the 1930s* (New York: Oxford University Press, 1996), 143–57.

[75] In Weinberg's characterization, "at a time of great international tension, reports of really routine German troop movements were mistaken as presaging an immediate attack on Czechoslovakia." In his opinion, the public rejoicing at Hitler's humiliation in the foreign press did not alter his timetable; it merely exacerbated his disposition. Gerhard Weinberg, *The Foreign Policy of Hitler's Germany*, 2: *Starting World War II, 1937–1938* (Chicago: University of Chicago Press, 1980), 367, 369.

free to secede and break up the Czechoslovak Republic if it suited their purpose or that of the German Reich to do so."[76] In fact, as we have seen, the Sudeten party was instructed to do precisely that.

Beneš tried to persuade the British Cabinet that Czechoslovak democracy offered its German community justice and fair play. He had used an interview with the *London Times* to demonstrate that the situation of the Sudeten Germans was not one of typically East European oppression of a minority. He offered facts. The Germans comprised 22 percent of the population of the country; yet the German – that is, the German-language – university in Prague received 24 percent of the state university budget. The German technical schools of Prague and Brno received 29 percent of the technical-school budget. There was in Czechoslovakia one Czech school for every 127 students; one German school for every 115 students. In Czechoslovakia there was one German school for every 862 Germans; in Prussia, one for every 1,112.[77]

The Chamberlain cabinet was not persuaded, and Chamberlain displayed once again his inclination to believe that only he could manage the situation. The consequence was the notorious Runciman mission. Lord (Walter) Runciman of Doxford was deputed to go to Czechoslovakia on a fact-finding mission that inevitably turned into a mission of mediation. Chamberlain had typically asked the Germans if they objected and asked the Czechoslovaks if they would accept the mission. He did not refer to the French, but the Czechoslovaks naturally did. There were few plausible reasons for refusing, and it was not refused.

Runciman was experienced in British politics, not in foreign affairs, and certainly not in the intricacies of the ethnography and politics of Eastern Europe. He spent approximately six weeks in Czechoslovakia, conferring chiefly with Henlein, while Henlein conferred with his Nazi managers in Germany. The British Cabinet, believing that Beneš rather than Hitler was the problem – as Sir Nevile Henderson, British ambassador in Berlin, put it, the solution lay not in Berlin but in Prague – was able to use Runciman to bring considerable pressure on Beneš to accept a radical compromise with Henlein.[78] On 7 September, Beneš capitulated and accepted, in what came to be known as the "Fourth Plan" (of concessions), the Karlsbad program itself. As one of the Sudeten German leaders lamented with astonishment, "My God, he's given us everything!" This development "sent the Sudeten

---

[76] Newton to Halifax, 10 May 1938; DBFP, 3rd series, 1: 277–80 (No. 201).

[77] 5 March 1938 interview, *Sunday Times; Documents on International Affairs, 1938*, 2: 119–20.

[78] On the Runciman mission, see Lukes, *Czechoslovakia Between Stalin and Hitler*, 179–90; *Survey of International Affairs, 1938*, 2: 206–62; Bruegel, *Czechoslovakia Before Munich*, 228–91.

Germans into a panicky search for excuses to break off negotiations."[79] They found it in a riot against the police that they helped to provoke in Moravská Ostrava.[80]

The farce of accommodation that played out in Beneš's acceptance and Henlein's rejection of the Fourth Plan was one transient consequence of the Runciman mission. The other was the "Runciman report." Although no such report had been charged to him, Runciman evidently felt that some such summary of his experience and findings was appropriate. It appears that he wrote up his opinions in a personal letter to Chamberlain and that Chamberlain then intervened to suggest the incorporation of his own revisions by the Foreign Office before the document was published. In any event, although Runciman had told the cabinet on his arrival that "there was a considerable percentage of people in the German area who did not wish to be incorporated in the Reich," there was no such suggestion in the published report, which, in fact, is a very vulnerable document[81]:

> In my opinion – and, I believe, in the opinion of the more responsible Sudeten leaders – [the Fourth Plan] embodied almost all the requirements of the Karlsbad 8 points, and with a little clarification and extension could have been made to cover them in their entirety. Negotiations should have at once been resumed on this favourable and hopeful basis; but little doubt remains in my mind that the very fact that they were so favourable operated against their chances, with the more extreme members of the Sudeten German party. It is my belief that the incident arising out of the visit of certain Sudeten German Deputies to investigate into the case of persons arrested for arms smuggling at Mährisch-Ostrau [Moravská Ostrava] was used in order to provide an excuse for the suspension, if not for the breaking off, of negotiations. The Czech Government, however, at once gave way to the demands of the Sudeten German party in this matter, and preliminary discussions of the 4th Plan were resumed on the 10th September. Again, I am convinced that this did not suit the policy of the Sudeten extremists, and that incidents were provoked and instigated on the 11th September and, with greater effect after Herr Hitler's speech, on the 12th September. As a result of the bloodshed and disturbance thus caused, the Sudeten delegation refused to meet the Czech authorities as had been arranged on the 13th September. Herr Henlein and Herr Frank presented a new series of demands – withdrawal of State police,

---

[79] Weinberg, *The Foreign Policy of Hitler's Germany*, 2: 420.

[80] Bruegel, *Czechoslovakia Before Munich*, 248; Parker, *Chamberlain and Appeasement*, 160.

[81] Bruegel, *Czechoslovakia before Munich*, 274–8 (quotation from cabinet papers); idem, "Dossier Jaromír Necas," in *Munich 1938: mythes et réalités*, 140. Bruegel has found discrepancies between the unpublished and published versions of the Runciman document and interviewed the Foreign Office author of the published version.

limitation of troops to their military duties, etc., which the Czechoslovak Government were again prepared to accept on the sole condition that a representative of the party came to Prague to discuss how order should be maintained. On the night of the 13th September this condition was refused by Herr Henlein, and all negotiations were completely broken off.

Responsibility for the final break must, in my opinion, rest upon Herr Henlein and Herr Frank and upon those of their supporters inside and outside the country who were urging them to extreme and unconstitutional action.

Evidently to balance the ledger of the assets and liabilities of the two parties in conflict, Runciman at this point turned his attention to the government's case in Prague. At this point, however, his remarkably concrete and factual presentation of the Sudeten brief turned conspicuously abstract and impressionistic. In fact, he rested his case on the word *impression*.

"I have much sympathy, however, with the Sudeten case. It is a hard thing to be ruled by an alien race; and I have been left with the impression that Czechoslovak rule in the Sudeten areas for the last twenty years, though not actively oppressive and certainly not 'terroristic', has been marked by tactlessness, lack of understanding, petty intolerance and discrimination, to a point where the resentment of the German population was inevitably moving in the direction of revolt."

Although Runciman had told the cabinet on his return that he had no recommendations to make, by the time of the composition of the report, recommendations had emerged, and they form a striking contrast to the thrust of his previous judgments:

1. That the Sudeten provinces "should be given full right of self-determination at once."
2. "That those parties and persons in Czechoslovakia who have been deliberately encouraging a policy antagonistic to Czechoslovakia's neighbours should be forbidden . . . to continue their agitations.
3. "That the Czechoslovak Government should so remodel her foreign relations as to give assurance to her neighbours that she will in no circumstances attack them or enter into any aggressive action against them arising from obligations to other States.
4. "That the principal Powers, acting in the interests of the peace of Europe, should give to Czechoslovakia guarantees of assistance in case of unprovoked aggression against her.
5. "That a representative of the Sudeten German people should have a permanent seat in the Czechoslovak Cabinet."[82]

---

[82] Runciman report: Runciman to Chamberlain, 21 September 1938; *Documents on International Affairs, 1938*, 2: 218–24.

In retrospect, points 2, 3, and 5 of these recommendations seem unavoidably ironic. In the first place, there were at the time three German ministers in the Czechoslovak cabinet of fifteen. Second, points 3 and 4 suggest, as Duff Cooper commented at the time, that "great brutal Czechoslovakia was bullying poor, peaceful Germany."[83] Cooper was at this time virtually alone in the cabinet in opposing further appeasement. As he put the choices facing Great Britain, it was not a question of war or peace; it was rather a question of war now or war later. He was not without supporters elsewhere, however. There was notoriously, of course, Churchill, but there were other voices, too. Sir Robert Vansittart, permanent undersecretary at the Foreign Office, had stood squarely against appeasement throughout, although it had cost him much influence. Colonel Josiah Wedgwood has been described as a maverick Labour member of Parliament. He warned the government, as if with clairvoyance, "Every time you sacrifice one of your potential allies to this pathetic desire to appease the tyrants, you merely bring nearer and make more inevitable that war which you pretend you are trying to avoid."[84] The government's men stood in the main, however, squarely for appeasement. The British ambassador in Paris was Sir Eric Phipps, a dedicated appeaser. As the crisis approached, Phipps wrote home to the Foreign Office that all that was best in France stood for peace at almost any price.[85] Perhaps more shockingly, the most notorious of the appeasers, Sir Nevile Henderson, wrote home the most amazing appeal: "I do wish it might be possible to get at any rate *The Times*, Camrose, Beaverbrook Press etc. to write up Hitler as the apostle of peace. It will be terribly short sighted if this is not done."[86]

By this time, however, Chamberlain was deeply involved in the conferences with Hitler at Berchtesgaden and Godesberg, negotiating over foreign property in which he had no direct interest without consulting the people who did. It left the Czechoslovaks unavoidably tense. It was only while Chamberlain was literally in the air on his way to Berchtesgaden that Henlein finally embraced the claim of self-determination – *Heim ins Reich* (Home in the Reich), he said.[87] Little could he have imagined the end result of that claim in 1945, the so-called Beneš decrees expelling the 3.5 million Sudeten Germans, with allied blessing, from Czechoslovakia.

The dependence of Soviet action on French cooperation and the dependence of French action on British cooperation continued to paralyze efforts to organize a genuine collective security. Litvinov made several

---

[83] Duff Cooper, *Old Men Forget* (New York: Dutton, 1954), 221.

[84] Commons debates, 26 July 1938; Hansard, 5th series, 338: col. 2994.

[85] Phipps to Halifax, 24 September 1938; DBFP, 3rd series, 2: 510 (No. 1076).

[86] Henderson to Cadogan, 26 July 1938; ibid.: 257 (No. 793).

[87] *Documents on International Affairs, 1938*, 2: 205–6.

tangible proposals to France, and through France to Great Britain, on 2 September. He suggested, first, that the League should be asked to consider the question of a German attack on Czechoslovakia under Article 16; second, that the three governments declare their commitment to oppose aggression in the Sudeten crisis; and, third, that the General Staffs of the three countries confer on common measures to take against the aggressor if Czechoslovakia were attacked.[88] For nine long days, no answer was forthcoming. On 11 September, Bonnet informed Litvinov in Geneva that London – and therefore France, of course – had turned down all three proposals.[89]

In the meantime, however, both the French and the Soviets were turning their attention to the cooperation of Romania in providing a feasible route for the intervention of Soviet forces to assist Czechoslovakia, and France in particular began to represent Romania as the last best hope of peace or war.

[88] Payart to Bonnet, 2 September 1938; DDF, 2nd series, 10: 934–5 (No. 534).
[89] Litvinov (Geneva) to Commissariat of Foreign Affairs, 11 September 1938; DVP SSSR, 21: 487–8 (No. 343).

Chapter 2

Soviet–Romanian Relations I: 1934–1938

During the bulk of the 1920s, Soviet diplomacy had dealt by preference with that other outcast of Europe, Germany, and attempted to play it off against the victors of Versailles and their somewhat cozy and complacent club, the League of Nations – "League of Imperialist Aggressors," as it was affectionately known in Moscow. When the Great Depression hit the continent in 1929, Moscow mistook it for the prelude to the revolution that had been so devoutly desired. To expedite the process, it refused to cooperate with the German centrist parties against the Nazis and Nationalists – the Comintern follies of the "Social–Fascist line" – and contributed thereby to a German revolution of quite a different kind. Hitler's Nazi regime was initially misread in the same myopic fashion as the prelude to the real one, and so the Social–Fascist line continued its merry way until it nearly provoked a similar Fascist revolution in republican France.

A series of four events forced Moscow to a sober reappraisal of the wisdom of its foreign policy. In diplomatic developments, the Germans and the Poles signed a nonaggression pact in January 1934. In April Moscow proposed and Germany rejected the idea of a more comprehensive Baltic security pact. In the meantime, developments in the domestic affairs of the continent were no more reassuring. In February 1934 the united front from below – the Social–Fascist line – triggered the Stavisky riots in Paris and nearly collapsed the Third Republic. Finally, Hitler's blood purge of the Nazi *Sturmabteilung* (Storm Troopers) on 30 June 1934 signaled the stabilization of his power. The sum of these events prompted the reversal of the outworn Comintern tactic and the introduction of the Popular Front. At the same time, as Germany dropped out of the League of Nations, the Soviet Union dropped in, and Maksim Litvinov began to preach there what in retrospect is recognized as the obvious wisdom – and the futile aspiration – of collective security.

As Litvinov looked west with a new Soviet perspective, he found in the expanse of the continent an already complex and nominally formidable

53

series of security arrangements designed to bolster the territorial status quo, especially against the presumed threat of German revisionism: the Franco–Polish alliance, the Franco–Czechoslovak alliance, the Little Entente, and the Locarno arrangements. It was instruments of this kind that he was concerned with developing and strengthening. In an unmistakably tangible sign of the new trend in Soviet foreign policy, Moscow established formal diplomatic relations with Romania and Czechoslovakia simultaneously on 9 June 1934. A more dramatic and more substantive manifestation of the new policy was the Franco–Soviet Mutual-Assistance Pact of 2 May and the subsequent similar Czechoslovak–Soviet Pact of 16 May 1935.

The most obvious liability of the Soviet–Czechoslovak Pact was the fact that Czechoslovakia and the Soviet Union had no common frontier. The two states were separated by Poland and Romania, and, as both of these powers had long experience of hosting Russian armies and paying the territorial price, neither was eager ever to do so again. Yet the issue of Red Army access to Czechoslovakia necessarily posed over and over again the question whether either of these countries might grant the Soviet forces transit rights.

Poland was the larger and the stronger country. It was also more vehemently anti-Russian as well as anticommunist. Its foreign policy, under the firm control of Colonel Józef Beck, was stubbornly maverick and independent. As Beck was uncooperative even with Paris, there was little hope of his collaborating with Moscow. Colonel Beck was convinced that France would constantly yield and never fight, and he was summarily skeptical of the idea of collective security. He was committed therefore – naively and tragically – to good relations with Germany.

Romania appeared, from the viewpoint of Soviet assistance to Czechoslovakia, a less serious obstacle, and Moscow clearly recognized its geographically crucial position in the Soviet security system. If Moscow's obligations to Czechoslovakia were to be turned from theory into practice, then some kind of understanding with Romania appeared indispensable.

The international circumstances of Romania in 1938 had been produced by World War I and Versailles. The war had brought an abundance of both bad fortune and good – in that order – to the young state (b. 1866) of Romania. The Russian Revolution and the peace of Brest-Litovsk – the collapse of the Eastern front – forced the Romanians to make a punitive peace with Germany in May 1918. A series of factors, however, soon reversed Romanian fortunes – the collapse of Austria–Hungary as well as of Russia, the defeat of Bulgaria, and the general European antagonism to the revolutionary regime of Béla Kun in Hungary. Romania was thus able to reenter the war and to emerge in possession of Greater Romania, annexing Transylvania, Bessarabia, Bukovina, and Dobrogea. Of course, these developments antagonized the victims of Romanian expansion and required the response of a Romanian security system. The formation of the Little Entente (Romania, Czechoslovakia, and Yugoslavia) in 1920–1921 was directed against Hungary. The Romanian–Polish alliance of 1921 was directed against the Soviet Union. The Balkan Entente of 1934 (Romania, Yugoslavia, Greece, and Turkey) was directed against Bulgaria. In the 1930s, in the face of German and Italian revisionism and the community of interests that these two powers naturally enjoyed with a Hungary aggrieved against Romania, Bucharest had every reason to support collective security, and it did so, especially in the wake of the Soviet pacts with France and Czechoslovakia.

The great statesman of Romanian foreign policy, Nicolae Titulescu, predicted in 1934 either the triumph of collective security or a German pact with the Soviets directed against Poland as a prelude to a new world war. As his successor, Nicolae Petrescu-Comnen, similarly foresaw in mid-1938, if Czechoslovakia were lost to the Germans, Poland would follow, and then would come the turn of Romania. The logic, then, of Soviet needs, Romanian needs, of collective security, and of the constellation of affairs on the continent more generally suggested the conclusion of some kind of military pact between Moscow and Bucharest.

There were three clear obstacles. Most generally, there was the widespread Romanian fear, on the part of the political parties and the public alike, of Soviet Communism. More specifically, there was the issue of Bessarabia. It had changed hands time after time, in 1812, 1856, 1878, and most recently in 1918, when the Russian Revolution had given the Romanians the opportunity to reclaim it. Moscow refused to recognize the Romanian annexation. Finally, there was the Romanian alliance with Poland, which was directed against the Soviet Union and clearly stipulated no alteration of either Polish or Romanian foreign policy in respect to the big Eastern neighbor without the prior agreement of the other signatory.

Of primary importance in the evolution of Soviet–Romanian relations was the Romanian regard for the personality who was the custodian of Soviet foreign policy. Fortunately, we have an authoritative account of the matter in the memoirs of a Romanian career diplomat who was minister of foreign affairs at the time of Munich, Nicolae Petrescu-Comnen. Comnen observed Maksim Litvinov over a period of more than ten years. First impressions were not good, but they evolved significantly. He saw Litvinov for the first time at the League Disarmament Conference in November 1927, and, as he records, the older delegates were curious about the novelty of the appearance of a Soviet delegation[1]:

> We had been informed, in fact, that Soviet Russia, having accepted to take part in the work of this Conference, was sending an important delegation under the leadership of one of her foremost diplomats: Maxim Litvinov.
>
> We were all eager to obtain information as precise as possible concerning the past, the capabilities, the behaviour of this man, for we were to assist at the first appearance of one of Bolshevism's big guns on the stage of the Genevan theatre.
>
> When he made his entry into the hall in which the Conference was meeting, all eyes were turned upon him. The first impression was disastrous.
>
> Somewhat small in height with a tendency to stoutness, a round, flabby, common face, slightly pitted by small-pox, was enlivened only by a pair of bright eyes hidden behind gold-rimmed spectacles, all crowned by a mass of unpleasant looking fuzzy grey hair.

The presence in the delegation of Minister of Education Anatol Lunacharskii, a cultured old Bolshevik of considerable experience in Western Europe, improved matters somewhat, although he himself gave the "impression of a provincial school-teacher, dressed in his Sunday clothes." The principals were accompanied by a "group of miserable looking secretaries with Mongolian faces." Mme. Lunacharskii, however, was strikingly different, "beautiful and elegant . . . , with her magnificent furs and fine jewels, [she] gave this rather repulsive-looking delegation a certain brightness and Slavonic fragrance reminiscent of the old czarist regime." Litvinov's behavior, on the other hand, matched his appearance:

> When Litvinov opened his mouth for the first time, he expressed himself in very uncertain English. His nervous throaty voice increased the unfavourable impression he had already made upon us. In addition, his speech, which was no more than propaganda, in which he advocated no less than universal and total disarmament, and the destruction of all war material (this already in 1927!), had a profoundly disquieting effect on the audience. [After his formal speech], Litvinov became reserved and displayed a certain amount of tact.

These first impressions were not lasting, however. Litvinov made adjustments, took the gauge of his new environment, and succeeded in it. He was to become one of the most respected, as well as one of the most

---

[1]   Nicolae Petrescu-Comnen, "Maxim Litvinov," in *Dust and Shadows: Unknown Pages of History*, 90–2, Hoover Institution Archive, Comnen Papers, Box 14, Folder 55. It is a long memoir of Petrescu-Comnen's career, one of several that he wrote in retirement (subsequently published in Italy under a somewhat different title, *Luci e ombre sull'Europa, 1914–1950* [Milan: Bompiani, 1957]). Comnen explains that he simply opened a trunk of personal documents in Florence in December 1955 and began to write.

prominent, players on the stage at Geneva, and at international diplomatic forums more generally. Comnen continues:

> He returned for the sessions of March 1928 and April 1929. Though his words retained a certain sharpness, it was evident that the violence of his tone diminished steadily, and his language became more diplomatic.
>
> In 1928, having been authorised by his Government to sign the Kellog [sic: Kellogg–Briand] Pact – which outlawed war – he won the favour of the English, of Briand, Benes and the Northern States.
>
> Speaking about him, Briand said to me: "Litvinov is making progress. You will see, he will become a great European". Benes described him as "the most Western of the Easterns". Titulesco [sic: Titulescu], more reserved, was however of the opinion that "perhaps one day we shall be able to discuss matters with this man".

These prophecies proved true, even the more flattering of them. Litvinov became, according to Comnen, one of the most influential people at Geneva. Everyone agreed that he was a very skillful negotiator:

> Thanks to him his country, which for many years had been placed under a ban by international society, regained its place as a great power.... His personal relations with the leading political personages and diplomats became close and confidential. In less than three years he had succeeded in becoming a star of the first magnitude in the international firmament. Henceforward he met with striking successes.
>
> His influence at times seemed almost to overshadow that of Briand, then at the summit of his career.... Likewise Benes, following Briand's example, ended by taking him completely on trust. Titulesco too, who had been amongst the last to re-establish diplomatic relations with the U.S.S.R. said to me once: 'As long as Litvinov is Minister, I shall not be afraid of Moscow.' [Titulescu's] trustfulness found many critics in Roumania, and also in certain quarters in France, Poland, Jugoslavia and Nazi Germany.

Litvinov's new policies after 1933–1934 made a no less striking and an even more substantive impression than had his personality at Geneva. In 1934, Titulescu and Litvinov negotiated informally what came to be known as the "gentleman's agreement," an understanding between themselves that in the transaction of their business the issue of Bessarabia was never to be mentioned. It was the indispensable *sine qua non* of the establishment of diplomatic relations without which they would inevitably have remained divided. This agreement and diplomatic recognition (9 June 1934) behind them, the obvious next step and the order of the day was the cementing of an accord to support collective security, and Titulescu set to work on it at once.

In the meantime, the Franco–Soviet Pact and the Soviet–Czechoslovak Pact of May 1935 had made a profound impression in Romania. For the most obvious reasons of geography and strategy, these pacts vastly increased the pressure on Romania to reach an agreement with Moscow and especially to define the conditions of Soviet military access to Czechoslovakia across Romanian territory. Immediately after the signing of the pact with Czechoslovakia, Soviet Commissar of Defense Kliment Voroshilov assured Czechoslovak President Edvard Beneš that the Red Army would come to the assistance of Czechoslovakia in the event of war *with* or *without* the consent of Romania. The following year, Czechoslovak Foreign Minister Kamil Krofta confirmed the Soviet promise. As French Minister Victor de Lacroix reported from Prague, Krofta said that Moscow "had declared in Prague that in case of an attack against Czechoslovakia, the Russian army would come to the assistance of this country across Romania with or without the consent of the Bucharest government." Furthermore, "M. Titulescu is aware of this intention and that . . . is one of the reasons that motivate him to sign a pact of mutual assistance with Russia. This treaty would regulate in particular the conditions of transit of the Russian army across the northern part of Romania."[2]

What has rarely or never been appreciated in this question is that the Romanian army, perhaps despairing of being able to defend the country from a serious Soviet challenge – not without reason, considering the Soviet invasion of June 1940 – supported Titulescu.

The Soviet minister in Bucharest, M. S. Ostrovskii, reported just such sentiments. A Romanian General Staff officer gave him a firsthand account of opinion around the army high command in early 1936. Major V. A. Semion was born in Imperial Russian Bessarabia and had studied at St. Petersburg University. He told Ostrovskii that there was a strong inclination among younger General Staff officers in favor of an alliance with the USSR. Their reasoning was logical and persuasive. The only great power even nominally an ally of Romania was France (Friendship Pact of 1926), which was alarmingly far away. At the same time, these officers found little consolation in contemplating the assistance of Romania's Little Entente allies. Yugoslavia's attention would be diverted, in time of war, by confronting Italy; and Czechoslovakia would be besieged from two sides, by Poland and Germany, simultaneously. Thus, without a Soviet alliance, the independence of Romania would almost certainly be forfeit. Semion's colleagues on the General Staff were studying Russian, he said, and they favored the stationing of a Romanian military attaché in Moscow.[3]

[2] Lacroix to Quai d'Orsay, 16 April 1936; DDF, 2nd series, 2: 139–40 (No. 84).
[3] Record of Ostrovskii's conversation with Major V. A. Semion, 26 February 1936; *Sovetsko-rumynskie otnosheniia, 1917–1941*, 2 vols. (Moscow: Mezhdunarodnye otnosheniia, 2000), 1: 62–3 (No. 26).

The Poles were worried about these developments, and the Polish military attaché in Bucharest, Jan Kowalski, monitored them carefully. He consistently reported the agreement of the Romanian army with Titulescu's policy.[4] In fact, Romanian General Staff documents from summer 1935 forward manifest a dramatic new attitude of which Western historiography remains, so far as I know, remarkably ignorant.[5] The two Soviet pacts, in the words of the General Staff, "changed the whole situation in the sense that a relaxation with Russia took place such that we could direct all our attention to the threatening western frontier." Accordingly the plan of operations drawn up for 1936, in response to the "removal of the Russian threat," entailed a dramatic redeployment of forces, leaving three to four divisions of infantry and a brigade of cavalry on the Southern (Bulgarian) front, sixteen divisions of infantry and two of cavalry on the Western (Hungarian) front, and a maximum of nine divisions of infantry on the Eastern (Russian) front, and "that only in the gravest case."[6]

In addition, and most dramatically, the document called clearly for the formulation of plans to permit the Red Army to cross Romania on its way to rendering to Czechoslovakia the assistance stipulated in the treaty of mutual defense: "If Russia remains allied with France and intends to support Czechoslovakia we will *need* to permit the Russian forces to cross Romania in order to assist the Czech army."[7] In fact, in June 1936, at a meeting of the Little Entente General Staffs in Bucharest, the Romanians informed their allies of the change of outlook, using virtually the same words. In the event of war, "if Russia remains allied with France and agrees to assist Czechoslovakia, we *will* permit Russian forces to traverse Romania in order to assist the Czech army."[8] The Romanian General Staff was ordered to construct an itinerary for the transfer of Soviet troops in the event of a decision, in common with France, to intervene in support of Czechoslovakia.[9] In the fall of 1937, King Carol II himself assured French Chief of Staff General Maurice Gamelin that in the event of war, "he

[4] Henryk Bułhak, "Polska a Rumunia, 1918–1939," in Janusz Żarnowski, ed., *Przyjaźnie i antagonizmy: stosunki polski z państwami sąsiednimi w latach 1918–1939* (Warsaw: Polish Academy of Science, 1977), 335.

[5] An exception is Larry L. Watts, "Romania as a Military Ally (Part I): Czechoslovakia in 1938," *Romanian Civilization* (Bucharest) 7 (1998): 21–54.

[6] Ioan Talpeş, "Măsuri şi acţiuni diplomatice şi militare in vederea întăririi capacitaţii de apărare a ţarii în faţa creşterii pericolelor Hitlerist şi revisionist," *File din istoria militară a poporului român* 8 (1980): 119–22.

[7] "Dacă Rusia rămâne aliată cu Franţa şi înţelege a ajuta Cehoslovacia noi vom trebui să permitem forţelor ruse să treacă prin România pentru a ajuta armata cehă." *Referate pentru întocmirea planului de campanie 1936*; AMR. Fond Marele stat major, Secţia I-a, Organizare şi mobilizare. Dosar 434: Planurile de campanie 1936, pp. 65–92, quote on p. 69.

[8] Ibid.

[9] Watts, "Romania as a Military Ally (Part I)," 44.

would allow the Russians to cross the northern part of his territory in order to reach Czechoslovakia. But he demanded that I keep it a secret, not wishing the question to be discussed in Romania. He would act at the desired moment."[10] In the spring of 1938, Carol sent a somewhat similar and somewhat different assurance to Daladier, who was told that Romania would "render assistance to Czechoslovakia," although what kind and how much was left undefined.[11]

Precisely this outlook continued to characterize Romanian military planning through 1938. The Romanian General Staff campaign plan for 1938 addressed the "degree of probability of war on the different fronts," East, West, and South, or Russian, Hungarian, and Bulgarian. The most threatening front was clearly the Western or Hungarian. The General Staff judged that, in view of Russia's treaty with France, Russian policy as enunciated at the League of Nations, and the attitude of the other powers, especially Hungary, "war on the eastern [front in 1938] appears little likely."[12] In 1937, approximately 90 percent of all military expenditures were devoted to the Western front, and in 1938, the number of divisions posted on the Eastern frontier was reduced to five.[13]

In the meantime, the Foreign Office naturally reflected the new prospects of cooperation with Soviet foreign policy as well. A Foreign Office policy paper of September 1936 addressed the question whether the League Pact obliged Romania as a member state to permit the passage of Soviet troops in the event of aggression. It concluded unequivocally that "member states of the League of Nations are obliged to authorize passage of States [sic] applying military sanctions under Article 16 of the Pact. They may not invoke their [own] non-participation in a military

---

[10]   Maurice Gustave Gamelin, *Servir*, 3 vols. (Paris: Plon, 1946–1947), 2: 279. Viorica Moisuc and Gheorghe Matei, "Politică externă a României în perioada Münchenului (martie 1938–martie 1939)," in Viorica Moisuc, ed., *Probleme de politică externă a României, 1919–1939* (Bucharest: Editură militară, 1971), 317. Both of these sources state that King Carol had previously made the same promise to former French Foreign Minister Joseph Paul-Boncour, both citing Paul-Boncour's memoirs, *Entre deux guerres: souvenirs sur la Troisième république*, 3 vols. (Paris: Plon 1945–1946). Boris Čelovsky, *Das Münchener Abkommen 1938* (Stuttgart: Deutsche Verlags-Anstalt, 1958), 204, repeats the statement, referring to Gamelin. I do not find the statement in Paul-Boncour's memoirs. According to Ioan Talpeş, *Diplomaţie şi apărare: coordonate ale politicii externe româneşti, 1933–1939* (Bucharest: Editură ştiinţifică şi enciclopedică, 1988), 181, it was on 15 October 1937 that King Carol made the commitment to Gamelin.

[11]   Surits (Soviet ambassador in Paris) to Commissariat of Foreign Affairs, 25 May 1938; DVP SSSR, 21: 287 (No. 198).

[12]   Memoriu pentru revederea şi punerea la curent a ipotezeilor de rasboi 1938; AMR. Fond Marele stat major, Secţia 3 operaţii. Dosar 1577: Studii în legătură cu planul de campanie 1938; Microfilm reel no. II.1.974, pp. 93–4 and passim.

[13]   Talpeş, *Diplomaţie şi apărare*, 195. Idem, "Date noi privind poziţia României în contextul contradicţiilor internaţionale din vara anului 1938," *Revista de istorie* 28 (1975): 1656.

action in order to free themselves from this obligation. Neither may they for this purpose take advantage of the absence of recommendations of the Council demanding such right of passage. The States' liberty of judgment [i.e., policy] exists only in reference to their pronouncing upon the determination [identification] of an aggressor."[14] Moreover, the General Staff concluded that, if the League authorized military sanctions against an aggressor and the Poles nevertheless defied a Soviet request for transit rights across Poland, Romania would thereby be relieved of its obligations in the 1921 mutual-defense pact with Poland.[15]

It was about this time that the machinations of Titulescu and Litvinov appeared to be moving collective security in Eastern Europe to a stunning victory. Titulescu had for some time advocated a treaty of mutual defense with Moscow, but King Carol refused. Eventually, the king gave his provisional consent. Such a treaty, he stipulated, was acceptable on three conditions: It must preserve Bessarabia, it must preserve the Polish alliance, and it must be directed against any attacker. In other words, it must avoid being directed explicitly against Germany. In November 1935, Titulescu initiated serious negotiations to this effect with Litvinov.[16] On 21 July 1936, the two of them, meeting at Montreux, drafted and initialed a pact that resolved most of the obstacles and served most of their needs.[17]

The document was drafted by Titulescu. Although it followed the inspiration of the Franco–Soviet Pact and the Soviet–Czechoslovak Pact, it differed from them in important particulars. Litvinov accepted three of the points without demur. Article 1 stipulated mutual assistance against *any* aggressor, not singling out Germany. Article 3 stipulated that neither

[14] Referat: Chestiunea trecerei peste teritoriul statelor membre ale societătei națiunilor a forțelor armate în aplicarea sancțiunilor militare prevăzute de articolul 16 al pactului, 9 September 1936; Romania. RMAE. Fond 71/U.R.S.S. 1920–1944. Vol. 52, Relații cu Cehoslovacia, pp. 417–33. A documentary record of Soviet–Romanian relations 1917–1941 has been published by historians and archivists of the two sides working together. I was given the first volume of the Romanian publication – *Relațiile româno-sovietice: documente*, I: *1917–1934* (Bucharest: Editură enciclopedică, 1999) at the Ministry of Foreign Affairs archive and was promised the second volume. So far as I can discover (i.e., Library of Congress, Ohio College Online Catalogue, correspondence with Romanian colleagues), the second volume has not appeared. Its Russian counterpart is available: *Sovetsko-rumynskie otnosheniia, 1917–1941*, 2 vols. (Moscow: Mezhdunarodnye otnosheniia, 2000). I have found the record in the Romanian archives to have superior authority, however, and I have therefore relied chiefly on it.

[15] Talpeș, "Date noi privind," 1652: "In the event that, availing themselves of Article 16 of the League of Nations Pact, the Russians should demand rights of passage over Poland in order to assist Czechoslovakia against German aggression, and the Poles refused, then Romania is no longer obliged to declare war on Russia even if the Russians enter Poland by force."

[16] Record of conversation of Ostrovskii with Titulescu, 27–28 November 1935; Litvinov to Ostrovskii, 29 November 1935; Litvinov to Ostrovskii, 13 December 1935; Litvinov to Ostrovskii, 13 January 1936; *Sovetsko-rumynskie otnosheniia*, 2: 44–9 (No. 19), 50 (No. 20), 51–4 (No. 21), 58–9 (No. 23).

[17] Draft treaty of mutual assistance, Montreux, 21 July 1936; ibid., 82–3 (No. 34).

army would cross the frontier and enter the other country without the express invitation of the country attacked. Article 4 stipulated that each side would withdraw its forces from the other country on request. Only Article 2 caused difficulties. Titulescu had written that the treaty would enter into force only when France entered the conflict. Litvinov objected that this article did not reflect Romania's own interests, as Romania did not have a treaty of mutual assistance with France, only the somewhat insubstantial moral alliance of a treaty of friendship of 1926. This question was deferred for further consideration. Titulescu hoped to address it in part by encouraging an alliance between France and the Little Entente. The document simply ignored the issue of the recognition of Bessarabia. The two statesmen planned to meet again in September for the formal signature of alliance.[18]

It is not surprising that problems developed in this implausibly rosy scenario. At this point, all the enemies of collective security abroad and all the enemies of Titulescu and of the Soviet connection at home coalesced to bring intolerable pressure on King Carol. The enemies at home were the liberals, the conservatives, and the nationalists, as well as the Iron Guard. The weightiest of the powers abroad was, for obvious reasons, Germany. Poland signaled, however, that if the treaty with Moscow were signed and ratified, it would denounce its own treaty of alliance with Romania – the terms of their treaty of alliance gave each power a veto over the formation of alliances with third parties.[19] In addition, in Yugoslavia – component of the Little Entente – the Stojadinović cabinet, no longer subject to the influence of King Alexander and Louis Barthou, both of whom had been assassinated in Marseille in 1934, was increasingly under the influence of the White Russian émigrés and hence more and more averse to dealing with Moscow. Finally, for the sake of collective security, Titulescu had taken a strong stand against the Italians in the Ethiopian crisis of 1935,[20] and they were his sworn enemies. The government of Romania was thus in a tough position, unable at the same time to retain its foreign minister and

---

[18] Dov B. Lungu, *Romania and the Great Powers, 1933–1940* (Durham, NC: Duke University Press, 1989), 80–2.

[19] Article 6: "Neither of the High Contracting Parties shall be at liberty to conclude an alliance with a third Power without having previously obtained the assent of the other Party." Arnold J. Toynbee, *Survey of International Affairs, 1920–1923* (New York: Oxford University Press, 1927), 504–5. The Poles in fact did not oppose a Soviet–Romanian Pact of nonaggression; they had had just such a pact of their own with Moscow since 1932. They objected vehemently, however, either to an alliance or to any permission for the transit of Soviet troops over Romania. As Marshal Eduard Śmigły-Rydz, Inspector General of the Army, explained, it would bring Soviet troops to another border of Poland. Talpeş, *Diplomaţie şi apărare*, 125–6.

[20] In fact, he was ready at the time to follow the lead of England even at the cost of a rupture with France. Ibid., 131. Romania provided more than half of Italy's oil imports.

the good will of four powers with crucial influence in Danubian Europe, two of which were its allies.

Titulescu had other weaknesses. He lacked – because he altogether neglected to cultivate – a plausible base of support for his policies in the give and take of Romanian party politics at home. He spent the bulk of his time traveling from one foreign chancery to another. He relied on logic, reason, and diplomatic finesse, on his personal persuasiveness, to win the consent of his cabinet collegues at home, and it was not enough to sustain his position. His colleagues in the cabinet thought that he attempted to play a role in the grand politics of European affairs beyond the scope of Romania's modest significance on the continent. In addition, they suspected him, perfectly reasonably, of keeping them in the dark about the business that he did abroad.[21] In fact, his conduct of the negotiations of the mutual-security pact with Litvinov were kept strictly secret from the cabinet.

In the event, Titulescu was dismissed, and his pact with Litvinov was never signed.[22] It was often observed that there were three sturdy pillars of the Little Entente, King Alexander of Yugoslavia, Titulescu of Romania, and Edvard Beneš of Czechoslovakia. From 1936 forward, only Beneš remained.

Moscow naturally suffered a sense of critical defeat. The Romanian government attempted to reassure it. As matters were explained to Soviet Minister M. S. Ostrovskii, their two countries were now – still – "on the same side of the barricades," and neutrality was in the circumstances "the product of intrinsic cretinism." Stalin's government of the latter 1930s was, however, hard to reassure. Ostrovskii responded to these comforting words by complaining of the curtailed circulation of the Soviet press in Romania and the censorship of Soviet films.[23] Litvinov asked the Romanians to hold to the course of Titulescu, specifically to loyalty to France, the Little Entente, and the League, and to good relations with the Soviet Union. What he saw in Bucharest instead, he complained, was a weakening of

---

[21] Litvinov (Geneva) to Ostrovskii, reporting conversation with the new foreign minister, Victor Antonescu, 20 September 1936; Ostrovskii to Litvinov, reporting conversation with Gheorge Tătărescu, 26 September 1936; *Sovetsko-rumynskie otnosheniia*, 2: 89–90 (No. 39) and 91–2 (No. 41).

[22] The best account is in Lungu, *Romania and the Great Powers, 1933–1940*, Chapter 5, "The Russian Connection and Its Enemies: The Causes of Titulescu's Fall." Lungu here argues, contrary to Talpes, in *Diplomație și apărare*, passim, that the dismissal of Titulescu did alter the direction of Romanian foreign policy. Titulescu, evidently for fear of playing into the hands of his enemies prematurely, did not communicate the text of the draft treaty to Bucharest. Lungu's source is a historical memoir written by Titulescu for King Carol that recapitulated Romanian policy toward Moscow (found in the archive of the Romanian Communist Party Central Committee).

[23] Ostrovskii to Litvinov, 20 January 1937; DVP SSSR, 20: 52–3 (No. 23).

the Little Entente and the growing influence of Germany and Poland, especially the latter.[24] These were the common themes of discussions between the two powers in spring and summer 1937, and the developing warmth of Romanian–Polish relations was the most conspicuous of them. In fact, Victor Antonescu,[25] the new foreign minister, on his way to another suspicious tête-à-tête in Warsaw, assured Ostrovskii that he was simply answering a French appeal to attempt to keep Poland out of the German orbit.[26] Returned from Poland, he continued that Romania would "hold to the course of Paris, London, and Moscow." Furthermore, as he said, "it is time for us to regulate our Bessarabian problem and our relations [in general] at the same time."[27] Some time later, Ostrovskii told the visiting Czechoslovak prime minister, Milan Hodža, that Moscow could not extend *de jure* recognition of Romanian Bessarabia without countenancing the principle of German claims on Prague, that is, the right of ethnic self-determination. He said, however, that the Soviets were willing to engage in a pact of mutual assistance with Bucharest, stipulating the withdrawal of Red Army troops behind the Dniestr on the cessation of hostilities.[28]

In conversation with visiting French Minister of Foreign Affairs Joseph Paul-Boncour, Ostrovskii elaborated Litvinov's plan of joining Moscow and Bucharest in an alliance to support collective security. Paul-Boncour reported this conversation of 15 May 1937 to his Romanian hosts:

> In the question of Bessarabia and in the absence of a pact of mutual assistance, [in particular] of dispositions concerning the retreat of the military forces of the two sides at the end of a possible common campaign, the Soviet minister spoke of a formula guaranteeing the inviolability of the Dniestr, the regime of which has already been agreed between the two countries by a common accord.
>
> He declared furthermore that [Moscow] is faithful to the conception of seeking a formula to implement the stipulations of the [League] Pact: on the one hand in the engagements of article 10 [inviolability of frontiers] of the Pact in order to give the reassurances that Romania would desire to obtain for the eastern frontier – and on the other hand in article 16 [military sanctions against an aggressor] where one could specify provisions permitting, in the event of hostilities, the regulation of concerted action of the two countries that would satisfy them equally.

[24] Litvinov to Ostrovskii, 22 February 1937; ibid., 92–4 (No. 53).
[25] Not to be confused with the leading military figure, General, later Marshal, Ion Antonescu, the *Conducător*, or *Führer*, of Romania during World War II.
[26] Ostrovskii to Litvinov, 1 March 1937; ibid., 94–100 (No. 55).
[27] Ibid., 28 April 1937; ibid., 207–12 (No. 131).
[28] Ibid., 16 June 1937; ibid., 312–16 (No. 203).

By way of reaching [such agreement], the Soviet minister seemed *disposed to negotiate, in all discretion, the delicate question of the passage of Soviet troops.*[29]

By this time, however, the fall of Titulescu had naturally altered the posture of the Romanian Foreign Office in respect to policy toward the Soviet Union and the question of Red Army rights of passage as stipulated under the League Covenant. A new Foreign Office paper addressed the familiar problem again: "The Present Intentions of the Soviet Government with Respect to the Conclusion of an Alliance with Romania." The paper observed that Soviet–Romanian relations were dominated at the time by two factors: Romanian interest in obtaining a formal recognition of the possession of Bessarabia and Soviet interest in obtaining the right of passage for Red Army troops in case of international war, in particular in the event of a German attack on Czechoslovakia. Referring to the conversations of Ostrovskii and Paul-Boncour of 15 May 1937, the ministry related that Ostrovskii had interesting ideas on composing these two factors. Ostrovskii thought that a proper formula to combine and reconcile them was to be found in Articles 10 and 16 of the League Pact. Article 10 would provide for securing the Eastern Frontier of Romania. Then the two countries must reach an understanding how to proceed jointly to implement Article 16 against an aggressor.[30] Here the document reverted to the old Litvinov–Titulescu "gentleman's agreement," according to which it was essential to avoid pronouncing on the judicial status of Bessarabia.[31] Romania recognized that it was already in possession of de facto claims to the province, and the problem seemed in any case sufficiently covered by the League Covenant. If Romania should proceed according to Ostrovskii's recommendations, then it would lose the right to choose whether or not to participate in military sanctions against an aggressor. Such a pact

---

[29] Extras din Referatul D-lui Ministru Al. Cretzianu din 8 Iulie 1937. Putem oare admite într'o formă sau alta dreptul de trecere a trupelor rusești? RMAE. Fond 71/U.R.S.S. 1920-1944. Volume 52: Relații cu Cehoslovacia, pp. 475–81. (Emphasis added.)

[30] Article 10: "The Members of the League undertake to respect and preserve as against external aggression the territorial integrity and existing political independence of all Members of the League. In case of any such aggression or in case of any threat or danger of such aggression the Council shall advise upon the means by which this obligation shall be fulfilled." Article 16 (excerpt): "The Members of the League agree, further, that they will mutually support one another in the financial and economic measures which are taken under this Article, in order to minimise the loss and inconvenience resulting from the above measures, and that they will mutually support one another in resisting any special measures aimed at one of their number by the covenant-breaking State, and that they will take the necessary steps to afford passage through their territory to the forces of any of the Members of the League which are co-operating to protect the covenants of the League." For fuller texts of the pertinent parts of the League Covenant, see Appendix 1.

[31] Titulescu and Litvinov had agreed not to raise the subject. It is recapitulated for the benefit of Comnen in Ciuntu to Comnen, 4 July 1938; RMAE. Fond 71/U.R.S.S. Vol. 85: Relații cu Romînia, anul 1938, pp. 302–4.

would also entail two great risks: (1) the occupation of the country by a foreign army imbued with a dangerous ideology and (2) transformation of the country into a theatre of operations. "We are entitled to ask ourselves whether the acquisition of indirect [*lăturalnică*] recognition of Bessarabia would compensate for such risks in the eyes of public opinion."[32] For the time being, the answer to the question was suspended in the limbo of studied ambiguity.

The torment continued, as the Foreign Office tried again in a new policy paper just two months later in July: "Can We Really Admit in One Form or Another the Right of Passage for Russian Troops?" Once again the 15 May conversations of Ostrovskii and Paul-Boncour served as the referential starting point. If Article 10 of the League Pact were judged adequate security for Romania's Eastern frontier, then it remained only to find a formula satisfactory to the two sides for regulating concerted military action in the event of hostilities. Here again the cardinal point was reviewed: Ostrovskii "seemed disposed to negotiate, in all discretion, the delicate question of the passage of [Soviet] troops."[33]

Several related questions were raised in the paper. One obstacle to the admission of the Red Army was the clear stipulation of Article 123 of the Romanian constitution: "No foreign armed force may be admitted into the service of the state nor enter or cross the territory of Romania except by virtue of a specific law." In the meantime, precedents set elsewhere by other League member states suggested an exit from the dilemma. During the Italo–Ethiopian crisis, Hungary, Austria, and Albania refused to comply with League sanctions against Italy, and the Belgian delegate to the League had announced in April 1937 the entire independence of his country in the question of subscribing to League military sanctions. Although the League was fully empowered to identify an aggressor, Belgium alone would reserve the right to grant or refuse the right of passage to foreign armies in the service of League policy. In conclusion, the Romanian paper argued, "we remain free to decide when and if we will permit the passage of foreign troops through our territory. It would, of course, be contrary to our interests to surrender, in the framework of an agreement with the Russian state, the liberty that we enjoy at present."[34]

The deteriorating prospects of Soviet–Romanian military cooperation were soon aggravated by a series of whimsically extraneous developments. In the winter of 1937–1938, the relations of Moscow and Bucharest entered

---

[32] Intenţiunile actuale ale Guvernului Sovietic cu privire la încheierea unui PACT cu ROMÂNIA, May 1937; RMAE. Fond 71/U.R.S.S. Vol. 84: Relaţii cu Romînia, anul 1937, pp. 222–4.

[33] Extras din Referatul D-lui Ministrul Al. Cretzianu din 8 Iulie 1937: Putem oare admite într'o formă sau alta dreptul de trecere a trupelor ruseşti? RMAE. Fond 71/U.R.S.S.. Vol. 52, pp. 475–81.

[34] Ibid.

a period of real crisis. On 28 December 1937, King Carol constituted a conservative and anti-Semitic government dominated by Octavian Goga and Alexandru Cuza (National Christian Party). The character of this cabinet was extremely repugnant to Moscow, close as it was to the Romanian Iron Guard and perhaps, as Moscow alleged, to the ruling party in Germany as well. Its fall on 11 February 1938, however, scarcely improved matters, as it led on 23 February to the scrapping of the constitution and the institution of the Royal Dictatorship. The new cabinet consisted of Patriarch Miron Cristea, Premier; Armand Călinescu (National Peasant Party), Interior; General Ion Antonescu, Defense; and Nicolae Petrescu-Comnen (career diplomat), Foreign Affairs. The new government was scarcely more to Moscow's taste than the old one. It may have been pure coincidence – although it is unlikely – that the chiefs of mission in both legations were recalled during these events.

The letter of recall of the Romanian minister in Moscow contained not a hint of political motivation. Premier Goga simply wrote that Minister Edmond Ciuntu's services were required in Bucharest.[35] Ciuntu said that his colleagues attributed his recall to a symbolic repudiation of the policy of Titulescu, to whom Ciuntu was regarded as close. The Moscow correspondent of Le Temps also interpreted the recall as political in nature. In Ciuntu's last conference at the Commissariat of Foreign Affairs, Potemkin assured him that the recall of M. S. Ostrovskii, Soviet minister plenipotentiary, was unrelated to the recall of the Romanian minister.[36]

Ostrovskii took formal leave of his post on 9 February. At the official banquet to mark the end of Ostrovskii's mission, Romanian Premier Goga made a customarily cordial speech, although he dropped one remark about Romania's "natural frontiers," obviously a reference to Bessarabia and the Dniestr.[37] Ostrovskii responded in warm and complimentary tones without any reference to issues dividing the two countries. The one remarkable comment that he made – in view of the fact that his recall may well have been as much motivated by the fact that he had fallen under suspicion of Trotskyism as by the wish to signal the displeasure of Moscow over Romanian politics – was his reference to FDR as the "grand homme d'état de nos temps."[38] If Stalin read the speech, it cannot have improved Ostrovskii's chances at Lubianka prison, which he did not, in fact, survive.

Ostrovskii was to have been replaced as chief of mission with the chargé d'affaires, Fedor Butenko, but Butenko had scarcely assumed his duties when he turned into a sensational scandal and the scandal turned into

---

[35] Goga to Moscow Legation, 27 January 1938; ibid., p. 60.
[36] Ciuntu to Ministry of Foreign Affairs, 30 January 1938; ibid., pp. 73–74.
[37] Ibid. Vol. 85, pp. 92–3.
[38] Ibid., pp. 94–7.

an ugly Soviet–Romanian confrontation. On 6 February 1938, Butenko simply disappeared mysteriously without a trace. It was alarming and embarrassing for the host country. For the Soviets, it was worse. The Soviet security organs, the GPU, were perhaps even more scrupulous in their surveillance of Soviet personnel abroad than of those at home, although of course they lacked the same comprehensive means of control in foreign diplomatic posts. The whole affair must naturally be understood in the context of the purges, which were taking an impressive toll on Maksim Litvinov's commissariat of foreign affairs.[39]

As the Soviet legation reported the facts of the case to the Romanian Ministry of Foreign Affairs, Butenko had been driven to his apartment by the legation chauffeur after work, did not respond to phone calls in the evening, and failed to come to work the following day. His colleagues went to look for him at home but failed to find him. The legation quite naturally asked for an investigation into Butenko's disappearance. Perhaps equally as naturally, given the Soviet style of the time, it lodged "the most categorical protest against the tragic fact [of his disappearance], unknown in the history of international relations," and imputed, without any apparent reason, "the entire responsibility" for the affair to the government of Romania.[40]

In fact, the Romanian government, altogether ignorant of the fate of Butenko, had dutifully reported the matter to Moscow. This report described suspicious spots on the stairway leading to Butenko's apartment, spots that led his colleagues to apprehend that a crime might have been committed against him. The Romanian police and the Procurator's office had then undertaken an intensive investigation, which immediately determined that the spots in question were not blood and promised to report further results as they were uncovered. "Our distinct impression is that we are dealing here with a [simple] case of disappearance. No one by the name of Butenko has crossed the frontier."[41]

The Soviet Commissariat of Foreign Affairs initially received this news surprisingly calmly. The Romanian minister plenipotentiary in Moscow, Ion Popescu-Pașcani, spoke with Vice-Commissar of Foreign Affairs, V. P. Potemkin, who expressed thanks for the information but suggested that it would be prudent to hold it for the time being in confidence. "I deduced from this request that Mr. Potemkin fears that Butenko might

---

[39]   Teddy J. Uldricks, "The Impact of the Great Purges on the People's Commissariat of Foreign Affairs," *Slavic Review* 36 (1977): 187–203.

[40]   Note-verbale, Légation de l'U.R.S.S., Bucharest, au Ministère Royal des Affaires étrangères, 8 February 1938; RMAE. Fond 71/U.R.S.S. 1920–1944. Vol. 135: Culegere de documente privind relații romîno-sovietice, 1933–1940, pp. 180–3.

[41]   Ministry of Foreign Affairs to the Romanian Legation, Moscow, 8 February 1938; ibid., Vol. 85: Relații cu Romînia, 1938, pp. 88–9.

have followed the example of other Soviet diplomats, who, facing the threat of being recalled and purged [*purificaţi*] at any moment, preferred exile from the 'felicity' of the fatherland."[42]

Potemkin's calm response to the news from Bucharest belied the tempestuous developments that the affair was soon to unleash. When the Romanian newspapers got wind of Butenko's disappearance, they began to have a good deal of amusement with it. They offered their readers a variety of hypothetical explanations of the matter. They suggested that Butenko had been kidnapped by the GPU, that he had been carrying on a clandestine love affair with the wife of a colleague in the Soviet legation, that he had simply gone abroad voluntarily, and, finally, that he was, in any case, a "lousy Russian Bolshevik [*rus parşâv bolşevic*]." The Soviet legation was grievously offended by these suggestions. It demanded that the Romanian foreign ministry bring the "mendacious" press under control.[43]

By the time the affair reached the newspapers, Potemkin's suggestion that it be handled discreetly had obviously become impossible, and the Soviet press soon responded to that of Romania in characteristically hysterical style. In an article entitled "Romanian Adventurists Overstep the Bounds," the "present leadership of the Romanian government" was held squarely responsible for the disappearance of Butenko. *Pravda* assessed the blame directly to the Goga–Cuza cabinet, which it described as a mere arm of Goebbels and the Nazi Party, a party whose goons had often called for the "physical destruction of Soviet state personnel." Such was the contemporary "national" quality of Romanian politics. The commentary continued in this spirit for some time.[44]

The tone of the Soviet diplomatic notes soon began to match the accusatory quality of the polemics in the press, whereas the Romanian government, always sensitive to the power and influence of its larger Eastern neighbor, and especially to its potential contribution to the policy of collective security, tried to restore an atmosphere of cordiality and confidence. Bucharest was naturally seriously alarmed by the deterioration of its relations with its large and unpredictable neighbor. Although the full facts on the Butenko case were several days yet in emerging, by the middle of February the Romanian Ministry of Foreign Affairs had clear evidence that the Soviet diplomat's disappearance had nothing to do with a criminal deed and that the Romanian government shared no responsibility for it. With considerable relief, the ministry addressed the Soviet legation accordingly. It announced the receipt of a letter from Butenko explaining

---

[42] Popescu-Paşcani to Ministry of Foreign Affairs, 9 February 1938; ibid., pp. 90–1.

[43] Soviet Legation, Bucharest, to Ministry of Foreign Affairs, 10 February 1938, Note verbale; ibid., Vol. 135, pp. 184–7.

[44] *Pravda*, 11 February 1938, p. 5.

that he had forsaken the Soviet diplomatic service and left Romania of his own free will. In view of that clear and important fact, the Romanian government complained that the Soviet accusations of Romanian complicity in the affair were unfounded and inappropriate, and it expressed the wish for the restoration of the good relations that had preceded this awkward development.[45]

In fact, Butenko had sent to the Romanian foreign minister a handwritten note in labored and awkward French to explain that he had left Romania "in order to search for asylum in a European country and to save myself from Bolshevism." He added that he had written a similar letter to the Soviet legation in Bucharest[46] – this latter letter has naturally never come to light. A few days later, the foreign minister received a longer note and a fuller explanation from Butenko, this time handwritten in his native Russian. He explained that he had long been disillusioned with Bolshevism and especially with the regime of terror that the purges had inflicted on the Soviet population. Having had the opportunity to travel in several European countries and to see for himself the freedom and prosperity that prevailed there, he had determined some time ago to escape the Soviet nightmare at the first opportunity. In the meantime, his decision to act was considerably expedited by the regime of surveillance with which the GPU had begun to surround him personally in Bucharest. In addition, he complained that, despite repeated requests, his wife and daughter had not been allowed to join him in Bucharest. They were held in Leningrad as hostages for his good behavior.

During the week before his departure, his situation had grown suddenly desperate. On 4 February, a GPU agent, one Tormanov, arrived from Vienna and, together with two other GPU agents resident in the Soviet legation, invited Butenko to take a drive with them to Sinaia, 120 kilometers north of Bucharest. More menacingly, they insisted on going without the embassy's regular chauffeur. "For me it became completely clear what fate awaited me, as well as other Soviet diplomats, only with this difference, that they were executed in Moscow, and it was proposed to destroy me in the vicinity of Bucharest." This development, of course, expedited Butenko's planned escape.[47]

With full documentation in hand, Comnen summoned the new chargé d'affaires of the Soviet Legation, Kukolev, showed him the facts and

---

[45] Hoover Institution Archive. Comnen Papers, Box 14, Folder 55, "Dust and Shadows: Unknown Pages of History," pp. 93–4. Royal Ministry of Foreign Affairs to Romanian Legation, Moscow, 16 February 1938; RMAE. Fond 71/U.R.S.S. 1920–1944. Vol. 135, pp. 196–7.

[46] Butenko to Minister of Foreign Affairs, undated and handwritten; Hoover Institution Archive. Comnen Papers, Box 3, Folder 16, photostat.

[47] Butenko to Minister of Foreign Affairs, undated and handwritten; ibid., photostat.

supporting documents, and asked him to communicate them to Moscow. At the same time, Comnen explained that Romania had no intention of exploiting the situation to the embarrassment of Moscow in any way. It would, in other words, handle the matter entirely confidentially for the sake of reestablishing harmony with its Eastern neighbor. "The Russian diplomat on hearing the message I desired him to deliver to his chief, became as white as a sheet and begged me to entrust the mission to our Minister at Moscow." Comnen, understanding the reason for his dismay, consented and said that he then considered the incident closed.[48]

He was mistaken. Confidentiality was soon breached. Comnen and Litvinov alike reckoned without the plans of Butenko himself and his co-conspirators, his Italian hosts. The diary of Italian Foreign Minister Galeazzo Ciano continues the story (12 February):

> A man describing himself as Butenko, the Soviet Chargé d'Affaires who disappeared from Bucharest, has given himself up at the *Questura* [police station] in Milan. He has no papers which prove his statements. He may simply be a lunatic or a mischief-maker. In any case I am having him sent on to Rome.[49]

On arrival in Rome, the newcomer requested an audience with the foreign minister. "I will only see him when he has been definitely identified. I have sent for an official of the Legation in Bucharest in order to make certain of his identity."[50] Butenko's identity confirmed, Ciano invited him to the ministry for an interview, and his account of the refugee and of his own plans for him explains the next turn of events:

> He doesn't seem to me a man of much character. But he was so confused and frightened that it would be premature to pass judgment on him. He even asked that the guards, instead of staying in the corridor, should take up permanent residence in his hotel bedroom. I have passed on his statements to the [papers] and by means of the foreign press, wireless, etc., I am building up the sensational news. It is a good piece of anti-Soviet propaganda, which must be properly exploited.[51]

On 17 February, Butenko's story appeared in the form of an interview in the Turin newspaper, *Gazzetta del Popolo*. His lurid exposé, preceded by sufficiently spectacular headlines and credible photographs, covered nearly

[48] "Dust and Shadows," p. 94; Hoover Institution Archive. Comnen Papers, Box 14, Folder 55.
[49] Entry of 12 February 1938; *Ciano's Diary, 1937–1938*, trans. Andreas Mayor (London: Methuen, 1952), 74.
[50] Ibid.
[51] Ibid., 76.

the entire front page:

BUTENKO SAFE IN ROME
REVEALS THE HORRORS OF THE STALINIST REGIME
How the ex-Soviet Diplomat Managed to Outwit the GPU Agents
and to Reach Rome after a Romantic Flight
Our Exclusive Interview with Teodoro Butenko

Butenko was disturbed by the exploitation of the peasants on collective farms, by the poverty of the workers in the new industries, by the insanity of the purges, and especially by the execution of all the best qualified chiefs of the army. He resented the fact that his wife and daughter were not allowed to join him. He related that both he himself and the former chief of the Soviet legation in Bucharest, M. S. Ostrovskii, had fallen under suspicion of Trotskyism. When the GPU agents proposed giving him a ride to Sinaia, he knew that he must take drastic measures at once. He therefore sought the protection of "another country," which obliged him by concealing him in Bucharest for five days. On 10 February, with a passport of "another country" and under a false name, he took the Simplon Orient Express for Milan, and from there he proceeded to Rome. He made it clear that his wife and daughter were not privy to his intentions, but, of course, he realized that they would not in any case be spared the attentions of the GPU.

He believed that Stalin's two recent military adventures, in Spain and in China, were designed chiefly to prepare the Red Army to support the worldwide Bolshevik Revolution. Stalin, he said, thought only of a new world war that would facilitate the triumph of Communism everywhere. The more difficult the internal situation of the Soviet Union grew, the more did the government turn its hopes onto world revolution. Butenko thought, however, that the country was in no condition to win a war and that war would shake the Stalinist regime itself. In particular, the purge of the military leaders had left the army disorganized and demoralized.

Finally, Butenko did not neglect to express his admiration for his hosts and especially for the *"genio di Mussolini."* It was, in the main, an impressive performance and, with the understandable exception of his flattery of the Italian government, plausible enough. It would undoubtedly be attended not only in the Nazi–Fascist camp but in the Anglo–French one as well, which fact made it all the more discomfiting. It would have embarrassed any country and any government, and of course the government in Moscow was more sensitive than most. Especially damaging, most likely, was the suggestion that the military might of the Red Army had been ruined, as respect for the army conditioned the value of a Soviet alliance as well as Soviet influence in Europe more generally.

Moscow's reaction to the revelations of Butenko's letters and interview was more imaginative than believable. Litvinov said to Popescu-Paşcani that either the alleged Butenko who turned up in Rome was an imposter or that he had been kidnapped and was being held under duress by anti-Soviet persons who were forcing him to write shameless lies about the Soviet Union. Popescu-Paşcani responded that it was implausible to think that everyone in Romania and Italy was lying about the matter. He posed the rather forceful question how it would serve the interests of Romania to engage in or cooperate in kidnapping a Soviet diplomat. Litvinov dismissed the question with a single word: Fascists.[52] Popescu-Paşcani added that he was sure that the Soviets were bluffing, that they understood perfectly well the ridiculous situation in which the defection of Butenko had left them but that they had no alternative to adhering to the dishonest interpretation of the affair that they had already adopted.

At this point, the attention of all the diplomatic offices of Europe was diverted by the *Anschluss*, Hitler's annexation of Austria, and the Butenko affair temporarily retreated from the urgent agenda of Soviet–Romanian relations. In the latter half of March, however, Litvinov returned to the subject in a carefully drafted document no less truculent than previous Soviet statements.

He complained that the Romanian investigation of Butenko's disappearance had not yielded any credible explanation of it. There was clearly a criminal element in the business, he said, and the Romanians were either unable or unwilling to uncover it. In a new wrinkle, the Romanians had evidently subjected Butenko's letters to graphological analysis and concluded that in fact the handwriting was his. Litvinov disputed it, entering into a long and tortuous rationalization of his opinion. He claimed that Butenko could not have sent letters from Budapest, where one of his letters was postmarked, to Bucharest, as the Simplon Express, his mode of flight, did not cross Hungarian territory.[53] This point was, of course, utterly irrelevant to Butenko's version of his escape, as he had told the *Gazzetta del Populo* explicitly that in order to throw the GPU off his track he had *caused the letters to be sent* – not that he himself had sent them – from Budapest.

Obviously Moscow was not amenable to conciliation, not even to reason, in this matter, and it too added a new wrinkle to an already tired altercation. In a classic expression of Soviet irritation, the GPU had begun to harass the personnel of the Romanian legation. Popescu-Paşcani

[52] Popescu-Paşcani to Ministry of Foreign Affairs, 17 February 1938; RMAE. Fond 71/U.R.S.S. 1920-1944. Vol. 135, pp. 198–201.
[53] Litvinov to Popescu-Paşcani (copy), Romanian translation from Russian, 17 March 1938; ibid., pp. 209–12.

reported an increase of flagrantly intrusive surveillance. Several persons having consular business at the legation had been detained and interrogated, and hence they had grown too frightened to return.

Somewhat later in the spring, Popescu-Pașcani turned to a more general analysis of Soviet–Romanian relations. He attributed the current chill to the fact that foreign policy was, in his opinion, under the influence of a clique that comprised the police – the "*éminence grise*," as he put it, of the government – and several influential members of the Politburo who were hostile to the political composition of the present Romanian government. This clique had used, he believed, the pretext of the Butenko affair "to give us a sample of their antagonism."[54]

Although it offers us no compelling proof, Comnen's memoirs suggest how portentous the events of the winter of 1937–1938 were to be in the long run. He writes that Moscow was disheartened first by the dismissal of Titulescu, then by the coming of the Goga–Cuza government, that the latter factor in particular prompted the recall of the Soviet minister plenipotentiary in Bucharest, M. S. Ostrovskii, and the ferocity of the Soviet reaction to the Butenko affair as well. In fact, he says that the vicious Soviet response to the affair helped to precipitate the formation of the Royal Dictatorship, which Moscow obviously found little more to its taste than its Goga–Cuza predecessor.[55]

Comnen does not take fully into account here the grand reach of Moscow's purge process, extending as it did far beyond the bounds of Romania, in fact, all over Europe and beyond. In spite of an enormous quantity of publication on the subject of the Soviet purges, both memoir material and historical literature, we have yet to find a plausible explanation of the phenomenon. In the wake of the Butenko affair, Litvinov, obviously frustrated by the decimation of his foreign-policy apparatus, took the decidedly daring step of appealing directly to Stalin about it.[56] He asked for the filling of the posts of *polpredy* (ambassadors) in Poland – where the Soviet minister, Iakov Davtian, had been recalled and purged in January 1937[57] – and Romania. The Romanians, he said, were urgently requesting it, specifically asking for someone who spoke French. Good

---

[54] Popescu-Pașcani to Comnen, 1 April 1938; ibid., pp. 215–16.

[55] "Dust and Shadows," pp. 94ff.; Hoover Institution Archive. Comnen Papers, Box 14, Folder 55. For details, see Hugh Ragsdale, "The Butenko Affair: Documents from Soviet-Romanian Relations in the Time of the Purges, Anschluss, and Munich," *Slavonic and East European Review* 79 (2001): 698–720.

[56] Litvinov to Stalin (copy), 29 May 1938 (copies to Molotov, Kaganovich, Voroshilov, Ezhov); RGVA, f. 33987, op. 3s, d. 1145, ss. 17–18.

[57] Jürgen Pagel, *Polen und die Sowjetunion 1938–1939: Die polnisch-sowjetischen Beziehungen in der Krisen der europäischen Politik am Vorabend des Zweiten Weltkrieges* (Stuttgart: Franz Steiner Verlag, 1992), 108, n. 79.

candidates were scarce, Litvinov admitted, but they were needed in the vacant posts in Spain, Hungary, Denmark, and Japan as well. In fact, they were needed in many other posts, including Finland, Latvia, Norway, Germany, Turkey, Afghanistan, Poland, and Mongolia.[58] M. S. Ostrovskii had hesitated to respond to his summons home but consented on the express assurance of his safety by Marshal Kliment Voroshilov. He was nevertheless arrested at the frontier. Among those who fled as Butenko did was F. F. Raskol'nikov, *polpred* in Bulgaria, who escaped to France and yet died there within a matter of months in suspicious circumstances, and Alexander Barmine of the legation in Athens, who lived to tell the story in a well-known memoir.[59] Barmine had married a foreign woman, and he relates, as Butenko did, the gradual closing of the GPU around him as well as its efforts to stay on his trail and eliminate him after his defection. What conceivable purpose these events served remains to be clarified.

Meanwhile, as Moscow pursued the dramatic diversions and decisive trivia of the Butenko business – to what purpose we can only try in vain to imagine – Hitler was with a different order of finesse pursuing Austria and Czechoslovakia. Before the Butenko affair passed, the *Anschluss* was accomplished and the Sudeten question posed, and, as everyone recognized, it focused the dilemmas of Soviet–Romanian relations even more clearly. If the purges were curious and destructive of Soviet advantages in so many general ways, in the Butenko affair they were even more so. Why should Moscow have ruined its relations with Bucharest in the midst of Hitler's expansionist moves in Eastern Europe, in the midst of its public efforts to sustain collective security? We may never know. In any event, Litvinov was soon hard at work to repair the situation, and before long he would declare himself satisfied with the results.

---

[58] Uldricks, "The Impact of the Great Purges on the People's Commissariat of Foreign Affairs," 188; idem, *Diplomacy and Ideology: The Origins of Soviet Foreign Relations, 1917–1930* (Beverly Hills: Sage, 1979), 169–88. See also Viktor Knoll, "Das Volkskommissariat für Auswärtige Angelegenheiten im Prozess aussenpolitischer Entscheidungsfindung in den zwanziger and dreissiger Jahren," in Ludmila Thomas und Viktor Knoll, eds., *Zwischen Tradition und Revolution: Determinanten und Strukturen sowjetischer Aussenpolitik 1917–1941* (Stuttgart: Franz Steiner Verlag, 2000), 73–155, and Rikke Haue, "Perzeption und Quellen: Zum Wandel des Dänemark-Bildes der sowjetischen Diplomatie in den dreissiger Jahren," ibid., 399–430.

[59] Alexander Barmine, *One Who Survived: The Life Story of a Russian Under the Soviets*, Intro. Max Eastman (New York: Putnam's, 1945), especially pp. 3–26.

Chapter 3

Soviet–Romanian Relations II: Summer 1938

The commitment of Czechoslovakia's Little Entente ally Romania to the preservation of Czech integrity and strength was part and parcel of its commitment to collective security more generally, which was hardly in doubt. Nor is there any logical reason why it should have been, given the territorial gains that it had realized in 1918 and the tacit conspiracy of its victims against it ever since. In the *Anschluss* crisis, Romania mobilized its army on the Western frontier.[1] At same time, French Minister Adrien Thierry was summoned to the Romanian Foreign Office and told that anything that affected the independence of Austria must be considered a *casus belli* but that it was up to the great powers to take the initiative.[2] The clear implication here is that Romania would have supported an Anglo–French war in the good cause, but it is equally clear that Romania was not in a position alone to face down the revisionists. As the French military attaché, Colonel Jean Delmas, reported about the same time, "Romania has long since declared that if it finds itself abandoned between the two enemy colossi, Soviet Russia and Germany, it will without hesitation opt for the latter for the sake of escaping communism."[3] A few weeks later, Minister Thierry reported to Paris his opinion that, in the case of war, Romania would be "with us" but that it would make no formal commitments in advance.[4] When French Foreign Minister Georges Bonnet queried Comnen at a League gathering in Geneva in May about the Romanian position in the event of a Czechoslovak crisis, Comnen repeated what the Romanians told the French over and over again, suggesting what thus appears to be official, though confidential, Romanian policy: irreversible decisions would

---

[1]   Larry Watts, "Romania as a Military Ally (Part I): Czechoslovakia in 1938," *Romanian Civilization (Bucharest)* 7 (1998): 31.

[2]   Thierry to Ministère des Affaires étrangères, 12 March 1938; DDF, 2nd series, 8: 749 (No. 399).

[3]   Colonel Delmas to Daladier, 20 March 1938; ibid., 8: 972–6 (No. 530).

[4]   Note du Département, 5 April 1938; ibid., 9: 215–16 (No. 112).

be postponed as long as possible. Citing Romanian obligations to the Polish alliance, to the Little Entente, and to the Balkan Entente, it was impossible, he said, for Romania to make a move without prior reference to its allies. Furthermore, he said, it served no one's interests, including those of France and Czechoslovakia, to jeopardize those alliances. If the British and the French were to fight in the event of a German challenge to Czechoslovakia, Romania and its allies would in all likelihood join them, but it could for the reasons stated take no position in advance.[5]

The Romanian position on the question of Soviet troop transit to Czechoslovakia was similarly cautious and ambiguous. When Bonnet raised the question at Geneva in May, Comnen said that no immediate response was possible. He observed that the public was hostile to the idea and that, without prior agreement with Poland, which was unlikely, the granting of such permission would result in the abrogation of the Polish alliance.[6] The government in Prague perfectly understood the delicacy of the Romanian situation and expressed its satisfaction with the Romanian policy position. Czechoslovak Foreign Minister Krofta realized that neither the internal nor the external situation of Romania admitted a bolder posture at the time. "From the Czechoslovak point of view it would be sufficient, in the immediate future," Krofta said, "to keep the question open, right up to the moment when its actual settlement became necessary or until Soviet–Rumanian relations are generally improved and harmonized."[7]

Ernst Urdăreanu, Romanian minister of the court, spoke more clearly and simply to the German minister, Wilhelm Fabricius. King Carol had told Edvard Beneš, Fabricius reported, that Romania would respond to a German–Czechoslovak conflict only in two circumstances. It would support Czechoslovakia under the terms of the Little Entente treaties, that is, if its ally were attacked by Hungary; or, in the event of world war, it would respond to its obligations under Article 16 of the League Covenant.[8] Given both the similarity and the divergences of interests among Romania and its allies, the Romanian position was entirely comprehensible, and the repetitive monotony of its policy position only delineates more clearly the poignant delicacy of its geostrategic situation.

At the height of the May crisis, as Europe apprehended a sudden German attack on Czechoslovakia, Romanian Foreign Minister Comnen

---

[5] Comnen (Geneva) to Ministry of Foreign Affairs, 12 May 1938; RMAE. Fond 71/U.R.S.S. Vol. 85, pp. 217–20.

[6] Ibid.

[7] Aleksandrovskii (Prague) to Litvinov, 30 May 1938; V. F. Klochko, ed., *New Documents on the History of Munich* (Prague: Orbis, 1958), 44–5 (No. 16).

[8] Fabricius to German Foreign Ministry, 24 May 1938; DGFP, D, 2: 337 (No. 205).

summoned the German Minister and informed him that the fate of Czechoslovakia was "of vital interest" to Romania and observed that an attack on Czechoslovakia would inevitably provoke a general European war.[9] Czechoslovak Foreign Minister Kamil Krofta expressed the official thanks of his government to Comnen: "Your initiative has moved the Czechoslovak government profoundly, which sees in it a new proof of friendship, which it has never doubted but which is especially precious manifested in present circumstances."[10] For all of its importance in the European military economy, especially its oil and wheat resources, Romania was, however, a conspicuously weak military power, and it is hard to imagine it exposing itself to the hostility of a great power such as Germany without the support of other great powers and especially those in which it had the greatest faith, France and Great Britain.

As the problem of Munich loomed, it was time, if there were ever to be such a time, for the Soviets and the Romanians to address the negotiations that had been sidelined by Butenko's disappearance. In the aftermath of the Butenko affair, and in the absence of senior diplomatic representation in Bucharest after the departure of both Ostrovskii and Butenko, Moscow sent its chief of the Prague legation, Sergei S. Aleksandrovskii, to Bucharest to deal with the problem. Comnen asked Aleksandrovskii to report to Litvinov that he saw no contradictions between Romanian and Soviet foreign-policy goals, which he described as collective security, strengthening the League, and the inviolability of present frontiers.[11] In June Litvinov received a joint visit of French Ambassador Robert Coulondre and Czechoslovak Ambassador Zdeněk Fierlinger and told them that Moscow was willing to engage itself, for the sake of a defensive pact with Romania, to withdraw behind the Dniestr on request at the end of possible hostilities.[12] Soviet–Romanian relations thus began, in the face of the urgency of the German threat and with the earnest efforts of the two foreign ministers, to recover a sense of common interests.

The question of Soviet military assistance to Czechoslovakia remained to be addressed, however, and it was a notoriously difficult matter. The government of Poland was suspicious of the Soviet Union at best and hostile to Czechoslovakia on account of the disputed district of Teschen as well as its Soviet alliance. Romania, on the other hand, was not only allied with the Czechs in the Little Entente but decidedly friendly to them. Yet the Romanian attitude toward the Soviets was apprehensive on the grounds of

---

[9] Thierry to Bonnet, 23 May 1938; DDF, 2nd series, 9: 85 (No. 422).

[10] Viorica Moisuc, *Diplomaţia României şi problema apărării suveranităţii şi independenţei naţionale în perioada martie 1938–mai 1940* (Bucharest: Editură Academiei, 1971), 53.

[11] Aleksandrovskii to Litvinov, 14 April 1938; DVP SSSR, 21: 196–7 (No. 132).

[12] Coulondre to Bonnet, 10 June 1938; DDF, 2nd series, 10: 7 (No. 6).

ideology, foreign policy, and Bessarabia alike. Still, soon after the *Anschluss*, as the urgency of the new crisis appeared unmistakably, Soviet–Romanian relations were repaired, and it was clear to everyone that the Romanian attitude toward the question of Soviet troop transit would play a significant role in the development of the situation.[13]

The prospect was, however, far from promising. As the crisis loomed, the French government queried the Romanians on the question, and as the French minister reported in July, "They have always given here the most categorical refusal to all suggestions in this matter." Furthermore, the new Romanian constitution of 27 February 1938 stipulated unequivocally, as the previous one had done, that no foreign military contingent would be admitted to Romania, even in the service of the country, without special legislation.[14]

The French, however, persisted. They began to bring considerable pressure on the Romanians for an explicit and positive response. Romanian Foreign Minister Comnen had pointed out to French Minister Adrien Thierry (22 May) that Romania could not take a position in the matter without consulting Poland and the Little Entente alike.[15] We have seen how the alliance with Poland, specifically formulated in 1921 against the Soviet Union, constrained Romanian policy. If the Romanian attitude toward Moscow underwent striking changes in the mid-1930s, the attitude of Poland remained as truculent as ever.[16] As tension developed, French Foreign Minister Georges Bonnet raised the question with Comnen again at a meeting of the League of Nations Council on 11 September. Comnen gave the same response.[17]

The Romanians maintained a stubborn and consistent position in this crucial question. The Poles were naturally concerned about it and made inquiries of their own. What they discovered is recorded in the diary of Under-Secretary for Foreign Affairs Jan Szembek: "The Romanians assured us categorically that they would not authorize the passage of Soviet troops. I judge that they will not for this reason, that in the contrary

[13] Much the best work known to me on Romanian foreign policy in this period is Dov B. Lungu, *Romania and the Great Powers, 1933–1940* (Durham, NC: Duke University Press, 1989). Lungu made extensive use of Romanian archival holdings.

[14] Adrien Thierry to Georges Bonnet, 9 July 1938; DDF, 2nd series, 10: 337.

[15] Moisuc, *Diplomaţia României şi problema apărării suveranităţii . . . martie 1938–mai 1940*, 58.

[16] N. P. Comnen, *Preludi del grande dramma: ricordi i documenti di un diplomatico* (Rome: Edizioni Leonardo, 1947), 39. Viorica Moisuc and Gheorghe Matei, "Politică externă a României in perioada Münchenului (martie 1938–martie 1939)," in Viorica Moisuc, ed., *Probleme de politică externă a României, 1919–1939* (Bucharest: Editură militară, 1971), 311.

[17] Georges Bonnet, *Défense de la paix*, 2 vols. (Paris: Éditions du cheval ailé, 1946–1948), 1: 201. Note du ministre (Bonnet), conversation avec M. Comnène, Geneva, 11 September 1938; DDF, 2nd series, 11: 161 (No. 96).

case, they would be obliged to demand whether it would be consonant with our alliance."[18] Similarly, "The ambassador of Romania declared to me . . . , again categorically, that there was no question of allowing the Soviet troops to pass over the territory of his country to assist Czechoslovakia."[19] Furthermore, Soviet Foreign Minister Litvinov said on more than one occasion that Soviet troops would not enter Romania without Romanian consent.[20]

Toward the end of May, the Romanians had given out several hints of the nature of their policy in the Sudeten crisis. According to the Soviet ambassador in Paris, Iakov Surits, King Carol had informed the French that Romania would "render assistance to Czechoslovakia," although what kind of assistance was not specified.[21] Bonnet told Surits that he believed Romania would assist Prague in the event that both London and Paris did so but would stand aside in the event of an isolated conflict.[22] Czechoslovak Foreign Minister Krofta confided to French Minister Victor de Lacroix that Comnen could not at that point declare rights of passage for Soviet troops but would reexamine the question in the event of a conflict. At the same time, Comnen refused to give Berlin assurance of the denial of Soviet passage.[23] Krofta expressed profound gratitude for Romania's position in the question.[24] About the same time, a rumor surfaced of a Polish–Romanian agreement to block Soviet army transit. Krofta raised the question with Comnen, who denied it and said that Bucharest would take a decision on the matter only when the occasion requiring a decision arose. Krofta said that he favored just such a policy.[25] The policy of postponing the making of such a decision until necessity required it became a settled and fixed element of the Romanian position. At the beginning of July, as a new Romanian minister took up his post at Prague, King Carol reiterated it.[26]

The Romanians appear to have been, in fact, somewhat surprised and somewhat frustrated at this time by the attention that the French Ministry

---

[18] Diary entry, 13 September 1938; Jan Szembek, *Journal, 1933–1939,* trans. J. Rzewuska and T. Zaleski, préface de Léon Noël (French ambassador) (Paris: Plon, 1952), 335. This translation is an abridgement of the longer manuscript later published as *Diariusz i teki Jana Szembeka, 1935–1945,* ed. Tytus Komarnicki, 4 vols. (London: Orbis, 1964–72).

[19] Diary entry, 20 September 1938; Jan Szembek, *Journal, 1933–1939,* 337.

[20] Bonnet, *Défense de la paix,* 2: 199, 200; Comnen, *Preludi del grande dramma,* 81.

[21] Surits to Commissariat of Foreign Affairs, 25 May 1938; DVP SSSR, 21: 287 (No. 198).

[22] Ibid., 27 May 1938; ibid., 292 (No. 203).

[23] Lacroix to Ministère des Affaires étrangères, 27 May 1938; DDF, 2nd series, 9: 923 (No. 467).

[24] Crutzescu (Prague Legation) to Romanian Ministry of Foreign Affairs, 29 May 1938; Hoover Institution Archive. Comnen Papers. Box 6, Folder 25.

[25] Aleksandrovskii (Prague Legation) to Commissariat of Foreign Afairs, 30 May 1938; DVP SSSR, 21: 295 (No. 206).

[26] Lacroix to Bonnet, 12 July 1938; DDF, 2nd series, 10: 357 (No. 194).

of Foreign Affairs wished to divert onto them. In a Europe dominated by great powers, they themselves, a modest power of Eastern Europe, were not the real fulcrum of political power plays. The heart of the matter was, in their opinion, the question whether the great powers in the West were willing to take a reasonable and firm stand in support of their own obligations and interests. Bucharest had communicated just such a point to Paris at the time of the *Anschluss*. At the end of July, it was repeated in a General Staff document: "Until such time as the great powers, and especially England, engage themselves in a categorical fashion to sustain Czechoslovakia, Germany will continue to agitate the Sudeten problem. At some time when the international situation is favorable, Germany will certainly use it as a pretext to put the Czechoslovak state to the test, the second stage of territorial expansion inscribed in Hitler's evangel to the German people, *Mein Kampf.*"[27] That, in fact, was the essence of the problem.

Although the French minister in Bucharest appeared to be unaware of the king's secret promise to Gamelin, he by no means despaired of eventual approval of Soviet troop transit. In spite of the many categorical refusals, he reported, "I get the impression that, a general war having once broken out, and in case of absolute necessity, it is certainly not impossible that the government will review [*revenir*] its present position."[28] Moscow, too, had long since had intimations that the Romanian position was more flexible than public statements suggested. As the intelligence section of the Red Army reported to Commissar of Defense Kliment Voroshilov in the spring, "Our resident in Bucharest [the *TASS* correspondent] has reported . . . that the Czech military attaché in Romania, Buda, has made the following communication to him: In conversation with the Romanian king on the developing situation in Europe, the latter is said to have assured him that 'In the event of passage of the Red Army across Romania, he [the king] will limit himself to a declaration of protest to the League of Nations, but Romania will remain on the side of the Czechs.' "[29] There was, after all, little more that the Romanian government could do in such a contingency, as the Soviet seizure of Bessarabia in summer 1940 would illustrate.

In addition, the Czech ambassador in Moscow, Zdeněk Fierlinger, had reported about the same time official discussion of the question how the

[27] Ioan Talpeş, *Diplomaţie şi apărare: coodonate ale politicii externe româneşti, 1933–1939* (Bucharest: Editură ştiintifă şi enciclopedică, 1988), 228.

[28] Thierry to Bonnet, 9 July 1938; DDF, 2nd series, 10: 339 (No. 182).

[29] Zam. nachal'nik Razvedyvatel'nogo upravleniia RKKA st. [starshii] maior Gos. bezopasnosti Gendin, Spetssoobshchenie . . . Tov. Voroshilovu, Sov. Sekretno, 2 April 1938; RGVA, f. 33987, op. 3s, d. 1145, s. 16.

Soviet Union would intervene militarily to assist the Czech ally with whom it did not share a common border. Litvinov was asked by a Reuters correspondent at a 15 March reception at the Iranian Embassy how his government would respond to such a necessity. Litvinov said that a corridor "would be found." A Polish correspondent asked Litvinov the same question at a similar reception on 17 March. Litvinov on this occasion said that such a corridor "had already been found."[30] As we shall see, a whole swarm of reports of the transfer of Soviet planes to the Czechs over Romania began a few weeks later. In the middle of September, Czechoslovak Foreign Minister Krofta told the American minister that "all was prepared for the passage of Soviet troops over Romania."[31] His conviction appears to have been shared by the Hungarians. They informed the Polish minister in Budapest that they had decided not to join a German attack on Czechoslovakia for fear that it would bring the Soviet army through Romania to the borders of Hungary.[32] As István Csáky, a senior official in the Hungarian Foreign Office, put it, the Hungarians had to feel their way in present circumstances with great care because the Romanians had taken a position very favorable to the Czechoslovaks, and it would be most awkward to throw them into the arms of the Russians. Budapest did not want to see a joint Soviet and Romanian army on the plains of Hungary.[33]

On 16 September, Litvinov told his friend, American journalist Louis Fischer, in Geneva that "the Romanians, not so hostile to the Czechs [as the Poles were], will probably let us pass."[34] In fact, Soviet–Romanian relations were growing warmer. The Romanians assured Litvinov on 20 September that they would not in any event, in case of war, be associated with an anti-Soviet side. Litvinov responded: "Never has Romania had

---

[30] Prague, Vojenský historický archív, 1938, dův. [důverny] čj. [čislo jednací] 319, karton 171: Zpráva čs. vyslanectví v Moskve o SSSR za I. čtvrtletí 1938 (39 listu).

[31] W. J. Carr to Secretary of State, 18 September 1938; *Foreign Relations of the United States, 1938*, 1: 615.

[32] Moisuc, *Diplomația României și problema apărării suveranității . . . martie 1938–mai 1940*, 65. Moisuc and Matei, "Politică externă a României in perioada Münchenului," 317–18.

[33] "Il était très nécessaire de n'avancer qu'en tâtant le terrain, car il n'aurait pas été opportun de voir les Roumains – qui, ces jours derniers, ont très nettement pris position en faveur de la Tchécoslovaquie – se précipiter dans les bras des Russes; en effet, nous n'avons aucune envie d'avoir à saluer les troupes roumaines et soviétiques dans la Grande Plaine de Hongrie." Report of Csáky on conversation with Sztójay, 16 September 1938; Magda Ádám, "Documents relatifs à la politique étrangère de la Hongrie dans la période de la crise tchécoslovaque (1938–1939)," *Acta historica Academiae scientiarum Hungaricae* 10 (1964):114–15.

[34] Louis Fischer, *Men and Politics: An Autobiography* (New York: Duell, Sloan and Pearce, 1941), 561.

better relations with the USSR than at the present moment."[35] In the latter half of September, the Czechoslovaks were reported to have received several hundred more Soviet planes over the Romanian route.[36]

The repeated denials of any intention to permit Soviet troop passage did not indicate, however, a complete indisposition of the Romanians to comfort and assist Germany's victims, Romania's allies, the Czechoslovaks. The clear assistance that the Romanian government rendered the Czechs in the matter of Soviet aircraft suggests that its attitude toward Soviet transit rights was not so categorical as its public statements. Comnen had foreseen – it did not require much foresight – that if Czechoslovakia fell to the Germans, Poland would be next, and Romania's turn would follow. As a Romanian historian has put it, the threat that irresistible German expansion posed to Romania forced the government to assume more obligations to Czechoslovakia than it was formally obliged to do, including "consent for transit of Soviet assistance" (*asentimentul pentru tranzitul ajutorului sovietic*).[37]

In fact, the presence of Soviet aircraft in Czechoslovakia was widely rumored throughout the summer, and yet precise details about the question have been as widely disputed subsequently as they were at the time. As early as April, Polish consuls began to report flights of Soviet planes over Romanian territory to Czechoslovakia. In the weeks and months that followed, the Poles first queried the Romanians, then protested the

---

[35] Moisuc, *Diplomația României și problema apărării suveranității... martie 1938–mai 1940*, 66. Readers who have followed the subject closely will be aware that we have for years now been in possession of a document in which Comnen allegedly gave to Litvinov formal approval of Soviet rights of passage: see Jiri Hochman, *The Soviet Union and the Failure of Collective Security, 1934–1938* (Ithaca, NY: Cornell University Press, 1984), Appendix C, 194–201. The document is more than suspect on several grounds. For a thorough examination of the issue of the authenticity of the document, see pp. 149–51.

[36] Moisuc and Matei, "Politică externă a României in perioada Münchenului," 315–16. The archive of the Central Committee of the Romanian Communist Party contains one intriguing document. According to a Comintern dispatch from Moscow, "The Romanian government declares its consent to the despatch of Soviet troops, in case of need, across the territory of your country to assist Czechoslovakia." There is no documentation of this allegation. Moisuc, *Diplomația României și problema apărării suveranității... martie 1938–mai 1940*, 66. Klement Gottwald claimed in an article in the Cominform organ, *For a Lasting Peace, for a People's Democracy*, 21 December 1949, that he had brought to President Beneš Stalin's assurance that the Soviets would support Czechoslovakia in the event of a German attack whether or not the French did. There is no documentation of this claim either. See the claim in Klement Gottwald, *O československé zahraniční politice* (Prague: SNPL, 1950), 134–5. According to Gottwald, Stalin said that he would render the Czechs assistance on two clear conditions: that they fought, and that they invited the assistance.

[37] Moisuc and Matei, "Politică externă a României in perioada Münchenului," 315. Moisuc, *Diplomația României și problema apărării suveranității*, 62 (the quotation); what kind of assistance is not specified.

overflights.[38] The question of the flights was taken quite seriously in Warsaw, such that Polish inspector general of armed forces, Marshal Edward Śmigly Rydz, raised it in conversation with the Romanian chief of staff, General E. Ionescu, on the latter's visit to Warsaw. Śmigly Rydz said that the Poles took a very negative view of the flights. Ionescu answered noncommitally.[39] In June, Czechoslovak Foreign Minister Kamil Krofta admitted to the Poles that his country had concluded an agreement with Romania to permit the overflights.[40] The Romanian Embassy in Prague subsequently informed the Poles that Czechoslovakia was purchasing the Soviet planes, that Romania consented to the overflights on the condition that the planes were unarmed, were not provided with photographic equipment, and were piloted by Czechoslovak personnel.[41]

Not surprisingly, the Germans were also interested in these developments. Reichsmarschall Hermann Göring himself inquired of the Romanian minister in Warsaw whether Soviet planes were being shipped to the Czechs overland. He was told that they were not; that it was possible, however, that Soviet planes were overflying Romania at altitudes above 4,000 meters. Göring remarked that at that altitude it was difficult to interfere with aircraft.[42] As the Polish chargé d'affaires reported of his conversation with German Embassy Counselor Kurt von Tippelskirch, "I sensed that the German government is quite alarmed at the possibility of Soviet assistance to Czechoslovakia."[43] In late August, Counselor von Tippelskirch brought to the Polish chargé in Moscow an interesting account of the matter. "[He] informed me confidentially that the Italian consul in Odessa has declared that for some time eleven Czech pilots are coming regularly through Tighina [Bendery]-Tiraspol each week to the USSR. As this same consul said that these pilots do not return to Czechoslovakia through Romania, the German embassy here is of the opinion that they are coming to the USSR not [for training] but exclusively in order to transport the next flight of Soviet planes purchased by Czechoslovakia over Romania."[44] In the middle of September, the Polish consul in Northern Bukovina reported increasing numbers of overflights. "The planes are supposed to have

---

[38] Jerzy Tomaszewski, "Polska korespondencja na temat wojskowej pomocy ZSSR dla Czechoslowacji w 1938 r. przez terytorium Rumanii," Z dziejów rozwoju państw socjalistycznych 1 (1983): No. 1: 162–70. I am grateful to Milan Hauner for providing me this series of documents.

[39] Tadeusz Kobylański (Vice-Director of Political Department, Ministry of Foreign Affairs) to Roger Raczyński (Polish Ambassador, Bucharest); ibid., 172.

[40] Kazimierz Papée (Prague) to Ministry of Foreign Affairs, 10 June 1938; ibid., 170. Talpeş, Diplomaţie şi apărării, 221.

[41] Papée to Józef Beck, 28 June 1938; "Polska korespondencja," 174–5.

[42] Jan Szembek to Polish Legation in Bucharest, 23 May 1938; ibid., 166–7.

[43] Tadeusz Jankowski (chargé in Moscow) to Józef Beck, 15 June 1938; ibid., 171.

[44] Jankowski to Beck, 30 August 1938; ibid., 175–6.

been observed several times by shepherds in the mountains in the region of Vijnita southeast of Czerniowce. According to reports, the flights occur regularly at about 4:00 AM and recur every several days."[45]

The Romanians informed the French that although their treaty obligations did not allow them to give formal permission for the overflights, their antiaircraft artillery would not reach planes flying at high altitudes and that in any event they would simply close their eyes to such flights.[46] At the end of August at the meeting of the Little Entente at Bled, Yugoslavia, Comnen told Czechoslovak Foreign Minister Krofta that, although the transit of Soviet troops was impossible, Romania would respond to Soviet overflights only by harmless protests.[47] Comnen wrote after the war that when these planes had engine trouble and made forced landings in Romania, the Romanians assisted in repairs and sent them on their way to Czechoslovakia.[48]

As substantial as the record of Soviet planes in Czechoslovakia appears from the indirect and somewhat remote testimony of the preceding evidence, we have few particulars from the Romanian archives. In fact, they are remarkably spare and elusive. So far as I know, no written record of the agreement between Bucharest and Prague to permit the overflights has come to light. We are in possession of one indubitable episode. On 16 June, the Romanian minister in Prague, Crutzescu, wrote to Comnen to request new arrangements for the expected arrival of a relatively large flight of Soviet planes in order to preserve confidentiality. "Our military attaché [Colonel Eftimie] has informed me that he has been instructed to take charge of the expected arrival in Czechoslovakia of 40 Soviet planes beginning today. The transfer that he will be obliged to make from Prague to the landing field in Slovakia will not escape the notice of foreign observers and will inevitably give rise to great suspicions." Comnen was requested therefore to intervene with the General Staff to relieve Colonel Eftimie of this duty, which would lend credence to the rumors, and leave the matter rather to the previously assigned Czech air force officer such as not to occasion political embarassment. Crutzescu also asked advice whether Warsaw was informed and how in any event to respond to whatever queries his Polish colleagues might make about the news.[49]

[45] Marian Uzdowski (consul in Chernovitsy) to Polish Legation, Bucharest, 19 September 1938; "Polska korespondencja," 181–2.

[46] Bonnet, *Défense de la paix*, 1: 202; 2: 408.

[47] Andreas Hillgruber, *Hitler, König Carol und Marshall Antonescu: Die deutsch–rumänishcen Beziehungen 1938–1944*, 2nd ed. (Wiesbaden, Germany: Franz Steiner, 1965), 20.

[48] Moisuc, *Diplomatia României și problema apărării suveranității*, 59. Moisuc and Matei, "Politică externă a României in perioada Münchenului," 312–13.

[49] Crutzescu (Prague) to Ministry of Foreign Affairs, 16 June 1938; RMAE. Fond 71/Romînia. Vol. 102, p. 116.

Comnen responded the following day. "It is true that the Czechoslovak government has requested authorization for the overflight of 40 planes purchased in the U.S.S.R. This request, complying with all the conditions of international agreements, has been approved by the General Staff, which has taken into account the conversations of Marshall Rydz Smigli [sic] and General Ionescu at Warsaw. The Polish military attaché at Bucharest has been informed of the above. It is preferable to speak of this question only if you are queried by the Polish legation. All of this information is completely confidential."[50]

Did these planes constitute a significant contribution to Czech military capacity? How many were there? In the contemporary German and French documents, there are many wild guesses, ranging up to several hundred planes. In fact, a reliable record of this perhaps overly celebrated – and disputed – question appears to be available only in recent Czech historiography. The Czechoslovak government had been interested for some time in the Soviet bomber SB-2 (*skorostnoi bombardirovshchik*, i.e., fast bomber). The SB-2, one of the more advanced aircraft of the day, was a two-engine plane, required a crew of three, was capable of a speed of 400 kilometers per hour, and carried a bomb load of 500–600 kilograms. It gave an impressive performance in the Spanish Civil War, where it went into combat without a fighter escort, as it was faster than most of the fighter planes of the time.

On 15 April 1937, the Czechoslovak government concluded with the Soviet government an agreement stipulating the purchase of 61 Soviet SB-2 bombers (Czech designation B-71) and a license to produce 161 more in Czechoslovak industries. The planes purchased were to be equipped in the Soviet Union with Czech engines and to be provided with armaments and photographic equipment only after being transported to Czechoslovakia. The transport itself posed significant problems. The rail route through Romania into Slovakia was not feasible, as the fuselage of the plane was too large to go through the multiple tunnels in Slovakia. The rail route through Poland or Hungary was not feasible, for the Czechs wished to keep the deal secret. And so the air route was the indispensable alternative.[51] Perhaps the most curious feature of this arrangement, given all of the speculation about Soviet planes sent to the assistance of Prague in the face of the Munich crisis, is that the original arrangements were made long before the Sudeten problem arose, and the planes themselves, purchased by the Czechs, did not constitute direct Soviet military assistance.

[50]   Comnen to Prague Legation, 17 June 1938; ibid., p. 133.

[51]   Miloslav John, *Československé letectvo v roce 1938* (Beroun: Baroko & Fox, 1996), 86–92, 99–101. The details that John gives for the dates of the flights differ from the reports of the Polish consuls as well as from those in the Romanian archives.

As the tension in Europe palpably increased, on 31 August, Georges Bonnet instructed the French chargé in Moscow, Jean Payart, in the absence of Ambassador Robert Coulondre, to query Litvinov under what conditions Prague could count on Soviet military assistance.[52] Litvinov was obviously not fully prepared for the question, and he turned at once directly to Stalin for an answer. As he wrote (1 September), "I absolutely do not know what line to take, as there has been no exchange of opinions on the question recently."[53] We do not have a record of Stalin's response – he usually did such business by phone – but we know, thanks to the recently published log of the visitors to Stalin's Kremlin office, that he received Litvinov on the day when the note was written,[54] and on the following day, 2 September, the foreign commissar was prepared to give Payart a relatively elaborate and definite answer[55]:

The people's commissar . . . confirmed his previous declarations of principle, according to which the U.S.S.R. has decided to fulfill by all *possible* means [my emphasis] the engagements stemming from the pact with Czechoslovakia on condition that France itself observes its own [obligations]. . . . M. Litvinov further indicated to me that given the negative attitude adopted by Warsaw and Bucharest, he sees only one practical way to proceed, that of appealing to the League of Nations. He mentioned, but only to exclude it *a priori*, the possibility of a forced passage of Soviet troops across Poland and Romania in the absence of a decision of Geneva. In his opinion, all measures should be taken in order to alert the Council of the League immediately, such that the procedure of Geneva might be ready to be activated from the moment when aggression occurs. If he excludes absolutely from his considerations the good will of Poland, he imagines on the contrary that a favorable [League] recommendation in regard to Czechoslovakia, even if it receives only a majority vote of the members of the Council [instead of the Charter's stipulated unanimity – HR], might exercise a positive psychological influence on the ultimate attitude of Romania, alarmed by the development of Hitler's dynamism.

He noted in this regard that M. Comnen said to M. Krofta at [the Little Entente conference at] Bled that if Romania objected to the passage of Soviet troops, it would on the contrary close its eyes to the flight of planes over its territory. He sees here a sign that Bucharest is less disposed to resist.

[52] Bonnet to Payart (chargé d'affaires), 31 August 1938; DDF, 2nd series, 10: 899–900 (No. 511).

[53] Litvinov to Stalin (copy), 1 September 1938; RGVA. Fond 33987, op. 3, d. 1146. Copy in Library of Congress, Manuscript Division. Volkogonov Collection, box 16 (reel 10), folder 2.

[54] *Istoricheskii arkhiv*, 1998, No. 4: "Posetiteli kremlevskogo kabineta I. V. Stalina: Zhurnaly (tetradi) zapisi lits, priniatykh pervym gensekom, 1924–1953 gg: Alfavitnyi ukazatel'," p. 109.

[55] Payart to Bonnet, 2 September 1938; DDF, 2nd series, 10: 934–5 (No. 534). Bonnet, *Défense de la paix*, 2: 408. Talpeş, *Diplomaţie şi apărăre*, 229–30.

This communication would seem to constitute exceptionally important evidence of Soviet intentions in respect to Romania and in respect to the crisis more generally. It is as close as we can come to the expression of Stalin's own opinion. At the same time, Litvinov sent his ambassador in London to Winston Churchill to elaborate the Soviet diplomatic plan. Churchill himself tells the story:

> In the afternoon of September 2, I received a message from the Soviet Ambassador that he would like to come down to Chartwell and see me at once upon a matter of urgency. I had for some time had friendly personal relations with M. Maisky. . . . I thereupon received the Ambassador, and . . . he told me in precise and formal detail the story set out below. Before he had got very far, I realised that he was making a declaration to me, a private person, because the Soviet Government preferred this channel to a direct offer to the Foreign Office which might have encountered a rebuff. It was clearly intended that I should report what I was told to His Majesty's Government. . . . It was implied by the fact that no request for secrecy was made [and] the matter struck me at once as being of the first importance.

Churchill thereupon wrote to Lord Halifax, the secretary for Foreign Affairs, and transmitted to him an account of Maiskii's conversation[56]:

> Yesterday, September 2, the French Chargé d'Affaires in Moscow (the Ambassador being on leave) called upon M. Litvinov and, in the name of the French Government, asked him what aid Russia would give to Czechoslovakia against a German attack, having regard particularly to the difficulties which might be created by the neutrality of Poland or Rumania. Litvinov asked in reply what the French would do themselves, pointing out that the French had a direct obligation, whereas the Russian obligation was dependent on the action of France. The French Chargé did not reply to this question. Nevertheless, Litvinov stated to him, first, that the Russian Soviet Union had resolved to fulfil their obligations. He recognised the difficulties created by the attitude of Poland and Rumania, but he thought that in the case of Rumania these could be overcome.
>
> In the last few months the policy of the Rumanian Government had been markedly friendly to Russia, and their relations had greatly improved. M. Litvinov thought that the best way to overcome the reluctance of Rumania would be through the agency of the League of Nations. If, for instance, the League decided that Czechoslovakia was the victim of aggression and that Germany was the aggressor, that would probably determine the action of Rumania in regard to allowing Russian troops and air forces to pass through her territory.

[56] Winston S. Churchill, *The Second World War*, 6 vols. (New York: Houghton Mifflin, 1948–1953), 1: 294–5.

The French Chargé d'Affaires raised the point that the Council might not be unanimous, and was answered that M. Litvinov thought a majority decision would be sufficient, and that Rumania would probably associate herself with the majority in the vote of the Council. M. Litvinov, therefore, advised that the Council of the League should be invoked under Article 11 [consideration of measures to avoid war in face of impending danger of it], on the ground that there was danger of war, and that the League Powers should consult together. He thought the sooner this was done the better, as time might be very short. He next proceeded to tell the French Chargé d'Affaires that staff conversations ought immediately to take place between Russia, France, and Czechoslovakia as to the means and measures of giving assistance. The Soviet Union was ready to join in such conversations at once.

Halifax replied, in the typically nonchalant idiom of appeasement, that he thought such action unnecessary at that time. Moscow in the meantime asked Paris to bring the Sudeten issue before the League Council, but the French refused.[57]

As the atmosphere of crisis developed, the Romanian General Staff drafted on 7 September a plan of mobilization designed to take into account the probable manner in which the nations of Eastern Europe would divide in the event of the outbreak of a general conflict. It foresaw Romanian solidarity with Czechoslovakia, France, and the Soviet Union and confessed failure to be able to anticipate Polish policy.[58] On September 9, however, the Romanian minister in Berlin, Radu Djuvara, told the Germans that Bucharest had recommended to Prague a conciliatory attitude in the Sudeten question. In addition, although he did not declare unambiguously that the Soviets would not be given permission to cross, he did say that it "was in the most vital interest of his country that Russia should be prevented from interfering via Romanian territory. In this connection Romania was at one with Poland."[59]

By this time the leading diplomats of Europe were gathering at Geneva for a meeting of the League. Comnen was naturally there and just as naturally in conference with Bonnet and Litvinov. Litvinov had proposed to Bonnet to bring the issue of Czechoslovakia before the League, and Comnen had told Bonnet that a League resolution would do nothing to dispose Romania to give the Red Army permission to pass. Comnen added that, without the consent of Poland, Romania was unable to change its position.[60] Bonnet refused in any event to bring the issue before the

[57] Fierlinger to Ministry of Foreign Affairs, 17 September 1938; *Dokumenty i materialy po istorii sovetsko–chekhoslovatskikh otnoshenii*, 5 vols. (Moscow: Nauka, 1973–88), 3: 498–503 (No. 339).

[58] Planul de mobilizare din punct de vedere operativ și al angaajamentelor luati fața de aliața, 7 September 1938; cited in Talpeș, "Date noi privind," 1661.

[59] Minute of State Secretary Weizsäcker, 9 September 1938; DGFP, Series D, 2: 725–6 (No. 447).

[60] Bonnet, *Défense de la paix*, 1: 200–1.

League. The French explained to the Czechoslovak minister in Moscow that they were afraid that the Soviets would use the complexities and delays of League procedure to shelter themselves from their obligations.[61] In fact, as we have seen, Litvinov was pressing the French to join Moscow in supporting precisely those obligations both through the League and through the General Staffs of the two nations.

On the following day, Comnen reported a long talk with Litvinov. They discussed the Butenko affair, the pending issue of establishing a commercial air route between Moscow and Prague over Romanian territory,[62] the resolution of border incidents along the Dniestr frontier, the surveillance of Romanian diplomats in Moscow, and the growing comity between Romania and Poland, as evidenced by the many exchanges of official state visits. The one pertinent item that was not mentioned was the issue of Red Army passage through Romania.[63] We know of no occasions when Moscow raised the question with the Romanians. Comnen reported from Geneva in the middle of September 1938 that he had a conversation of an hour and a half with Litvinov during which, however, Litvinov made no reference to the question.[64] Bonnet persisted, however, in a fashion that Litvinov declined to do, to deal with the issue of Soviet troop passage. According to Comnen's memoirs, "While France continued to make efforts to obtain reassuring declarations on this matter from Poland and Romania; and at Geneva the French delegates, Georges Bonnet, Paul Boncour [sic: Joseph Paul-Boncour], and [Édouard] Herriot assailed us with requests, Litvinov, whom I saw almost daily, either at meetings of the Council, or the Assembly or during official lunches and dinners, maintained an attitude of reserve. . . . During that session of the League of Nations which proved to be one of the most tragic in its brief existence, although my meeetings with Litvinov were of almost daily occurrence, he spoke to me of many other matters but never of that primary condition on which he insisted for the intervention of his country. He preferred to leave it for our French friends to enlighten us on this matter." Litvinov repeated to

---

[61] Fierlinger to Ministry of Foreign Affairs, 17 September 1938; *Dokumenty i materialy po istorii sovetsko–chekhoslovatskikh otnoshenii*, 3: 498–503 (No. 339).

[62] The Russians and the Czechoslovaks had long before concluded an agreement to establish such an air service, but it naturally had to cross the territory of either Poland or Romania. The Romanians were not averse to cooperating in the venture, but the negotiations hit a stone wall when the issue of specifying a precise route of the flights was raised. The problem consisted in the terminology of defining the Soviet–Romanian frontier. The Romanians naturally wanted the Dniestr identified as that frontier, and the Soviets refused. On this issue, the negotiations stalemated throughout the 1930s. The archives at RMAE are virtually awash in documentation of the issue.

[63] Comnen (Geneva) to Ministry of Foreign Affairs "for H. M. the King," 12 September 1938; RMAE. Fond 71/U.R.S.S. Vol. 85, pp. 443–6.

[64] Comnen, Geneva, to Ministry of Foreign Affairs "for H. M. the King," 12 September 1938; RMAE. Fond 71/U.R.S.S. Vol. 135, pp. 298–301.

Comnen that Moscow would not intervene unless the French did and would not in any case enter Romania without Romanian consent.[65] He also recounted to Comnen his recent conversation with the German ambassador in Moscow, Count von der Schulenburg, in which the latter had inquired of the Soviet attitude in the event of the outbreak of hostilities over Czechoslovakia. Litvinov repeated what he had said to Schulenburg, that, if Germany attacked, Britain and France would certainly intervene and that the Soviets would fulfill all their obligations.[66]

In spite of avoiding altogether in his conversations with Comnen in Geneva the subject of Soviet troop transit, Litvinov was mysteriously reported soon afterwards to be satisfied about the question. As the Romanian minister in Prague described the matter to Comnen, "The Soviet minister [here] has said to M. Krofta that Litvinov is very satisfied with the conversations that he had with Your Excellency at Geneva on the problem of Czechoslovakia and that he has the impression that we have only to find the means of approving Russian assistance [că nu am mai căuta decât formula care să îngăduie sprijunul rusesc]."[67]

Only days later (15 September), Comnen told the British delegate at the meeting, Count de la Warr, that, in the event of war, "supplies would probably pass [from Russia] through Romania to Czechoslovakia and he thought there would be no difficulty in such a case in allowing transit, especially for aeroplanes." For ground troops and their supplies, on the other hand, the outlook was bleak on account of poor communications. The natural line of communications between Russia and Czechoslovakia ran through Poland. The "Foreign Minister stated that if Czechoslovakia collapsed now it would be Poland's turn next and then that of Romania." Still, Romania was not in a position to march alone in support of Czechoslovakia. It was obliged to wait on the cooperation of Poland and Yugoslavia. He expressed natural reluctance to welcome Russian troops into Romania, for "throughout history, whenever there had been association with Russia that country had managed to secure large portions of Romanian territory for herself."[68]

The Romanian historian Al. Gh. Savu has argued, in a fashion that I find to be entirely consonant with the documentation, that the government of Romania could have overcome its natural fear of Communism and concluded an alliance with Moscow if such an agreement might have

[65] Comnen, "Dust and Shadows," 3–4, 7; Hoover Institution Archive. Comnen Collection, Box 14, Folder 55.

[66] Comnen, Geneva, to Ministry of Foreign Affairs "for H. M. the King," 12 September 1938; RMAE. Fond 71/U.R.S.S. Vol. 135, pp. 298–301.

[67] Crutzescu (Prague) to Comnen, 18 September 1938; RMAS. Fond 71/U.R.S.S. Vol. 103, pp. 152–3.

[68] Lord de la Warr to Foreign Office, 15 September 1938; DBFP, 3rd series, 2: 354–5 (No. 898).

taken place in a larger system of alliances, that is, in a collective-security arrangement including Britain and France.[69]

In summary, if we consider the unhappy, tormented dilemma of Romania in the context of the crisis, it seems eminently fair to conclude that it had an altogether reasonable fear of the intervention of the Red Army in Czechslovakia across Bessarabia and was eager to avoid it, yet was powerless to prevent it and thus would have consented under pressure, as it did in 1940, whenever that intervention was unavoidable.

By this time, Neville Chamberlain had become the driving force of whatever motley coalition of interests the designs of Hitler challenged. If Czechoslovakia was a country, in his deplorable phrase, "of which we know nothing," how much more so was Romania; how much less did it figure in his calculations. Totally unprepared to confront Hitler in person and utterly oblivious of the interests of the crucial powers of Eastern Europe, he nevertheless considered himself the appropriate person to address the problem, and the mosaic texture of conflicting interests among the powers great and small provided him the opportunity to which they all silently consented.

[69] Al. Gh. Savu, *Dictatură regală (1938–1940)* (Bucharest: Editură politică, 1970), 205.

PART TWO

Foreground: Climax of the Crisis

Chapter 4

East Awaiting West: Berchtesgaden
to Godesberg

And so, at this point, British Prime Minister Neville Chamberlain arose –
or perhaps he descended – to take the initiative to save the peace of the
continent – temporarily – at almost whatever price Hitler demanded.
Hitler later told Polish Ambassador Józef Lipski that he was "taken aback
to a certain extent by Chamberlain's proposition to come to Berchtesgaden. It was, of course, impossible for him not to receive the British
Prime Minister. He thought Chamberlain was coming to make a solemn
declaration that Great Britain was ready to march."[1] He need not have
worried.

The French Cabinet, it is true, was invited to London several times for
extensive discussions, consultations, for the formulation of joint policy.
And yet the most substantive British initiatives – the Runciman mission,
the meetings at Berchtesgaden and Godesberg – were taken without consultation with the French. The French meekly consented. For all the wisdom of Daladier's speech at the first Anglo–French meeting in London on
28–29 April, he was eventually maneuvered by the wiles of Chamberlain
into a compromise of which he was deeply ashamed. Conscious of their
own military weakness and without any confidence in their Polish or Soviet allies, who in turn had no confidence in the French, they placed their
hope entirely in the uncertain prospect of unity with the British Cabinet.

As tension began to swell and the threat of war seemed ever more likely,
Daladier on 13 September proposed to Chamberlain the convocation of a
meeting of British, French, and German heads of state. Chamberlain declined, convinced that he himself had a better idea. This was his notorious
"Plan Z." That is, he proposed to *invite himself* to a meeting with Hitler in

---

[1]   Wacław Jedrzejewicz, ed., *The Papers and Memoirs of Józef Lipski, Ambassador of Poland, Diplomat in
      Berlin 1933–1939* (New York: Columbia University Press, 1968), 408.

Germany *without* the French.[2] According to Duff Cooper, Chamberlain dispatched the telegram embodying this unprecedented proposal to Hitler and only subsequently informed the cabinet.[3] According to Sir Robert Vansittart, chief diplomatic adviser to the foreign secretary, it was "going to Canossa."[4]

In some respects, it was worse than going to Canossa, as one of the casualties of the announcement of Chamberlain's trip to Berchtesgaden was the collapse of the plans of the military conspirators against Hitler. This plot had originally formed around General Ludwig Beck, chief of the General Staff. Beck was one of those ardently dutiful, totally dedicated officers of adamantine integrity, of the old Prussian type who were never comfortable with the likes of the Nazi regime in Germany. He and officers like him were in complete sympathy with Hitler's *minimum* program of territorial revision in the East, but they were convinced both that the time was not ripe and that Hitler would blunder into another two-front war and condemn Germany to a more costly loss than that of 1918. Through the spring of 1938, Beck wrote one memorandum after another to persuade his chief, defense minister and commander in chief of the army, General Walther von Brauchitsch, to persuade Hitler that his plans against Czechoslovakia were mad. Brauchitsch was himself persuaded, but he was timid and hesitant, a pliable state servant. He passed along a good deal of Beck's criticism to Hitler, but he pulled punches, too. Even so, Hitler soon tired of Beck's resistance, Beck despaired of success, and he resigned (18 August). He had already, however, begun to form the conspiracy that now fell upon the shoulders of his successor, General Franz Halder.[5]

Neither Halder nor Beck had the temperament of conspirators, and neither proved willing to subordinate all other considerations of an officer's traditional conception of honor to the goal at hand. Many of their lieutenants, however, did. In particular, there was General Erwin von

[2] Anthony Adamthwaite, *France and the Coming of the Second World War, 1936–1939* (London: Frank Cass, 1977), 210–11; Jean-Baptiste Duroselle, *La décadence, 1932–1939* (Paris: Imprimerie nationale, 1985), 345; Élisabeth du Réau, *Édouard Daladier, 1884–1970* (Paris: Fayard, 1993), 256.

[3] Alfred Duff Cooper, *Old Men Forget* (New York: Dutton, 1954), 228.

[4] Telford Taylor, *Munich: The Price of Peace* (New York: Vintage, 1980), 671; Keith Middlemas, *The Diplomacy of Illusion: The British Government and Germany, 1937–1939* (London: Gregg Revivals, 1991), 339. The reference is to the humiliation of Emperor Henry IV at the feet of Pope Gregory VII at Canossa in the Investiture Controversy of 1077, an act of prostration and self-humiliation.

[5] Peter Hoffmann, *The History of the German Resistance, 1933–1945,* trans. Richard Barry (Cambridge, MA: MIT Press, 1977), Chapter 6: "Beck's Plans," 69–80, and Chapter 7: "Halder's Plans," 81–96; and Joachim Fest, *Plotting Hitler's Death: The Story of the German Resistance,* trans. Bruce Little (New York: Henry Hold, 1996), Chapter 3: "The September Plot," 71–101.

Witzleben, an absolutely key figure, as he commanded the army corps of the III Military District headquartered in Berlin. He professed total ignorance of politics, but he said that he knew what it was necessary to do with Hitler.

Younger and more junior officers were sure that they knew, too. In particular, while the more conservative older officers considered a suitable fate for Hitler once he was seized, a coterie that gathered around Captain Friedrich Wilhelm Heinz formed a conspiracy within the conspiracy, one determined to kill Hitler at the first opportunity in order to preempt the necessary backlash that could be expected in a military that had taken an oath of personal loyalty to the Führer. They had arranged to have some of their colleagues prepare to open the great double doors of the Reich Chancellery Building to admit a squad of assassins equipped with firearms, grenades, and other explosives. They awaited only word that war was declared, and that is what Chamberlain's announced flight to Berchtesgaden denied them. At that point the conspiracy collapsed.

Of the reams of print on the meeting at Berchtesgaden, we need here only a spare account of the essentials, and the record itself is spare enough. Three persons were present, Chamberlain, Hitler, and Hitler's interpreter, Paul Schmidt. The only record kept at the time consists of Schmidt's notes, although Chamberlain later wrote a compatible summary.[6]

Chamberlain opened with general queries as to how the state of Anglo–German relations could be improved. Hitler responded that the Sudeten question was at the moment so urgent as to supersede all more general considerations. Chamberlain took up this challenge remarkably boldly. He posed the critical question at once: Were the Sudetens the ultimate objective or merely a phase in the process of German expansion? Hitler, utterly unruffled, indicated that the Sudetens were not the end of the matter, as the wishes of the Poles, the Hungarians, and the Ukrainians had to be taken into account. Why did this grim suggestion of how much more trouble Hitler had up his sleeve not make more impression on Chamberlain? We have no way of knowing. He may have missed the implication of that remark, as he then asked whether Czechoslovakia would remain dangerous to Germany once a resolution of the Sudeten problem was reached. Hitler said that Czechoslovakia would remain dangerous so long as it retained alliances with other countries that menaced Germany. Chamberlain asked whether, if the Czechoslovak treaty with the Soviet Union were abrogated, it would allay Hitler's concern. Hitler said – another foreboding portent

---

[6]   We have in the British and the German documents two different translations of Schmidt's German original: DGFP, Series D, 2: 786–98 (No. 487); DBFP, 3rd series, 2: 342–51 (No. 896).

overlooked – that Czechoslovakia would in any event at some point disappear, as the Slovaks were even then attempting to detach themselves from the country. Chamberlain wanted to know if the transfer to Germany of Czech districts that were 80 percent German would satisfy Hitler's demands. Hitler said no, that districts 50 percent German would have to be transferred. Chamberlain queried whether it would not be possible to encourage the two parties in the area to negotiate their differences in a quieter atmosphere. Hitler said no, as atrocities against Germans were occurring there, "and I do not care whether there is a world war or not, I am determined to settle it soon." Chamberlain, evidently somewhat taken aback by this aggressive tone, asked "why the Führer had let him come to Germany when the Führer was apparently determined to proceed in one definite direction and would not consider an armistice." Totally unfazed by this intervention of sweet reason and peaceful motif, Hitler said he simply wanted to know whether his demands would be met or not. Chamberlain said that "he must naturally also consult France and Lord Runciman. But he could give it as his personal view . . . that he admitted the principle of the separation of the Sudeten areas. . . . He wished, therefore, to return to England in order to report to the Government and to obtain their approval of his personal attitude." Hitler said that he would accommodate the prime minister's convenience by meeting next time in the Rhineland, perhaps at Cologne or Godesberg. Hitler promised to withhold military action, except in extreme circumstances, until they met again. He said that he hoped that a peaceful resolution of the problem could be found and that an improvement in Anglo–German relations might follow. "The attitude of England and France was incomprehensible to him. While England had given the Irish their freedom without a war, and while the French . . . had allowed the Saar to be returned to Germany, there was talk in both countries of warlike developments in an affair which was to them after all by no means a direct interest. France had allowed a plebiscite to take place in the Saar, but when a plebiscite was to take place in the Sudeten area, was she ready to go to war with Germany, a war which would naturally be a question of life and death?"

Here was what a later age would denominate a summit meeting, and it must be admitted that Chamberlain approached it with a disastrous deficiency of skills as a negotiator, accepting in principle what appeared at the time to be Hitler's maximum demands *before* presenting them to his own cabinet or that of the Czechs – whose territory alone was at issue – and the French. The cabinet convened to hear his report on the following day, discussed what was to be done in a bewildered and desultory fashion, and finally agreed that nothing further could be done without additional consultations with the French – no reference here to the exclusive property holders, the Czechs. And so on the morning of 18 September the French came back to London.[7]

Chamberlain opened the meeting by giving a résumé of his talk with Hitler and concluded with the observation that only the fulfillment of the principle of self-determination could avert a war. He then asked Daladier to express the views of the French government. In fact, the two parties engaged in a considerable amount of verbal fencing for a while, each side trying to prompt the other to take a position first. Chamberlain brought an end to this impasse by pointing out that, as only the French had a treaty obligation in the Sudetenland, they were compelled to decide whether they could accept the principle of self-determination. Daladier said that it was a very dangerous principle in Czechoslovakia, as both the Poles and the Hungarians would claim a piece of the pie and thus contribute to the destruction of the Czechoslovak state, a point that Hitler had made at Berchtesgaden. Chamberlain asked Daladier if he had any alternative to the acceptance of self-determination to propose. Daladier had none. Halifax intervened to say that even in the event of a victorious war, it probably did not make sense to reconstitute Czechoslovakia in so troublesome and unstable a condition as the present one. In any event, it was up to the French to state whether their treaty allowed them to accept the principle of self-determination.

Fatigue and monotony suggested an adjournment for lunch. Daladier and Chamberlain lunched together. Although no record of the talk exists, it was apparently at this lunch that Daladier introduced confidentially a strictly secret proposal from President Beneš himself, the now-notorious Nečas memorandum.

Here we find the intrusion of an affair that was tortured, clandestine, disputed, and deliberately obscure. In fact, Beneš himself took the initiative in the most secretive fashion to propose the cession of carefully limited parts of the Sudeten territories. He had apparently been contemplating some such plan – scientific politics by nature, of course – for some time, and it first surfaced, so far as we know, in a conversation with the French minister in Prague.

M. de Lacroix had made a call on Beneš on official business and spontaneously began to engage him in unofficial matters of conversation. He recognized, he said, the exceptionally perplexing nature of the current problem, and he appealed to the celebrated diplomatic skills of Beneš to suggest a solution, or at least an approach to a solution.

---

[7] Record of Anglo–French conversations held at No. 10 Downing Street on September 18, 1938; DGFP, 3rd series, 2: 373–99 (No. 928); Compte rendu des conversations franco-brittaniques du 18 septembre 1938; DDF, 2nd series, 11: 309–33 (No. 212).

Beneš, "not without great hesitation," pulled out of his files the sketch of just such an approach. He had foreseen something of the present problem as long ago as the conference of Versailles, he said. He had in mind the cession of three bits of border territory in Northwest Bohemia, several thousand square kilometers populated by 800,000–900,000 Germans, delineated such as to leave Czechoslovak border fortifications intact. Beneš assumed that a part of the Germans inhabiting these territories would voluntarily move east into predominantly Czech Bohemia to avoid the Nazi regime. They could be exchanged, then, for the transfer of hardened Sudeten-Deutsch partisans, according to a previously negotiated agreement, whose emigration would thereby relieve the scale of ethnic conflict in Czech territory proper. For reciprocity, he would expect a concession on the part of the German government, specifically that it should agree to accept approximately 1 million more Sudeten Germans. The German minority remaining in Czechoslovakia would thus be reduced to 1–1.2 million persons, of whom at least half were Jews or Social Democrats naturally opposed to Nazism. This remaining minority would not constitute a danger threatening the integrity of the state.[8]

This thought was apparently the prelude to the notorious Nečas memorandum. Beneš selected a trusted colleague in the cabinet, Jaromír Nečas, a Social Democrat, to be the bearer of a special confidential communication to the former French Socialist premier, Léon Blum, who would, it was obviously assumed, forward it to current Premier Édouard Daladier.[9]

Monsieur le Ministre Nečas,

1. Do not allow anyone to suppose that this plan comes from Czechoslovaks.
2. Hold it in the most absolute secrecy; nothing may be published from it.
3. The terms [of the note] should be negotiated secretly between France and England after a rigorous delineation *on our part* of the territorial *extent* that it would be possible for us to cede, because there is reason to fear that, once we admit the principle [of cession], these powers would retreat in the face of Hitler and *abandon the whole as a bloc.*

---

[8] De Lacroix to Bonnet, 17 September 1938; DDF, 2nd series, 2: 273–5 (No. 180). Beneš had made similar proposals to Hungary soon after the conclusion of the Versailles Conference in 1920, the cession of purely Magyar areas of Southern Slovakia in exchange for a population transfer and rights for the Slovak minority remaining in Hungary, a far-reaching economic agreement, and Hungarian renunciation of all further claims on Czechoslovakia. Hungarian revisionism was, however, more ambitious. C. J. Macartney and A. W. Palmer, *Independent Eastern Europe: A History* (London: Macmillan, 1962), 265–6.

[9] Note de Beneš à Nečas; *Munich 1938; mythes et réalités* (Paris: Institut national d'études slaves, 1979), 138.

4. Thereafter, once the whole plan is agreed upon, it must be *imposed* on Hitler as the *last concession* among others.

5. This would concede to Germany so many thousands of kilometers of territory (personally I do not know just how many but probably something between 4000 and 6000 square kilometers; don't commit yourself on this point) on the condition that [Germany] take a minimum of 1,000,000 to 2,000,000 inhabitants of German speech. In other words, a transfer of population, the democrats, the socialists, and the Jews remaining a part of the [Czech] community.

6. [Any] other solution would be impossible because it would pose the question of the partition pure and simple of the Republic. *This is why the whole idea is extremely dangerous.* If it is approached without deliberation, it would be a catastrophe.

7. Be careful. They can play a trick on you [*on pourrait vous jouer quelque tour déloyal*]. One never knows.

8. On the subject of the plebiscite, [you must] indicate that it can lead us into a situation in which President Beneš would send several hundreds of thousands of democrats, socialists and Jews to a massacre, as occurred in Austria and elsewhere, to the barbarity of humiliations and of antisemitic murders, in the concentration camps.

This he will not do. And if they attempt to protect them [sic – by other means], note that this would create a new problem of nationality. From the announcement of the plebiscite, all the democrats, the socialists, the Jews, etc., will leave [the territory in question], we will have an *internal* emigration and, moreover, the problem of nationalities will not be solved.

A plebiscite is completely impossible from the technical, legal, or political point of view. Demonstrate on a map the form of our state and the position of Germany as a result of a plebiscite.

Do not reveal that all of this comes from me.

Do not breathe a word of it to [Ambassador Štefan] Osuský and demand that no one speak of it to him.[10]

Destroy these notes.

Blum later testified that he received from Beneš a map and a note: "I am sending you the map on which Daladier can see [*lire*] by the location of our military works and our fortifications the extreme limit beyond which we would consider Czechoslovakia surrendered [*livrée*] and lost."[11] Blum

---

[10] Beneš and Osuský did not have a trusting and confidential relationship and subsequently became bitter enemies. Osuský's papers at the Hoover Institution Archive contain an abundant record of it.

[11] Testimony of Blum, 30 July 1947; Commission d'enquête parlementaire, *Les événements survenus en France de 1933 à 1945*, 9 vols. (Paris: Presses universitaires de France, 1951–1952), 9: 256.

sent these messages to Daladier, who received them 17 September just before leaving for London to confer with the British cabinet on Chamberlain's meeting with Hitler at Berchtesgaden. As Daladier later testified, "On the eve of my departure for London, it would have been better not to receive a proposition from Prague," especially as it constituted "an additional argument in favor of the London point of view [*thèse de Londres*]." He nevertheless informed Chamberlain of the memorandum "*dans une conversation intime,*" and Chamberlain responded just as Daladier had apparently apprehended that he would: "You see very well that we can do nothing. Prague itself recognizes it."[12] The memorandum was evidently not shared with the cabinet of either country. There is no record of the conversation, no reference to it, nor to the Nečas memorandum at all, in British sources. And it is anybody's guess how well these two men, who understood each other, each other's cultures, and each other's languages, so poorly might have understood, based on their own unaided conversation, a relatively complicated and ambitious plan – or, more importantly, the import of it.[13]

Although this paper was obviously composed in great haste and entirely lacks the character of finesse and sophistication usually associated with Beneš's diplomatic documents, there are elements of real misfortune in the fate of the idea. It was imaginative, creative in the most positive sense of the reputation for diplomatic skill that Lacroix imputed to Beneš. The dismissive reaction to it of both Daladier, who regretted it, and of Chamberlain, who welcomed it, was crude in the extreme. Neither appreciated its possibilities, that is, that it formed the basis for an agreement of Prague, Paris, and London – and, perhaps, even Moscow – and thus the basis for presenting to Hitler a diplomatic united front, one which he would have found far more imposing than the set of circumstances that actually brought him to Munich later.

In any event, from the time of the resumption of the Anglo–French Cabinet conference, the idea of the integrity of Czechoslovakia, the wholeness of the Czechoslovakia of the design of Versailles, was a lost cause. In fact, from the outset of the renewed discussions, it was Daladier who took the initiative in the question of Czechoslovak sacrifices. He opened with the simple statement that the Czechoslovaks must be persuaded to cede something. The idea had come, after all, from Prague itself. It was agreed in

---

[12] Testimony of Daladier, 21 May 1947; ibid., 33–4. See also du Réau, *Édouard Daladier,* 257–8; Yvon Lacaze, *La France et Munich: étude d'un processus décisionnel en matière de relations internationales* (Bern, Switzerland: Peter Lang, 1992), 198–200; Taylor, *Munich,* 1025 (notes).

[13] Testimony of Blum, 30 July 1947; testimony of Daladier, 21 May 1947; *Les événements survenus en France de 1933 à 1945,* 9: 256, 33–4.; du Réau, *Édouard Daladier,* 258.

the course of the afternoon that areas containing more than 50 percent of Germans must be ceded. Daladier proposed assigning the drawing of such a line of demarcation to an international commission. Chamberlain approved. Daladier then said that the obligations of the French in the question obliged them to issue a security guarantee to the remainder of Czechoslovakia and that he would like to see Britain associated with the guarantee. Chamberlain said that such an idea represented a major departure from the traditions of British foreign policy. Daladier said that "if he were certain that Herr Hitler were speaking the truth when he repeated the usual Nazi propaganda to the effect that nothing more was wanted than the Sudeten Germans and that German aims stopped there, then he would not insist upon a British guarantee, but he was convinced in his heart that Germany was aiming at something far greater. It was clear from 'Mein Kampf' that Herr Hitler did not regard himself in the light of a second Emperor William II, but that he was rather aiming at dominating Europe as Napoleon had done." Halifax suggested that if Britain engaged in a guarantee of Czechoslovak security, the Czechoslovaks would have to accept British advice in foreign policy. The French did not respond. Chamberlain then said that he and his colleagues needed to retire to discuss the idea, and so they did.

The meeting resumed after a considerable break at 7:30 in the evening. Chamberlain said that Britain would join the French in extending to Czechoslovakia a security guarantee. In addition, he brought the draft of a communication to be made to Prague, subject to French consent, setting out what the two powers would require of the Czechoslovak government. The meeting then adjourned to give the French ministers time to consider the document. When it resumed at 10:30 P.M., the French consented to the draft subject only to the approval of the entire cabinet the next day. A response was promised by noon.

The French Cabinet approved Chamberlain's draft, and it was communicated to Prague, where it struck with the force of a body blow. This was the notorious "virtual ultimatum" from a presumably faithful ally and friendly associated power. It stipulated that the Sudeten districts of 50-percent German population must be ceded with or without a plebiscite. An international commission would supervise the procedure. If the Czechoslovaks complied, they would receive a security guarantee of the British and French governments for the remaining territories of Czechoslovakia, provided only that Prague cancel its treaties of military alliance, which is to say, the treaties of mutual assistance with the Soviet Union and the Little Entente states. Often noted is the irony that the Anglo–French were ready – although only rhetorically, as we shall see – to guarantee an indefensible form of a state whose defensible form they were abandoning. Finally, the note required an early response, as Chamberlain needed to resume his negotiations with Hitler.[14]

The Czechoslovaks, of course, felt betrayed, especially by their French ally. The cabinet in Prague wriggled and squirmed, equivocated, and appealed to the Locarno treaties of abitration.[15] Premier Milan Hodža of the Slovak Peasant Party demanded a real Anglo–French ultimatum in order to justify capitulation in the eyes of Czechoslovak public opinion.[16] That threat was forthcoming in notes jointly presented by the British and the French in Prague in the early morning of 21 September. The two governments instructed Prague to accept the conditions that had been forwarded on 19 September or be abandoned to its fate.[17] At that point, Prague accepted. The mood in the city may easily be imagined. It was expressed graphically by one Czech citizen writing to a French friend. The Anglo–French terms were "the biggest disappointment of my life. All of us, Czechs and German democrats, desire peace. But we are convinced that it cannot be achieved by sacrificing our country, which we love as much as you love France, to Nazism.... our sacrifice will substantially fortify... Hitlerism... and intensify all the more his policy of blackmail by violence.... Don't abandon us."[18]

Chamberlain was not concerned, however, with the sentiments of a faraway country of which Britain was ignorant. He was thus able, after Berchtesgaden and his consultations with the cabinet and the French, to embark on his next tête-à-tête with Hitler at Godesberg on 23–24 September with precisely the offer that Hitler had demanded of him at Berchtesgaden just a week before. A rude surprise awaited him there, however.

Chamberlain reported that he had brought the approval of the British, the French, and the Czechoslovak governments of the conditions that Hitler had posed at Berchtesgaden. He then proceeded to outline measures designed to protect Czechs, Jews, and German Social Democrats in the territories to be occupied or the interests of such people who wanted to emigrate. He made the point that a plebiscite would take time to organize and that it could not be conducted fairly in conditions of (German) military occupation. In addition, he wanted to discuss German compensation

[14] Halifax to Newton (Prague), 19 September 1938; DBFP, 3rd series, 2: 404–6 (No. 937); also DDF, 2nd series, 11: 334–6 (No. 213).
[15] Note from Czechoslovak Government to British Legation, Prague, 20 September 1938; DBFP, 3rd series, 2: 434–6 (No. 987); Note du ministre, 20 September 1938; DDF, 2nd series, 11: 355–6 (No. 225) and Lacroix to Bonnet, 20 September 1938; ibid., 359 (No. 229).
[16] M. de Lacroix (Prague) to Bonnet, 20 September 1938; DDF, 2nd series, 11: 361 (No. 232).
[17] Halifax to Newton, 21 September 1938; DBFP, 3rd series, 2: 437–38 (No. 991); Note de Département, 21 September 1938 (by telephone to Prague); DDF, 2nd series, 11: 394 (No. 249).
[18] Pierre Le Goyet, Munich, "un traquenard"? (Paris: France-Empire, 1988), 346.

for public property acquired in the transfer of territory, but Hitler cut him short. In his own words, "*Es tut mir leid, aber das geht nicht mehr*" (I am sorry, but that is no longer acceptable). Whereas Hitler at Berchtesgaden insisted on subordinating all larger issues to the very specific question of the Sudetenland, now that Chamberlain had addressed all of his claims on that issue, Hitler reversed priorities, insisting that the Sudetenland was but a part of larger problems. He objected that the Polish and Hungarian claims had to be addressed before peace could be arranged, and he said that Germany must occupy the disputed districts at once.[19] On the previous day, the British Cabinet, feeling that the very limit of concessions had been reached, had instructed Chamberlain to break off talks at once if either of these conditions were posed,[20] but he did not. Instead, he asked for a document setting out the whole of Hitler's claims in writing. The document was duly provided – the notorious "Godesberg memorandum" – and it administered another shock. Here was a substantial inventory of entirely new demands:

1. The withdrawal of the entire Czechoslovak administrative apparatus from the Sudeten districts by 1 October.
2. *No private property or capital assets were to be evacuated by Czechs departing from the territory in dispute, including food products and livestock, and no compensation would be paid for property forsaken.*
3. Sudeten citizens were to be discharged from the Czechoslovak armed forces.
4. All "political prisoners of German race" were to be released from detention.
5. A plebiscite was to be conducted before 25 November in districts of uncertain ethnic composition.
6. Military installations, public utilities, and transport facilities in the Sudeten territories were to be handed over intact.
7. All further details were to be handled not by an international commission but by a German–Czechoslovak commission.[21]

No provisions were made for the protection in the Sudeten territories of Czechs, Jews, and German Social Democrats, the kind of protection that Hitler had demanded – dishonestly – for Germans in the former Czech territories.

---

[19] Minutes of the conversation between the Führer and the Prime Minister, Godesberg, 22 September 1938; DGFP, Series D, 2: 870–9 (No. 562); and DBFP, 3rd series, 2: 463–73 (No. 1033).
[20] Taylor, *Munich*, 808.
[21] Memorandum of the Führer to the Prime Minister, 24 September 1938; DGFP, Series D, 2: 908–10 (No. 584); British delegation, Godesberg, to Newton (Prague), 24 September 1938; DBFP, 3rd series, 2: 495–6 (No. 1068). (My emphasis.)

This was the sad prospect that Chamberlain was forced to bring back to his cabinet in London. When the terms of the Godesberg memorandum were published, British opinion stiffened noticeably, and it was soon reflected in the cabinet. In fact, the cabinet split into three groups, one disposed to continue appeasement, one opposed, and one that was ambivalent. Remarkably, Halifax's position shifted to those opposed to further concessions.[22]

The next order of business in London was to invite another visit of the French ministers for consideration of the evolving situation. They came on 25 September. It was a grim meeting, a good deal shorter than the previous ones. Chamberlain described the new situation. Daladier reported that the French Cabinet had rejected the Godesberg memorandum unanimously.[23] He proposed to return to the position taken by the Anglo–French conference of 18 September. And what to do, Chamberlain queried, if that position were rejected by Germany? Daladier: "in that case each of us would have to do his duty."[24]

The Czech Cabinet, too, rejected the Godesberg ultimatum, also unanimously. Ambassador Jan Masaryk described his government's position to Halifax:

> My Government is amazed at the contents of the memorandum. The proposals go far beyond what we agreed to in the so-called Anglo–French plan. They deprive us of every safeguard for our national existence. We are to yield up large proportions of our carefully prepared defences and admit the German armies deep into our country before we have been able to organize it on the new basis or make any preparations for its defence. Our national and economic independence would automatically disappear. . . . The whole process of moving the population is to be reduced to panic flight on the part of those who will not accept the German Nazi regime. They have to leave their homes without even the right to take their personal belongings or even, in the case of peasants, their cow. My Government wish me to declare in all solemnity that Herr Hitler's demands in their present form are absolutely and unconditionally unacceptable. . . . We rely upon the two great Western democracies, whose wishes we have followed much against our own judgment, to stand by us in our hour of trial.[25]

In the meantime, wiser heads in France were suggesting to Daladier the better part of wisdom. On 22 September, while Chamberlain was away as

[22] Taylor, *Munich,* 812–5, has a good summary.
[23] Jean Zay, *Carnets secrets (de Munich à la guerre)* (Paris: Éditions de France, 1942), 37.
[24] Record of an Anglo-French conversation held at No. 10 Downing Street, 25 September 1938; DBFP, 3rd series, 2: 520–35 (No. 1093); also DDF, 2nd series, 11: 537–48 (No. 356).
[25] Jan Masaryk (London) to Halifax, 25 September 1938; DBFP, 3rd series, 2: 518–19 (No. 1092).

Hitler's guest, again without Daladier, one of the seasoned elder academic statesmen of Slavic and East European studies in France wrote to Daladier, again a letter that he may well have been too distracted to consider carefully. This was André Mazon, professor at the Collège de France and president of the Institut d'études slaves:

Monsieur le Président[26]

I am obliged . . . to tell you in all loyalty my opinion on the events of these last few days.

The solution that your Government, in association with that of M. Chamberlain, is imposing upon the Czechoslovak Government, under a pressure more imperious than friendly, is not justified either by history or by the political and economic conditions of the present. The transfer to the Reich by the shifting of a millenial frontier does not correspond either to the will of the majority of Sudeten Germans or to their interests. If it satisfies several thousands of young people comprising the activist element of the masses that Henlein has assembled . . . , it surrenders to Hitler's regime on the other hand several hundreds of thousands of German workers, peasants, and middle-class people, half a million Czechs, and some fifty thousand Jews. Far from solving the problem, this solution [sic] aggravates it. . . . There is no historian, be he even a German historian, who does not know that Bohemia is a whole, and that carving it up will only ruin it.

But if the solution is ruinous for the State compelled to accept it, it is no less disastrous for our country. Political and military disaster, whereby we lose our last alliances on the continent and confidence in our own strength. Moral disaster: . . . the undermining of the trust that a whole people has placed in us, the people of Masaryk and Beneš, who share our democratic ideal. . . . The dishonor, Monsieur le Président, for our country – and for Germany, a Sedan[27] that will not have cost a single life.

These impressions, Monsieur le Président, are those of a great number of French people, of all those among us, certainly, who have dedicated themselves to the study of central and eastern Europe. And I will draw the conclusion: you will not have saved the peace . . . by sacrificing the only one of our continental allies that has remained true to us. It is in taking our stand that our country will avoid war and not in shrinking from it.[28]

Litvinov was making a similar point in the quite public forum of the League in Geneva. One of his more impressive performances in the cause of collective security was his address to the League of Nations on

---

[26] That is, Président du Conseil des ministres or premier.

[27] Sedan was the great Prussian victory on 1 September 1870 that cost France the Franco–Prussian War and Napoleon III his throne.

[28] Mazon to Daladier, 22 September 1938; *Munich 1938: mythes et réalités*, 13.

21 September 1938. The League was given birth, Litvinov reminded his hearers, by the horror of the world war, and its original purpose was to make any repetition of such an experience impossible by replacing the system of military alliances with "the collective organization of assistance to the victims of aggression." The results, however, had not been encouraging: "In this sphere the League has done nothing. Two States – Ethiopia and Austria – have lost their independent existence in consequence of violent aggression. A third State, China, is now a victim of aggression and foreign invasion for the second time in seven years, and a fourth State, Spain, is in the third year of a sanguinary war, owing to the armed intervention of two aggressors in its internal affairs." The League failed in its duties to all these states. "At the present time a fifth State, Czechoslovakia, is suffering interference in its internal affairs at the hands of a neighbouring State, and is publicly and loudly menaced with attack." He recalled the role of the present president of Czechoslovakia, Edvard Beneš, in the founding of the League, and he taunted the League members by reminding them that the most pressing question in European international affairs, the Sudeten conflict, was not so much as *mentioned* in its current agenda. The prelude to the present crisis, *Anschluss*, also "passed unnoticed by the League. Realizing the significance of this event for the fate of the whole of Europe, and particularly of Czechoslovakia, the Soviet Government, immediately after the *Anschluss*, officially approached the other European Great Powers with a proposal for an immediate collective deliberation on the possible consequences of that event, in order to adopt collective preventive measures." Regrettably, there was no response. The Soviet Union was, of course, bound to Czechoslovakia by a pact of mutual assistance. "When, a few days before I left for Geneva, the French Government for the first time enquired as to our attitude in the event of an attack on Czechoslovakia," Litvinov replied unambiguously. "We intend to fulfil our obligations under the pact and, together with France, to afford assistance to Czechoslovakia by the ways open to us. Our War Department [sic] is ready immediately to participate in a conference with representatives of the French and Czechoslovak War Departments, in order to discuss the measures appropriate to the moment." At the same time, Litvinov had advised that the question should be placed on the agenda of the League. "It was only two days ago that the Czechoslovak Government addressed a formal enquiry to my Government whether the U.S.S.R. was prepared in accordance with the Soviet–Czech pact to render Czechoslovakia immediate and effective aid if France, loyal to her obligations, rendered similar assistance, to which my Government gave a clear answer in the affirmative." Finally, "to avoid a problematic war to-day and receive in return a certain and large-scale war tomorrow, moreover at the price of assuaging the appetites of insatiable aggressors and of the destruction or mutilation of

sovereign States, is not to act in the spirit of the Covenant of the League of Nations.... The Soviet Government... has invariably pursued the principles of the two pacts.... Nor has it any intention of abandoning them in the future... it is impossible otherwise to safeguard a genuine peace."[29] Hindsight could not more resoundingly ratify the wisdom of foresight.

If the lethargy and inertia of diplomatic jousts and feints continued in Western Europe, in the East matters appeared to be growing distinctly more desperate. It may well have been Chamberlain's trip to Berchtesgaden – in any case, it was at that time, and we have no other explanation of the timing – that prompted in Romanian Foreign Minister Comnen an unusual sense of urgency. On 16 September, he sent a rather extraordinary dispatch to the Ministry of Foreign Affairs with instructions to refer it at once to the king: "In the face of the threat of a total revision of the map of the European situation, the question arises whether it is not necessary that Poland and the members of the Balkan [sic] Entente speak out strongly in Paris and London, declaring loudly [*respicat*] that we [*Statele noastre*] are disposed to take part in any action to save the peace but that we will not take part in any meeting that would subscribe to a program of territorial revision and that we would oppose solidly with all our power any such efforts." He was opposed to any signs of weakness or to raising any question of ethnic politics in the countries concerned. He asked for deliberation of his proposal in the Romanian cabinet and a response.[30]

On 19 September, the Romanian General Staff issued orders to complete all preparations to defend the country's Western Frontier. On 23 September, it issued its prognosis on the probable grouping of Central and Eastern European powers in the event of the outbreak of war[31]:

Group 1 is represented by the interests of Germany, Poland, and Hungary which, through the amputation which they attempt to apply to Czechoslovakia, wish to create a dangerous precedent favorable to the idea of the revision of frontiers.

Group 2 is represented by Czechoslovakia, Yugoslavia, and Romania which are obliged to intervene if Hungary will force the Czech frontier with its army. We would then find ourselves confronting a causus [sic] foederis which

[29] Litvinov at the League, 21 September 1938; *New Documents on the History of Munich* (Prague: Orbis, 1958), 104–8 (No. 46).

[30] Comnen to Ministry of Foreign Affairs, 16 September 1938; RMAE. Fond 71/Romînia. Vol. 103, pp. 130–1.

[31] Talpeş, "Date noi privind poziţia României în contextul contradicţiilor internaţionale din vara anului 1938," *Revista de istorie* 28 (1975): 1664. Watts, "Romania as a Military Ally (Part I): Czechoslovakia in 1938," *Romanian Civilization* 7 (1998): 38.

is at the basis of the military conventions of the Little Entente. In this last case, Soviet Russia, which has consistently and continues to support Czechoslovakia, would enter into the sphere of coincident interests of the states of the Little Entente, which are the representatives of the same idea.

At the same time, Comnen was ordered to return home immediately for urgent discussions, which we will take up in due course.

In the meantime, as Comnen reacted to the events at Berchtesgaden, so did Litvinov apparently react to those of Godesberg. In any event, on 23 September, in Geneva for the meeting of the League, as his conferences with various leaders of the other nations and the downward spiral of events around them gradually induced in him a more and more pessimistic view of the impending threat, he evidently experienced a moment of near panic, and he wrote home to the commissariat of foreign affairs an uncharacteristic note. "Although Hitler has so committed himself as to make it difficult for him to retreat, I think nevertheless that he would draw back if he were assured in advance of the possibility of a joint Soviet–Franco–English [*declaration*] against him. At present no kinds of declarations, not even joint ones, or convocations, will produce an impression on him. More persuasive demonstrations are needed. Considering that a European war into which we will be drawn is not in our interests and that it is necessary to do everything to prevent it, I pose the question should we not announce even a partial mobilization and carry on a press campaign such as to force Hitler and Beck to believe in the possibility of a big war with our participation. De la Warr [British delegate to the League] said to me that the disposition of France is growing stronger. Perhaps France would agree to a simultaneous announcement of partial mobilization. It is necessary to act quickly."[32] This note repeats what was more and more conspicuous in Litvinov's motivation as matters deteriorated: His most important objective was not to incite a war that Moscow could stay out of; it was rather how to avoid war altogether.

One dramatic development on the Czech frontier contributed to the growing tension. The Sudeten Freikorps attacked and took possession of two cantons in Northwest Czechoslovakia, Eger and Asch, and at reports of the assistance of the SA and SS in the enterprise, the British and French officially withdrew on the evening of 22 September their objection to Czechoslovak mobilization.[33] Mobilization immediately followed. Of course, here was a German blunder that spoiled the prospect of at least

---

[32] Litvinov to Commissariat of Foreign Affairs, Geneva, 23 September 1938; DVP SSSR, 21: 520 (No. 369).
[33] Halifax to Newton, 22 September 1938; DBFP, 3rd series, 2: 461 (No. 1027).

partial surprise. More and more, diplomatic talk appeared to be giving way to military developments.

And so, as diplomacy appeared in the wake of Godesberg to have reached a stalemate, we find the armies mobilizing, the German army, the Romanian army, and the Czechoslovak army. On 21–22 September, the Red Army mobilized, too, and before the crisis ran its course, the French army and the British navy were to follow suit.

Chapter 5

The Red Army Mobilizes

On 19 September, President Beneš, in receipt now of the increasingly bad news from the Western capitals, where the fate of Czechoslovakia was being decided in his absence, summoned Soviet Ambassador Sergei Aleksandrovskii and asked him to put two questions to Moscow: (1) Would Moscow render military assistance to Czechoslovakia if Hitler attacked and if France rendered such assistance, and (2) would Moscow otherwise render such assistance if it were approved by the League of Nations under Article 16?[1] On the following day, V. P. Potemkin responded, in Litvinov's absence in Geneva, with an unqualified affirmative to both questions.[2]

The shuttle diplomacy of Neville Chamberlain was by this time quite publicly apparent, everywhere the subject of the headlines, and it ratcheted up both the focus of attention and the pace of diplomatic – and other – developments. On 22 September, as Chamberlain flew to Berchtesgaden, Czechoslovak Foreign Minister Kamil Krofta summoned Aleksandrovskii again. This time he reported that the Poles were concentrating a large military force on the border of Czechoslovakia, and he asked Moscow to warn them that an attack on Czechoslovakia would automatically void, according to Article 2, the Polish–Soviet Non-Aggression Treaty of 1932.[3] On the following day, the Soviet government issued precisely such a warning to the Polish Embassy in Moscow and followed it with a public declaration to the same effect: If the Poles attacked Czechoslovakia, Moscow would denounce the nonaggression pact.[4]

---

[1] Aleksandrovskii to Commissariat of Foreign Affairs, 19 September 1938; DVP SSSR, 21: 498–9 (No. 354).

[2] Potemkin to Aleksandrovskii, 20 September 1938; ibid., 500 (No. 356).

[3] Aleksandrovskii to Commissariat, 22 September 1938; ibid., 515–16 (No. 365).

[4] Declaration and record of interview of Potemkin with Polish Chargé d'Affaires Jankowski, 23 September 1938; ibid., 516–17 (Nos. 366, 367).

In the meantime, the Czechoslovak ambassador in Moscow, Zdeněk Fierlinger, informed Potemkin of the Anglo–French terms accepted now by the Beneš government (before Godesberg), and Potemkin, who was already aware of the terms, posed the question, why Prague had not called on Moscow for military assistance! Fierlinger explained that it had to do with the geographical obstacles to such assistance.[5] Both the question and the answer are strange, as it is obvious that, in accepting the Anglo–French terms, the Czechoslovak government had consented to the abrogation of its mutual-assistance pact with Moscow. Litvinov, however, addressed precisely this point in a fashion at least as surprising. Speaking at the League in Geneva again on 23 September, Litvinov said that Prague's acceptance of the Anglo–French terms clearly gave Moscow the moral right to consider itself relieved of the obligations that the pact stipulated. Here, in other words – Litvinov did not say so – was the perfect opportunity for Moscow to do what legions of skeptical historians have thought that it was seeking to do, that is, to disemburden itself of the now moribund duties of collective security. Yet Moscow was not looking, Litvinov said, for any such pretexts and continued to regard the original terms of the treaty as *valid*.[6] In the meantime, Radio Moscow was announcing over all its media outlets, including the speakers hanging all over public places in the country – the public parks "of Rest and Culture" in particular – that it was prepared to defend Czechoslovakia.[7]

By this time, the Red Army was mobilizing. This is precisely the development of which both the contemporaries and the historians of the Munich crisis have been so skeptical. It is, then, a somewhat fine and a decidedly controversial point, and hence it must be pursued here with some concentration. The published Soviet documentation is by no means spare; Western historians have simply paid little attention to it.

The question of Soviet military policy and intent at the time of Munich was reopened recently but only to provoke the usual controversy about it. In particular, the memoirs of Marshal M. V. Zakharov have been cited to detail Soviet military preparations evidently intended for assistance to Czechoslovakia.[8] Zakharov should be a good authority in the question, as he was at the time of Munich assistant to Chief of the General Staff B. M. Shaposhnikov, and when he wrote his memoirs in 1969, he was

---

5   Coulondre (reporting Fierlinger) to Bonnet, 22 September 1938; DDF, 2nd series, 11: 446–7 (No. 292).

6   DVP SSSR, 21: 517–20 (No. 368).

7   Coulondre to Bonnet, 26 September 1938; DDF, 2nd series, 11: 557 (No. 367).

8   G. Jukes, "The Red Army and the Munich Crisis," *Journal of Contemporary History* 26 (1991): 195–214.

himself Chief of the General Staff, although the book was published only twenty years later. Zakharov gives impressive particulars[9]:

At 1800 hours on 21 September 1938 the Kiev Special Military District was ordered to mobilize and deploy in the regions of Volochinsk, Proskurov (later named Khmel'nitskii), and Kamenets-Podol'skii a group of forces consisting of the Vinnitsa army group, the 4th Cavalry Corps (34th, 32th, and 9th Cavalry Divisions), the 25th Tank Corps, the 17th Infantry Corps (96th, 97th, and 72nd Infantry Divisions), and the 23rd and 26th Light Tank Brigades. At the same time, the infantry divisions called up 8,000 reservists per division as well as their required complement of horses, and the 2nd Cavalry Corps was moved to the Polish border. Three fighter-plane regiments, three regiments of light bombers, and one regiment of heavy bombers as well as the district's own air forces were attached to these formations, and two air bases called up reserves. The following day the headquarters staff in Kiev reported that these orders were being implemented. Simultaneously, the commander of the Kiev Special Military District, (later Marshal) S. K. Timoshenko, together with his staff, transferred headquarters from Kiev to Proskurov.

At 2345 hours on 23 September the commissariat of defense issued similar orders to the Belorussian Special Military District. These measures mobilized still more substantial forces: around Polotsk the 50th Infantry Division along with a division of armored trains and the 5th Infantry Division; around Lepel' the 24th Cavalry Division, the 16th Tank Brigade, and the 79th Infantry Division; around Minsk the 36th Cavalry Division, the 100th Infantry Division, the 2nd Infantry Division, the 21st Tank Brigade, the 7th Cavalry Division, and the 13th Infantry Division; around Slutsk the 4th Cavalry Division. These dispositions were to be completed on 24 September. To accompany these deployments, fighter-plane squadrons were ordered to move to forward bases near the frontiers to cover the Sebezhsk, Polotsk, Minsk, and Slutsk sectors; light bombers were stationed at Vitebsk and Orsha, while heavy bombers were to operate from their usual airfields. The aviation was to begin moving on the morning of 24 September. At 1055 hours, 24 September, Belorussian Special Military District headquarters reported that the orders were being implemented.

On 23 September the Kalinin Military District was ordered to move the 67th Infantry Division to the Western frontier. At the same time the antiaircraft forces were brought into combat readiness in the Leningrad, Kalinin, Belorussian, Kiev, Kharkov, and Moscow Military Districts. All of these dispositions were accompanied by a call-up of reserves, and on

---

[9] M. V. Zakharov, *General'nyi shtab v predvoennye gody* (Moscow: Voenizdat, 1989), 112–15.

28 September, the General Staff suspended the discharge of all personnel whose terms of service had expired in all European Military Districts as well as those in the Caucasus.

Zakharov, in short, cited substantial preparations: the mobilization and deployment along the Western Soviet frontier of sixty infantry divisions, sixteen cavalry divisions, three tank corps, and twenty-two tank and seventeen air brigades.

This account has been disputed, however. As Zakharov's memoir contains not a hint of documentary evidence, not a single archival reference, skeptics have attacked it.[10] We have been referred, in particular, to the motoring tour through the Ukraine, where the bulk of the mobilization was to have taken place, of a German diplomat in the Moscow Embassy, a man pretty obviously on a mission of intelligence and reconnaissance, Hans von Herwarth. Herwarth observed that he "got considerable information on the stationing of Soviet troops but found no indications that they were preparing to move."[11] This point is, in fact, irrelevant, as Herwarth writes plainly that he took this trip "in late July," and "in August 1938, I went to Berlin."[12] He was therefore in the area seven or eight weeks before the issuance of the orders of 21–28 September that, according to Zakharov, set the Soviet military machine in motion.

If these alleged developments are to be clarified, we must look for further evidence. In fact, there is much intriguing evidence that has not been hitherto taken into account in Western historical literature. A good example is the Soviet Ministry of Defense's official history of World War II, *Istoriia vtoroi mirovoi voiny, 1939–1945.*[13] Volume 2 describes much the same measures in September that Zakharov's memoirs detailed later: Substantial forces in the Kiev Special Military District were ordered to mobilize and move to the frontier; reserves were called up; horses were drafted; military aviation was brought to full combat readiness; and Commander S. K. Timoshenko and staff relocated to Proskurov. On 23 September, orders were issued to form two army groups in the Belorussian Special Military District. One was deployed on the frontier in the region of Polotsk and Lepel'; the other reinforced Minsk. These movements were initiated on the 24th, and they were accompanied by the forward stationing of both fighter and bomber aircraft and the call-up of engineering battalions. The total scale of these preparations included thirty infantry and ten cavalry

---

[10] Igor Lukes, "Stalin and Beneš at the End of September 1938: New Evidence from the Prague Archives," *Slavic Review* 52 (1993): 29, n. 5. See also, idem, *Czechoslovakia Between Stalin and Hitler: The Diplomacy of Edvard Beneš in the 1930s* (New York: Oxford University Press, 1996).

[11] Hans-Heinrich Herwarth von Bittenfeld, *Against Two Evils: Memoirs of a Diplomat-Soldier During the Third Reich* (New York: Rawson, Wade, 1981), 123.

[12] Ibid., 122–3.

[13] A. A. Grechko., ed., *Istoriia vtoroi mirovoi voiny, 1939–1945*, 12 vols. (Moscow: Voenizdat, 1973–1982).

divisions, seven tank and motorized infantry brigades, twelve brigades of fighter planes and bombers, and two corps, one division, six brigades, and thirty-one regiments of antiaircraft forces. Meanwhile the discharge of all personnel in these military districts was deferred.

Further orders were issued on 29 September to the Kiev, Belorussian, Leningrad, and Kalinin Military Districts to call up from reserve and form seventeen additional infantry divisions, the command staffs (*upravleniia*) of three tank corps, twenty-two tank and three motorized infantry brigades, and thirty-four air bases. In addition to the forces prepared and deployed along the Western frontiers, a considerable second echelon of forces was formed in the interior of the country: thirty infantry divisions, six cavalry divisions, two tank corps, fifteen additional tank brigades, and thirty-four air bases. This account of military preparations differs from Zakharov's in one important particular: Here there is explicit and abundant documentary reference to Ministry of Defense archival sources.[14]

Similarly detailed accounts of Soviet military preparations in the face of Munich are older yet.[15] With minor exceptions, all the information presented in a variety of Soviet publications, serious and academic or semipopular and transient, and including the official history of World War II – the statistics, the military units cited, the dates in the calendar and the hours of the day, the locations from which and to which military units were moved, and the excerpts quoted from documents – is identical, and several of them cite the same specific archival sources.[16]

This is a rather impressive accumulation of particulars, but can we corroborate them in a broader spectrum of evidence? If we consider the historical literature of Czechoslovakia itself, the obvious work to take into account is the official military history of the country, *Vojenské dějiny Československa*.[17] It is a very full account and appears to be careful and authoritative, though it lacks documentary notes. Although the pertinent volume (three) was published in the era of *glasnost'* (1987), it was obviously in preparation and likely nearly complete before the Gorbachev era, and it retains the flavor and viewpoint of traditional Soviet bloc historiography. It follows literally and in detail the account of Soviet military preparations

[14] Ibid., 2: 104–7. The citations specify *fondy* (document groups), *opisi* (inventories, catalogues, finding aids), *dela* (volumes), and *listy* (pages).

[15] For example, A. N. Grylev, "Nakanune i v dni Miunkhena," in S. I. Prasolov and P. I. Rezonov, eds., *Sovetsko–chekhoslovatskie otnosheniia mezhdu dvumia voinami, 1918–1939: iz istorii gosudarstvennykh, diplomaticheskikh, ekonomicheskikh i kul'turnykh sviazei* (Moscow: Nauka, 1968), 220–7.

[16] There is a brief summary of these measures in English, without documentation, in Oleg Rzheshevskii, *Europe 1939: Was War Inevitable?* (Moscow: Progress Publishers, 1989), 103–7.

[17] Zdeněk Procházka, ed., *Vojenské dějiny Československa*, 5 vols. (Prague: Naše vojsko, 1985–1989), 3: *1919–1939*.

given in the official Soviet history of World War II.[18] Thus although it offers us no new data, it does represent another significant source of information on Soviet military preparations.

The Poles also had a large stake in these developments, as they were preparing in favorable circumstances to seize the disputed district of Teschen from Czechoslovakia. They were thus very sensitive to Soviet policy in the fate of Czechoslovakia, and Polish historiography takes into account Soviet military measures before Munich. In fact, the distinguished Polish historian Marian Zgórniak has contributed an ambitious work on the military situation in Europe in 1938–1939. He concludes, somewhat cautiously, that "the [Soviet mobilization and deployment] seems to indicate the readiness of the Soviet Union to discharge its alliance obligations to Czechoslovakia and France."[19] Zgórniak relies on standard Soviet literature and documentary publications, especially on *Istoriia vtoroi mirovoi voiny*. Obviously information on Soviet military preparations before Munich is widely available in a number of East European languages. In fact, the bulk of the story was told in a previous work of Zgórniak that is now more than thirty years old.[20]

Are there unused documentary sources? The most obvious place to look is in the major Soviet collection of documents on Soviet–Czech relations between the wars.[21] And here is the directive from Minister of Defense K. E. Voroshilov to the Kiev Special Military District, dated 21 September 1938, ordering the mobilization of its forces and their deployment to the frontier.[22] It is long and detailed, full of the apparently original

---

[18]   Ibid., 523–6. In June 1996, I specifically asked several authorities on Czech military history at the Historical Institute of the Czech Army whether this work is, in spite of its somewhat dated and skewed point of view, factually reliable. They considered the question thoughtfully and agreed that it was.

[19]   Marian Zgórniak, *Europa w przededniu wojny: sytuacja militarna w latach 1938–1939* (Kraków: Księgarnia akademicka, 1993), 225–7. I am grateful to Dr. Jaroslav Valenta of the Historical Institute of the Czech Academy of Sciences for bringing this work to my attention.

[20]   *Wojskowe aspekty kryzysu czechosłowackiego 1938 roku* (Kraków: Zeszyty Naukowe Uniwersytetu Jagiellonskiego, 1966).

[21]   *Dokumenty i materialy po istorii sovetsko–chekhoslovatskikh otnoshenii*, 5 vols. (Moscow: Nauka, 1973–1988).

[22]   Direktiva narodnogo komissara oborony SSSR K. E. Voroshilova o provedenii voennykh uchenii v raione gosudarstvennoi granitsy, Moscow, No. 75212, 21 September 1938; ibid., 3: 515–17 (No. 352). This is the most important published document on the subject. The collection in which it appears is ignored entirely by Jukes, in his article "The Red Army and the Munich Crisis" and by Jiri Hochman, *The Soviet Union and the Failure of Collective Security, 1934–1938* (Ithaca, NY: Cornell University Press, 1984), and Lukes misses the military documents in the collection in his other works on the subject, i.e., *Czechoslovakia Between Stalin and Hitler*; idem, "Stalin and Beneš at the End of September 1938," and idem, "Did Stalin Desire War in 1938? A New Look at Soviet Behaviour during the May and September Crises," *Diplomacy and Statecraft* 2 (1991): 3–53, as does Ivan Pfaff, whose most recent work is *Die Sowjetunion und die Verteidigung der Tschechoslowakei: Versuch der Revision einer Legende* (Cologne: Böhlau, 1996). The entire collection was published in

abbreviations, and yet the only source reference is the cryptic annotation "publikuetsia po arkh" (i.e., published from archival sources). It is followed by a response acknowledging receipt of the order and reporting the progress of its execution.[23] A note in a subsequent document summarizes the military measures taken both in the Kiev District and elsewhere and cites as reference *Istoriia vtoroi mirovoi voiny*. These two important documents are also published in the Czech edition of the collection and the more important of them, Voroshilov's order to the Kiev Military District, was published in both the Soviet and the Czech collection of documents devoted to the Munich crisis. Thus although the Voroshilov directive was in print in four publications in two languages by 1979,[24] so far as I know, there is passing reference to it in only three Western works, the books of Jonathan Haslam, Jürgen Pagel, and Geoffrey Roberts.[25]

One of the documents ordering the supplementary mobilization of 29 September, as related by Zakharov, has also been published. These orders were given to the Belorussian, Kievan, Leningrad, and Kalinin Military Districts. They called for the additional preparation of airfields, new tank and motorized infantry brigades, the formation of new command and staff headquarters within five days, call-up of reserves, and the organization of motor transport. Voroshilov requested a report on the execution of the orders at 0800 and 2100 hours every day and designated the code in which the reports were to be made.[26]

If the Soviet mobilization and frontier deployment actually occurred on the scale alleged, it should have been apparent to the intelligence operations of the other powers. Yet one of the stranger features of this episode is

---

Czech as well: *Dokumenty a materialy k dějinam československo-sovetských vztahů*, ed. Čestmír Amort., 5 vols. (Prague: Academia, 1975–1984); the numeration of the documents is the same, although pagination differs.

[23] Donesenie komandovaniia Kievskim osobym voennym okrugom nachal'niku general'nogo shtaba RKKA o khode podgotovitel'nykh meropriiatii k voennym ucheniiam i sosredotochenii voisk, Kiev, 22 September 1938; *Dokumenty i materialy po istorii sovetsko–chekhoslovatskikh otnoshenii*, 3: 518 (No. 354).

[24] The Soviet collection of documents on Munich is *Dokumenty po istorii miunkhenskogo sgovora, 1937–1939*, ed. V. F. Mal'tsev (Moscow: Politizdat, 1979); Voroshilov's 21 September directive to the Kiev District is on pp. 254–6. The Czech edition is *Dokumenty k historii mnichovského diktátu, 1937–1939*, ed. Hana Tichá (Prague: Svoboda, 1979).

[25] Jonathan Haslam, *The Soviet Union and the Struggle for Collective Security in Europe, 1933–39* (London: Macmillan, 1984), 186 and 278, n. 129. Jürgen Pagel, *Polen und die Sowjetunion 1938–1939: die polnisch-sowjetischen Beziehungen in den Krisen der europäischen Politik am Vorabend des Zweiten Weltkrieges* (Stuttgart: Franz Steiner Verlag, 1992), 154, n. 265; Geoffrey Roberts, *The Soviet Union and the Origins of the Second World War: Russo–German Relations and the Road to War, 1933–1941* (New York: St. Martin's, 1995), 56, 160, n. 36.

[26] Direktiva General'nogo shtaba RKKA Voennym sovetam okrugov, 28 September 1938, and Direktiva Narodnogo komissara oborony SSSR Voennomu sovetu Belorusskogo osobogo voennogo okruga, 29 September 1938; *Dokumenty po istorii miunkhenskogo sgovora, 1937–1939* (Moscow: Politizdat, 1979), 314–15 (Nos. 205, 206).

Measures Taken by the Soviet Union to Extend Military Assistance to Czechoslovakia in 1938.

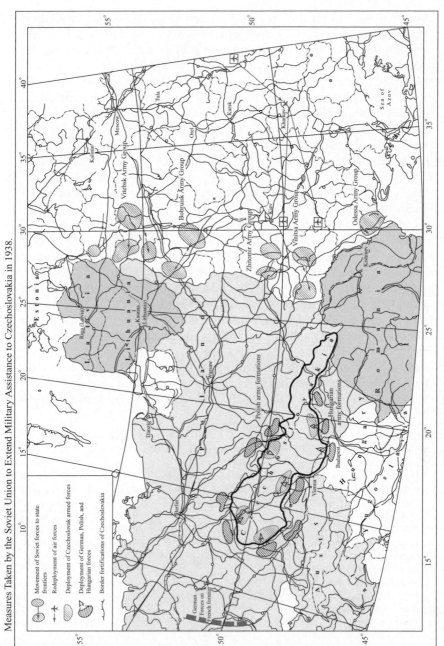

Map 1. Disposition of military forces, September 1938.

that, although the nations of Europe were increasingly anxious about the outbreak of war, the military intelligence organs of Britain, France, and Germany appear *not to have noticed* any Soviet measures of mobilization.[27] In fact, the German counselor of the embassy in Moscow reported that Moscow *failed to take even preliminary measures of mobilization*.[28] Moscow did inform its French allies, although in a distinctly understated fashion, reporting the preparation of only thirty divisions plus complementary aircraft.[29] Military movements of this size, however, were of course not difficult for the neighboring countries to detect, and the Soviet movements were carefully observed and recorded by the Polish consuls stationed in the area. The Minsk consulate reported that "on 24 [September] the majority of the local garrisons moved out in the direction of the frontier. In Minsk state of alert introduced [sic], which continues."[30] The Polish Embassy in Prague reported similar news: "In the past few days the activity of Moscow in the course of mounting support for Czechoslovakia has increased and has a feverish character." The report spoke of "the intensive activity of all Soviet radio stations" as well as the increased tempo of Soviet propaganda inside Czechoslovakia.[31]

The Poles were also preparing a force to intervene in Czechoslovakia. Soviet intelligence reported on 10 September extensive Polish army maneuvers along the Soviet frontiers, including the evacuation of families from border areas. When the Poles discovered the massive mobilization of the Kiev and the Belorussian Military Districts, they responded with similar countermoves. Vice-Commissar of Foreign Affairs V. P. Potemkin reported to Stalin on 23 September a conversation with Polish Chargé d'Affaires Tadeusz Jankowski, who complained of the Soviet maneuvers.

---

[27] Wesley K. Wark, *The Ultimate Enemy: British Intelligence and Nazi Germany, 1933–1939* (London: Tauris, 1985), especially 102–10; F. H. Hinsley, *British Intelligence in the Second World War: Its Influence on Strategy and Operations*, 4 vols. (Cambridge, England: Cambridge University Press, 1979–1988); Jacques Benoist-Méchin, *Histoire de l'armée allemande, 1918–1939*, 2 vols. (Paris: Robert Laffont, 1984); Rudolf Absolon, *Die Wehrmacht im Dritten Reich*, 6 vols. (Boppard am Rhein, Germany: Harald Boldt Verlag, 1969–1995); Wolfgang Schumann and Gerhart Hass (of Akademie der Wissenschaften, DDR), eds., *Deutschland im Zweiten Weltkrieg*, 6 vols. (Cologne, Germany: Pahl-Rugenstein, 1974–1985). I am told that there is no reliable history of the Abwehr; I owe advice on this point to Gerhard Weinberg and Jaroslav Hrbek.

[28] Counselor von Tippelskirch to Counselor of Legation Schliep, 3 and 10 October 1938; DGFP, Series D, 4: 602–7 (Nos. 476, 477).

[29] Commissariat of Defense to Soviet military attaché in Paris, 25 September 1938; *Dokumenty i materialy po istorii sovetsko-chekhoslovatskikh otnoshenii*, 3: 535–6 (No. 374); Note du Directeur politique: Démarche de l'attaché militaire soviétique, 26 September 1938; DDF, 2nd series, 11: 581 (No. 380).

[30] Telegram szyfrowy nr 2 Okonskiego o ruchach wojsk radzieckich, Tajne, 26 September 1938, Minsk; Zbigniew Landau and Jerzy Tomaszewski, eds., *Monachium [Munich] 1938: Polskie dokumenty dyplomatyczne* (Warsaw: Panstwowe Wydawnictwo Naukowe, 1985), 419 (No. 351).

[31] Telegram szyfrowy nr 158 K. Papée o dążeniu ZSRR do umocnienia oporu Czechosłowacji wobec III Rzeszy, 30 September 1938, Prague; ibid., 491 (No. 441).

Potemkin responded that the military moves of the Soviet government were prompted by the measures introduced by Poland on the Czechoslovak frontier.[32]

Czech documentary collections provide additional corroborating items. In his memoirs General Jaroslav Fajfr related arrangements for the Soviet air force to come to the assistance of Czechoslovakia. He was sent secretly to Moscow in September and spent three days negotiating an agreement stipulating the immediate dispatch to the Czechs of 700 planes on the preparation of suitable airfield facilities and appropriate antiaircraft defenses for them.[33] General Fajfr recalled that in the latter half of September Soviet officers arrived in Czechoslovakia to oversee preparation of these facilities at sites in Spiška Nová Ves (near Košice) and several other places in Slovakia.[34]

According to published Soviet sources, preparation to transfer these aircraft was soon proceeding. Voroshilov reported on 28 September that by 30 September the USSR would be prepared to dispatch, "in case of necessity," a substantial contingent of planes to Czechoslovakia: 123 light bombers from the Belorussian Military District, 62 light bombers from the Kiev District, 246 from the Kharkov District, 151 fighter planes from the Belorussian District, and 151 fighter planes from the Kiev District; a grand total of 548 planes.[35]

In sum, the evidence accumulated here constitutes an unambiguous contradiction of conventional wisdom in this question: It suggests that the Soviets were preparing and were on the move. Still, it must be admitted that the evidence presented thus far may not dispose of one common form of suspicion and evidentiary weakness: All Soviet bloc publications were subject to the influence of comprehensive forms of Soviet censorship and control. Perfectly cogent corroboration of these developments must come then from unedited and unpublished sources.

Genuinely cogent documentation, therefore, requires work in the Soviet military archives, and, in fact, the unedited documents that corroborate the published ones actually are there. Most important is the telegram of 21 September 1938 from Commissar of Defense Voroshilov embodying the orders to mobilize the Kiev Military District, and it is identical to the

---

[32] Record of Potemkin's conversation with Polish Chargé Jankowski, 23 September 1938; *Dokumenty i materialy po istorii sovetsko–pol'skikh otnoshenii*, 12 vols. (Moscow: USSR Academy of Sciences, 1963–1986), 6: 364 (No. 259).

[33] According to the official Czech military history, it was in August that General Fajfr was in Moscow to negotiate this arrangement. *Vojenské dějiny Československa*, 3: 523.

[34] Čestmír Amort, ed., *Na pomoc Československému lidu: dokumenty o československo-sovetském přatelství z let 1938–1945* (Prague: Nakladatelství Československé akademie věd, 1960), 180.

[35] Report of Commissar of Defense Voroshilov to the Politbiuro and the Council of Commissars, 28 September 1938; *Dokumenty po istorii miunkhenskogo sgovora, 1937–1939*, 312–13 (No. 204).

published document.[36] In addition, however, is documentation whose very nature has unaccountably never been published. There are copies of NKVD reports of the proceedings of what were evidently *agitprop* meetings – meetings devoted, as the Russian name suggests, to agitation and propaganda – among the military units posted to the Western Soviet frontier. As one soldier put it, "We have a treaty with Czechoslovakia, and if Germany attacks Czechoslovakia, the Soviet Union will help it beat the Germans as we beat the Japanese on the heights of Zaozernaia [Lake Khasan]."[37] Another soldier commented in similar fashion: "We cannot break the treaty. Let everyone understand this. If it is necessary we will advance as one man to protect Czechoslovakia."[38] At this point, skepticism must yield: Soviet military preparations as previously described in Soviet historical literature and documentary publications did take place.

The Soviet press of the time, while presenting rather full and accurate coverage of the *foreign* news of the Munich crisis, presented only modest and indirect coverage of the mobilization of Soviet forces. The government paper, *Izvestiia*, published on page one of 22 September the full text of Litvinov's speech of the day before at the League. On 26 and 27 September, the same paper carried photos – page one and page three respectively – of Soviet troops on "tactical maneuvers" in the Ukraine, and *Pravda*, the party paper, followed on 28 September with similar photos on pages two and six.

It is tempting to consider what decisions took place in the Politbiuro concerning the Soviet mobilization, what the intentions of the government

---

[36] Commissariat of Defensive Directive No. 75212, 22 September 1938; RGVA, f. 37977, op. 5c, d. 479, ss. 11–17.

[37] The Sudeten crisis was not the only major threat that faced the Soviet Union at the time. It is worth remembering that during most of the period of the last four great crises leading to World War II – the *Anschluss* in March 1938, Munich in September 1938, Prague in March 1939, and the Polish corridor in September 1939 – the Soviet Union was involved in a relatively large though obscure war with Japan along the frontier of Mongolia and Manchuria. Two large battles were fought in that war, Lake Khasan, 29 July–11 August 1938, and Khalkin Gol, 17–30 August 1939. At Lake Khasan, the two sides together deployed perhaps 40,000 troops. The Red Army committed 150 planes, including four–engine heavy bombers, and 200 tanks. The Japanese were outgunned and withdrew. "Khasan," in *Sovetskaia istoricheskaia entsiklopediia*, 16 vols. (Moscow: Sovetskaia Entsiklopediia, 1961–1976), 16: 543; John Erickson, *The Soviet High Command: A Military-Political History, 1918–1941* (London: Macmillan, 1962), 494–9; Alvin D. Coox, "The Lake Khasan Affair of 1938: Overview and Lessons," *Soviet Studies* 25 (1975): 51–65; idem, *The Anatomy of a Small War: The Soviet-Japanese Struggle for Changkufeng/Khasan, 1938* (Westport, CT: Greenwood, 1977). The Soviet account in *Krasnoznamennyi dal'nevostochnyi: istoriia Krasnoznamennogo dal'nevostochnogo voennogo okruga* (Moscow: Voenizdat, 1971), 137–51, is strictly narrative, rabidly patriotic, and does not give information on numbers involved. See also Jonathan Haslam, *The Soviet Union and the Threat from the East, 1933–41* (Pittsburgh: University of Pittsburgh Press, 1992), Chapter 5: "Frontier Fighting: Lake Khasan (1938) and Khalkhin-Gol (1939)."

[38] Copy of Major Shapiro of Ukrainian NKVD to Voroshilov, 25 September 1938; RGVA, f. 33987, op. 3, d. 1147, ss. 110–16.

were, what use it intended to make of the mobilized army. On the subject of defense affairs, however, the old party archive, known at the time of this research as RTsKhIDNI,[39] was closed to research on subjects subsequent to 1934. It is only apparent through finding aids that defense affairs were discussed twice at Politbiuro meetings on the day before the orders to mobilize were issued.[40]

Disappointing as conditions of access to archival records in Moscow sometimes still are, perhaps research conditions would be more promising in the now-liberated, former fraternal republics. What about the records in Prague, in particular? Perhaps most illuminating would be the dispatches of the Czech military attaché in Moscow during the 1930s, Colonel František Dastich. The researcher in Prague naturally turns to the Historical Institute of the Czech Army and the Institute of History of the Czech Academy of Sciences.[41]

At the Czech archive of military history, the Vojenský historický archív, it quickly becomes apparent that most such materials were destroyed on the entrance of the Wehrmacht into Czechoslovakia in March 1939.[42] None of Colonel Dastich's dispatches survive from the period of Munich, and his name does not appear in the index of names of the military chancery of the president's office.[43] The military archive preserves one lengthy dispatch of the Czechoslovak ambassador in Moscow, Zdeněk Fierlinger.[44] It dates to April 1938, and it is of some interest chiefly for political affairs.[45]

---

[39]　That is, Rossiiskii tsentr khraneniia i izucheniia dokumentov noveishei istorii (Russian Center of the Preservation and Study of Documents of Modern History).

[40]　Protokoly Politbiuro, 20 September 1938; ibid., f. 17, op. 3, d. 1001.

[41]　In particular, I am grateful for advice and assistance to Dr. Antonín Klimek, a biographer of Eduard Beneš, and Dr. Jaroslav Hrbek, a specialist in World War II, at the former and to Dr. Jaroslav Valenta at the latter.

[42]　I was assisted in orientation at the Vojenský historický archív by Mr. Vaclav Sluka. It is surmised there that both the Wehrmacht and the Red Army may also have evacuated whatever evidence survived the Czech destruction of materials in March 1939. It may also be surmised that any records dealing with Soviet affairs were subject to review and the disposition of the Soviet Big Brother during the years before the coming down of the wall. See Lukes, *Czechoslovakia Between Stalin and Hitler*, 207 n. 21.

[43]　Vojenský historický archív; Vojenská kancelář presidenta republiky, 1938, číslo jednací 450, karton 173.

[44]　Zpráva čs. vyslanectví v Moskve o SSSR za I. čtvrtletí 1938 (39 listu), 18 April 1938; ibid., čislo jednací 319, karton 171.

[45]　Despite the destruction of the Czechoslovak military records, there is nevertheless in the Czech Republic a revisionist trend of historiography. The Czechs continue to rehash the trauma of Munich, the "Munich complex," as well as that of February 1948, and the role of President Edvard Beneš at the center of both. Typical of the genre are Karel Bartosek, "Could We Have Fought? – The 'Munich Complex' in Czech Policies and Czech Thinking" and Edward Taborsky, "President Edvard Beneš and the Czechoslovak Crises of 1938 and 1948," both in Norman Stone and Eduard Strouhal, eds., *Czechoslovakia: Crossroads and Crises, 1918–1988* (Basingstoke, England: Macmillan and BBC, 1989), 101–19 and 120–44, respectively, and "Munich from the Czech Perspective:

There are, however, useful references to Colonel Dastich in other materials of Soviet derivation. In the Volkogonov papers in the Library of Congress Manuscript Division, there are copies of notes of two conversations in which Czech Chief of Staff General Ludvík Krejčí complained to visiting Soviet military delegations of the virtual ostracism of Colonel Dastich by his Soviet colleagues in Moscow as well as the obtrusive surveillance of him by the NKVD.[46] Colonel, later General, Dastich, incidentally, emigrated to the United States in 1948 and died in Queens, New York, in 1964. There are evidently no surviving papers.

At this somewhat discouraging point in the development of this research, a series of significant documents entered the picture in a most fortuitously happy fashion. A colleague furnished me a fascinating series of documents that prompted me to take my inquiry in a new direction. This was a collection of Polish consular reports from the region of the Romanian–Soviet frontier in the summer of 1938.[47]

The Soviet border with Romania was in September 1938 an intriguing place. The Polish consular service was as alert as ever to Soviet troop and supply movements. Thus a report from Kishinev, in the heart of Bessarabia, 15 September: "Rumors are circulating that Soviet forces are crossing Bessarabia to Czechoslovakia, probably through Tighina [Bendery], and that the Romanian government is not alarmed. The authorities here

Roundtable," *East Central Europe* 8 (1981): 63–96. The revisionist trend among Czech historians suggests now that it would have been better to have fought in 1938. See, e.g., Milan Hauner, "Září 1938: kapitulovat či bojovat?" *Svědectví* 13 (1975):151–68. Best known among more recent work reflecting this line of argument is Václav Kural, "Vojenský moment česko-německého vztahů v roce 1938," *Historické studie* 22 (1987): 66–112, reprinted in Václav Kural, Jan Anger, and Klaus-Jürgen Müller, *Rok 1938: mohli jsme se bránit?* (Prague: Naše vojsko, 1992). A variety of Western studies are supportive of this line of argument. For an interesting, and remarkably positive, assessment by a British officer in Czechoslovakia, see H. C. T. Stronge, "The Czechoslovak Army and the Munich Crisis: A Personal Memorandum," *War and Society* 1 (1975): 162–77. On the significant difference between the views of Stronge at the time and later, see Milan Hauner, "Ein Bericht des britischen Militärattachés in Prag vom 4. April 1938 über seine Reise zur Besichtigung der tschechischen Grenzbefestigungen," *Militärgeschichtliche Mitteilungen* 2 (1978): 125–36. Probably the most balanced and best informed analysis of Czech strength in 1938 is Jonathan Zorach, "Czechoslovakia's Fortifications: Their Development and Role in the 1938 Munich Crisis," *Militärgeschichtliche Mitteilungen* 2 (1976): 81–94. A very useful and stimulating study, although uneven in quality and quite weak on East Europe, is Williamson Murray, *The Change in the European Balance of Power, 1938–1939* (Princeton, NJ: Princeton University Press, 1984). Murray argues, without authoritative reference to East European materials, that the balance against Hitler was stronger in 1938 than in 1939. I find the argument convincing.

[46] Komandir Kulik to Commissariat of Defense, 28 March 1938; Library of Congress. Volkogonov Papers, Reel 10, Box 16, Folder 5 (Czechoslovak Situation Reports, RGVA); Major Kashuba to Commissariat, 4 April 1938; ibid.

[47] I am grateful to Milan Hauner for supplying me the series edited by Jerzy Tomaszewski, "Polska korespondencja dyplomatyczna na temat wojskowej pomocy ZSRR dla Czechoslowacji w 1938 r. przez terytorium Rumunii," *Z dziejów rozwoju państw socjalistycznych* 1 (1), (1983): 159–84.

are showing no concern. Lack of preventive instructions or preparations [sic]."[48]

A more substantial report followed from Kishinev on 20 September:

> From several border posts come reports of the presence of Soviet forces on the left bank of the Dniestr.
>
> From a position on the Dniestr around the locality of Rezina [fifty miles northeast of Kishinev] a great movement of Soviet forces is already visible since early [today?] on the opposite bank, i.e., in the region of Rybnica. Apparently large maneuvers are taking place there. Artillery fire can be heard. This intelligence comes from a reliable source. The railroad bridge at Rezina, partly destroyed (in 1919), has not been rebuilt.
>
> Apparently movements of Soviet forces have been observed farther south as well at Vadului Voda [Vadalui, south of Soviet town of Dubosary, twenty miles northeast of Kishinev; underlining in original]. This intelligence comes from a less reliable source and requires confirmation.
>
> Several months ago the Romanian authorities began a small number of evacuations, however, of localities (of fishermen) from the frontier islets of the mouth of the Dniestr between Karolina and Bugaz [underlining in original].[49]

A week later, 27 September, the news from Kishinev grew yet more interesting:

> Transports of military matériel continue to go both through Cainari-Besarabiasca as well as [through] Kishinev. Thus far the contents of these shipments have consisted of, among other things, tanks, machine guns, gas masks, and covered freight cars of unknown cargo (marked "explosives," thus probably ammunition). From well informed sources (railway employees), I have intelligence that until the 25th of this month around 600 freight cars passed through Kishinev with Soviet military matériel for Czechoslovakia.
>
> The Soviet trains move through Kishinev exclusively during the night, maintain extensive [security] precautions, for example prohibiting in several places nighttime access to tracks and stations. The railroad worker is ordered to maintain the greatest discretion and under threat of termination of employment is forbidden to mention the passing Soviet transports. The above exceptional measures of security are prompting, on one hand, the spread of numerous alarming rumors.... This is particularly true of the rumor of alleged sightings of Soviet soldiers. In spite of the number of such rumors, I

---

[48] Aleksandr Poncet de Sandon to Ministry of Foreign Affairs; "Polska korespondencja," 179.

[49] Probably Aleksandr Poncet de Sandon to Polish Embassy in Bucharest, 20 September 1938; "Polska korespondencja," 182–3. It is significant that this report *preceded* the issuance of Voroshilov's mobilization orders by a day.

judge, however, that thus far there have been no [Soviet] troop trains (besides those engaged in the maintenance of military vehicles). . . .

On 21st and 22nd September two shipments of tanks passed through Kishinev on several [*kilkunasta*, i.e., from 13 to 19] flatcars.

- Approximately 6 tanks at present, according to an eyewitness, are sighted on a flatcar at Vesternicei station [location ??]. Here there is no doubt that we are dealing with Soviet tanks (reliable intelligence).
- Recently numerous freight trains consisting of covered cars containing some kind of Czech cargoes have passed Kishinev during the night hours.
- Shipments of Soviet tanks seen among other [places] at the Causani station [approximately ten miles due south of Bender on way to Cainar]. Shipments of machine guns seen at Zloti station [location ??] (reliable intelligence).
- 24 September, a train of Soviet troops in Czech uniforms stood in a field in the vicinity of Kishinev (doubtful intelligence).
- A large Soviet troop transport allegedly seen last week at Roman station [approximately 100 miles west of Kishinev on railway].
- Much talk of massive overflights of Soviet planes north of Bessarabia and Bukovina, 450–480 planes in the course of several days.[50]

By 30 September, on the other hand, all was quiet on the Ukrainian front. The Polish consul in Kiev was traveling that day from the border to his post. As he reported, "On the railroad line from the border to Kiev I did not meet any military transport. Around Slavuta [150 miles due west of Kiev] fortification works are visible. In Kiev the mood is apathetic, there is no special press campaign against Poland. I confirm an aggravation of provisioning in the market."[51]

These documents not only nourished my research in a phase of it that had grown discouraging; they also suggested a clear new orientation of it. I was frankly impressed by the explicit particulars in the reports, but I was disturbed by the fact that all the evidence of this sort came from one utterly unique documentary source. I was certain that if movements of Soviet military equipment on the scale here reported had actually taken place, they would have been observed and reported far more fully and more frequently by the Romanian army. As if to dramatize the acquisition of this information, I soon discovered that by the time when these documents were generated, the Romanian army had received orders to mobilize on

[50] Aleksandr Poncet de Sandon to Polish Embassy in Bucharest, 27 September 1938; ibid., 182–3.
[51] Telegram szyfrowy nr 10/6 Jerzego Matusinskiego do Ministerstwa Spraw Zagranicznych, 30 September 1938; ibid., 184.

its *western, Hungarian frontier* (19 September)[52]; and at 2100 hours on the evening of 25 September, a Czechoslovak officer, followed by six soldiers, arrived at the railway station of Sighet on the Romanian–Czechoslovak frontier and said that "following the mobilization of the Czechoslovak army, he had received the order to come to the frontier post in order to 'cooperate in the regulation of traffic.' "[53]

Here, it seemed, was something like the Red Army coming to the rescue. Could it be real? Obviously, given the closed nature of Soviet records on the subject, the answer could only come from the observations of the border guards and the work of the intelligence section of the general staff of the Romanian army. And so, having exhausted the prospects of research in Moscow and having confronted a dead end in Prague, it was obvious that the development of the research depended on turning to Bucharest.

Before considering more carefully, however, the question how prepared the Red Army was to intervene and what kind of aims its intervention might have had, we must take account of the climax of that series of events that led to Moscow's *not being asked to intervene*.

---

[52] Ioan Talpeş, *Diplomaţie şi apărăre: coordonate ale politicii externe româneşti, 1933–1939* (Bucharest: Editură ştiinţifică şi enciclopedică, 1988), 216–18, 235.

[53] Comnen Papers, Hoover Institution Archive. Box 4-A, Folder 3.

Chapter 6

Dénouement

It is worth recalling, as we consider the prospect of a German attack on Czechoslovakia, the Soviet reaction to a somewhat similar challenge to the Versailles system, the remilitarization of the Rhineland in March 1936. At that time, U.S. Ambassador William Bullitt had asked Litvinov if he hoped that the French would send troops into the Rhineland, and Litvinov had replied "that he did not as that would mean immediate war."[1] In the meantime, in the direct aftermath of the *Anschluss*, Litvinov communicated to London, Paris, Prague, and Washington – and published in the Soviet press – a Soviet offer "to participate in collective actions... to stop the further development of aggression and to remove the growing dangers of a new worldwide carnage. [Moscow] is ready to enter at once into discussion of practical measures [toward that end] with other powers in the League of Nations or outside of it."[2]

In the wake of the *Anschluss* the prospect of war had obviously moved closer to the Soviet frontier, and adjustments in Soviet policy seemed to be in order. The Soviet minister in Prague, Sergei Aleksandrovskii, was summoned home to report on circumstances in Czechoslovakia. He had a meeting in the Kremlin with Stalin, Commissar of Defense Voroshilov, Commissar of Foreign Affairs Litvinov, and two of Stalin's closest associates, Viacheslav Molotov, and Lazar Kaganovich, and he was authorized to assure President Beneš of the assistance of the Soviet army and air force.[3]

As Munich approached, Litvinov had to explain Soviet policy carefully to Aleksandrovskii, who was evidently dissatisfied with the subtle

[1] Bullitt to Secretary of State, 7 March 1938; *Foreign Relations of the United States: Diplomatic Papers, 1936*, 5 vols. (Washington, DC: Government Printing Office, 1953), 1: 212–13.
[2] Litvinov to Maiskii, Surits, Aleksandrovskii, Troianovskii (ambassador in the United States), 17 March 1938; DVP SSSR, 21: 127–8 (No. 81). Litvinov interview with members of the press, 17 March, 1938; ibid., 128–9 (No. 82).
[3] Fierlinger to Krofta, 23 April 1938; *Dokumenty i materialy po istorii sovetsko–chekhoslovatskikh otnoshenii*, 5 vols. (Moscow: Nauka, 1973–1988), 3: 402 (No. 271).

ambiguities of Soviet policy and asked for a clearer line of support.[4] Litvinov instructed Aleksandrovskii not to discuss in Prague any hypothetical question of Soviet assistance independently of that of France. All military questions were to be dealt with jointly by the General Staffs of the three countries:

> We are not going to be too forthcoming in offering such talks and you must not raise this question . . . With such a raging pressure being put upon Czechoslovakia by England and France, you should of course reinforce the spirit of the Czechs and their resistance to that pressure. You should not forget, however, that we are not at all interested in the forcible solution of the problem of the Sudeten Germans and we should offer no objection at all to such measures, which, while preserving Czechoslovakia's full political independence, would be able to diffuse [sic] the tension and prevent the danger of a military confrontation . . . You should not object to Anglo–French suggestions concerning some extension of the rights of the Sudeten Germans, the sending of observers and so on.[5]

As in the case of the Rhineland, contrary to the common assumption that Moscow sought to provoke a war between the victors and the vanquished of Versailles,[6] this evidence argues in favor of the Soviet wish to see the continuation of peace.

Late in the summer, Litvinov explained to Aleksandrovskii the Soviet aim of preserving Czechoslovakia chiefly as a means of blocking German expansion; yet quite realistically he nearly despaired of achieving the aim without the cooperation of the Anglo–French: "We are extremely interested in the preservation of Czechoslovakia's independence, in the hindrance of the Hitlerite drive to the south-east, but without the Western powers it is doubtful whether we would be able to do anything serious, and those powers do not consider it necessary to seek our assistance, [they] ignore us and decide everything concerning the German-Czechoslovak conflict among themselves. We are not aware of Czechoslovakia herself ever pointing out to her Western 'friends' the necessity of bringing in the Soviet Union."[7] Somewhat later, Litvinov reiterated the same frustration: "I continue to think that, if we are to speak about any serious help to

---

[4] Zara Steiner, "The Soviet Commissariat of Foreign Affairs and the Czechoslovakian Crisis in 1938: New Materials from the Soviet Archives," *The Historical Journal* 42 (1999): 762–3.

[5] Quoted note of Litvinov to Aleksandrovskii, 11 June 1938, in ibid., 758.

[6] A very familiar argument in the older literature on Soviet foreign policy before World War II most recently and aggressively argued by Igor Lukes, *Czechoslovakia Between Stalin and Hitler: The Diplomacy of Edvard Beneš in the 1930s* (New York: Oxford University Press, 1996), passim.

[7] Note of Litvinov to Aleksandrovskii, 11 August 1938 in Steiner, "The Soviet Commissariat of Foreign Affairs and the Czechoslovakian Crisis," 759.

Czechoslovakia, it would be difficult to go without serious negotiations with France."[8]

About the same time, Litvinov gave a revealing explanation of Soviet foreign policy to quite a different person with quite a different point of view, German Ambassador Count Friedrich Werner von der Schulenburg. Litvinov said that "the Soviet Union regarded the Sudeten German question as an internal affair of Czechoslovakia. The *Soviet Union* [sic] had not interfered in any way, and had not given the Czech Government any advice either in one direction or the other." Germany, Litvinov said, "was not so much concerned about the Sudeten Germans; she aimed at the annihilation of Czechoslovakia as a whole." He thought that if Germany attacked, the Anglo–French would come to the assistance of the Czechs, however reluctantly in the case of Britain, and the Soviet Union would certainly keep her word to the Czechs, too. Schulenburg asked whether the powers would really engage in a major war for the sake of Czechoslovakia. Litvinov said that Czechoslovakia was not the issue: The issue was power politics. "The Soviet Union bore no responsibility for the creation and composition of the Czechoslovak State; she had not sat at Versailles; on the other hand, she must combat any increase in power of National Socialist Germany in her violence and desire for attack. Litvinov added, *"If the old democratic Germany had still existed, the Czechoslovak question would have assumed quite a different aspect for the Soviet Union. The Soviets had always been in favor of the right of self-determination of peoples."*[9]

Schulenburg repeatedly asked what form Soviet aid to Czechoslovakia would take, and Litvinov stubbornly evaded answering the question. In view of Litvinov's insistence that Moscow would, in Schulenburg's words, "keep her word and do her best," Schulenburg felt obliged to consult with his embassy's military and naval attachés and to sketch an estimate of what it might in fact do.

1. Moscow wanted France and Britain to take the initiative, but it might have arrived at some agreement with them about joint assistance.
2. Moscow would not attack Germany, because there was no common frontier. It would, however, mobilize the Western Military Districts.
3. It could attack Germany from the air.
4. Its submarines and minelayers could interrupt shipments of iron ore from Norway and Sweden.

---

[8] Note of Litvinov to Aleksandrovskii, ca. 27–28 August 1938, in ibid., 762.
[9] Schulenburg to Auswärtiges Amt, 26 August 1938; DGFP, D, 2: 629–31 (No. 396) (my emphasis). General Ernst Köstring to Counsellor of Embassy Tippelskirch, 29 August 1938; Hermann Teske, *General Ernst Köstring: Der militärische Mittler zwischen dem deutschen Reich und der Sowjet-Union, 1921–1941* (Frankfurt am Main: Mittler, 1965), 205.

5. It could attack East Prussia by land and sea.
6. It would supply Czechoslovakia with massive war materials, but the sending of troops was difficult.

Finally, "the overwhelming conviction of the Diplomatic Corps here is that, in the event of a German–Czech armed conflict, France would attack Germany, and Great Britain would be at France's side. The members of the British and French Embassies here have repeatedly told us this. As far as the Soviet Union is concerned, my colleagues here believe that she will do so as little as possible, so that at the end of the war she will have an intact army at her disposal. In consequence, the Soviet Union would in the end be the only one to gain. Characteristic of this is the following remark of my French colleague here [Robert Coulondre]: 'I hope, with all my heart, that it will not come to a German–French conflict. You know, as well as I do, for whom we are working if we come to blows.' "[10]

On 23 September – by which time the bad news of Godesberg was abroad on the continent – Romanian Foreign Minister Comnen was suddenly ordered home from Geneva. The king requested him to return by the first available train – without an evidently previously planned stopover in Belgrade – to take part in a government council at Sinaia to review the critical juncture of affairs in Europe.[11] The news that Comnen brought there was fateful. It was evidently his report to the council of Sinaia that prompted a revolution of Romanian policy, the beginning of a considerable about-face in Bucharest. Litvinov, according to Comnen, had proposed bringing the Sudeten issue before the League of Nations, but he found no support for the idea even in France. To make matters worse, Comnen related that the British delegate at the League meeting had moved, and the League had accepted the proposal to abrogate the provisions of the Covenant on applying military sanctions to an aggressor (Article 16).

This move at the League really amounted to public proclamation of what had been sneakingly apparent for some time. The League members had already been declaring one by one their own independence of the compulsion of military sanctions. Now they were led by the most influential great power that remained a member of the League, the British. Count de la Warr, the British delegate at the League, had addressed the subject there in late July. He said that the provisions of Article 16 stipulating punitive measures against an aggressor were unfortunate, that the League had sometimes

---

[10]   Schulenburg to Auswärtiges Amt, 26 August 1938; DGFP, D, 2: 629–31 (No. 396).
[11]   Ministry of Foreign Affairs to Comnen (Geneva), 23 September 1938; RMAE. Fond 71/Romînia. Vol. 103, p. 234.

defended the status quo *too rigidly*[12] (when, where?!). On 23 September, in the very froth of the crisis, R. A. Butler, under-secretary of state for foreign affairs, addressed the League in a fashion all too familiar in the idiom of appeasement: "The circumstances in which occasion for international action under Article 16 may arise, the possibility of taking such action and the nature of the action to be taken cannot be determined in advance: each case must be considered on its merits. In consequence, while the right of any Member of the League to take any measures of the kind contemplated by Article 16 remains intact, no unconditional obligation exists to take such measures." League members must consult with each other, he said, before determining what common measures to take in the event of need: "In the course of such consultation, each Member of the League would be the judge of the extent to which its own position would allow it to participate in any measures which might be proposed, and, in so doing, it would no doubt be influenced by the extent to which other members were prepared to take action."[13] The British initiative was followed by a rush of other national representatives to agree: Luxembourg, Belgium, Denmark, Finland, The Netherlands, Norway, Sweden, and others. The Political Committee then reported to the Assembly that "there is general agreement that the military measures contemplated in Article 16 are not compulsory." By this time, there was an unseemly stampede of flight from Article 16 – devil take the hindmost – and it must have been obvious to everyone that it was a dead letter, although the British resolution to kill it was adopted by the Assembly only too ironically on 30 September, the day of the Czechoslovak acceptance of the Munich *Diktat!*[14] It was left, more ironically, to the Polish delegate – Colonel Beck must have felt a sense of foolish satisfaction – to observe that "the League of Nations has ceased to be an organisation of States which can hope to take decisions having a general application."[15]

And so, by majority vote, the League Covenant was itself abrogated, and the issue to be addressed at Munich was never brought before the council at all. The great powers – which comprised whatever real muscle of international policy was left at the disposal of a League badly battered after its failures in the Manchurian crisis, the Spanish Civil War, and the Italo–Ethiopian problem – had suddenly gone on record as deserting the

[12] *League of Nations Official Journal. Special Supplement No. 183: Records of the Nineteenth Ordinary Session of the Assembly: Plenary Meetings, Text of the Debates* (Geneva, 1938). Library of Congress microfilm reel no. 61, 1938, pp. 42–5. (My emphasis.)

[13] Ibid., *Special Supplement No. 189. Records of the Nineteenth Ordinary Session of the Assembly: Meetings of the Committees: Minutes of the Sixth Committee (Political Questions)*, Library of Congress microfilm reel 61, 1938, p. 25.

[14] Ibid., p. 103, Annex 3.

[15] Ibid., p. 47.

principle at the very heart of the conception of the Covenant. At that point, the poor allies and dependents in Eastern Europe of the League leaders in Western Europe realized that they had been abandoned and their hopes betrayed, and they began to scramble to make such accommodations as they could with the now unavoidable aspirations of the aggressor in Berlin.[16]

This series of events apparently helped to precipitate the Romanian change of front. Yet there was evidently another factor that played into the Romanian decision as well. Prague's acceptance of the Anglo–French terms of 19 September included the stipulation of the abrogation of all of Czechoslovakia's Eastern alliances – with both Moscow and the Little Entente powers – in favor of the Anglo–French guarantee. The Romanians were informed of this development only on 26 September and only by the French, whereas the treaty in question (16 February 1933) required that all such acts influencing treaty obligations receive the consent of all three powers of the Entente. So the obligations of the Romanians to their Czechoslovak allies under the Little Entente treaties were effectively abrogated by the Czechoslovaks themselves![17]

On September 26, as the League was preparing virtually to abolish itself and Bucharest discovered that Prague had unilaterally suspended the Little Entente, the council at Sinaia decided to take up a neutral stance on the Sudeten issue, and at that point, apparently, the preparations for mobilization on the Western frontier of the country were suspended.[18] That same evening, Hitler made another grand speech – public festival, forensic carnival – in the Berlin Sportpalast, and he repeated again that the

[16] There is an authoritative summary account, quoting the British resolution in *Monthly Summary of the League of Nations* 18 (1938), 221–4. I am unaware that the British move to abrogate Article 16 has been taken into account in any of the literature on British foreign policy in the period. There is a teasingly allusive description in F. P. Walters (an officer of the League), *A History of the League of Nations*, 2 vols. (London: Royal Institute of International Affairs and Oxford University Press, 1951), 2: Chapter 63: "The League Abandons the Covenant," 777–83.

[17] Comnen, "Dust and Shadows," 1–2; Hoover Institution Archive. Comnen Papers. Box 5, Folder 21. To complete the rout of collective-security arrangements, when the Poles sent to Prague their ultimatum on the occupation and annexation of Teschen, they did so without prior consultation with the Romanians, and that act effectively terminated the Romanian–Polish alliance of 1921, as it had required prior consultation and agreement before major foreign-policy initiatives. Ultimatum of 30 September 1938; *Monachium 1938: polskie dokumenty dyplomatyczne*, Zbigniew Landau and Jerzy Tomaszewski, eds. (Warsaw: Panstwowe Wydawnictwo Naukowe, 1985), 496–8 (No. 449); Viorica Moisuc, *Diplomația României și problema apărării suveranității și independenței naționale in perioada martie 1938–mai 1940* (Bucharest: Editură Academiei Republicii Socialiste România, 1971), 72.

[18] Al. Gh. Savu, *Dictatură regală (1938–1940)* (Bucharest: Editură politică, 1970), Chapter 9: "Münchenul și situația României," 197–231, especially p. 210; Dov B. Lungu, *Romania and the Great Powers, 1933–1940* (Durham, NC: Duke University Press, 1989), 134–5; Ioan Talpeș, *Diplomație și apărăre: coordonate ale politicii externe românești, 1933–1939* (Bucharest: Editură științifică și enciclopedică, 1988), 235–6, 241.

Sudeten provinces were "the last territorial claim which I have to make in Europe."[19]

In the meantime, Chamberlain, having done so much to dissolve all the League and collective-security arrangements that might have strengthened the cause that the malevolence of Hitler would eventually force him unavoidably to embrace, was driven by his adversary's intransigence, by Daladier's firmness, and by British public opinion, to take that strong stand that might have spared the continent so much had it been done in time. He dispatched to Berlin special emissary Sir Horace Wilson to convey to Hitler in person the newly agreed Anglo–French position. "The French Government have informed us that, if the Czechs reject the Godesberg memorandum and Germany attacks Czechoslovakia, they will fulfil their obligations to Czechoslovakia. Should the forces of France in consequence become engaged in active hostilities against Germany, we shall feel obliged to support them."[20] Wilson went to Berlin, where he weasled characteristically – hesitated, equivocated, tergiversated – but eventually delivered the message on 27 September.[21] Ambassador Henderson reported from Berlin that Hitler had previously issued a 2:00 P.M. 28 September deadline for the Czechoslovaks to accept the memorandum, failing which Germany would march.[22] About an hour before the expiration of the deadline, Mussolini persuaded Hitler to postpone the attack by a day. In the meantime, Hitler, having been thus deserted by Italy, having been assured unambiguously that both the French and the British would fight, had watched as the movement of his troops through Berlin on the way to the Eastern frontier elicited only sullen silence from the public there. The Czechoslovak army had been mobilized and posted to the frontier fortifications since 23 September, and the German army thus lost the advantage of surprise. The French began calling up reserves on the 27th, and the British fleet was mobilized on the 28th. It was enough; he was sufficiently impressed; and he consented to postpone the attack. When the Italians, responding to appeals from both Chamberlain and Roosevelt, suggested the meeting at Munich, he consented.

What, now, was that mastermind of scientific politics, the captain of the Czechoslovak ship of state, thinking? We have an intimate portrait from Sergei Aleksandrovskii, the Soviet minister in Prague.

Aleksandrovskii was summoned by phone to Beneš's office around 6:00 P.M. on 21 September. There were on the street outside the building many

[19] *The Speeches of Adolf Hitler, April 1922–August 1939*, ed. Norman H. Baynes, 2 vols. (New York: Oxford University Press, 1942), 2: 1517.

[20] Middlemas, *Diplomacy of Illusion*, 387 (referring to unpublished cabinet papers).

[21] Notes of talk of Wilson and Hitler, 27 September 1938; DBFP, 3rd series, 2: 566 (No. 1129).

[22] Henderson to Halifax, 27 September 1938; DBFP, 3rd series, 2: 574 (No. 1142).

demonstrators demanding resistance to Germany. Beneš was very calm and confident. "When he asked questions about the Red Army's passage through Romanian territory or about our reaction to the possibility of a Polish attack on Czechoslovakia, there was no sign of doubt in his tone about our resolve to pass through Romania or Poland even if we had to fight. He said clearly enough that he considered Romania a country belonging to the anti-German bloc . . . and believed that Poland was in league with Germany. Furthermore, it was perfectly clear that he regarded the French refusal to help as no more than a threat and still believed that at the last minute France, followed by Britain, would have to make common cause with Czechoslovakia and the Soviet Union against Germany. . . . He made it perfectly clear this time as well that the French General Staff was entirely at one with him and could be relied on without qualification."[23]

If this report is reliable, it is remarkable to find Beneš, reputed to be a realist, so full of illusions, perhaps misled by his own vanity. After all, it was about this time that he was broadcasting to the nation that he had a plan for every eventuality.

On 22 September, Aleksandrovskii reported to Moscow that popular demonstrations were demanding resistance to Germany, that both Beneš and Hodža were being followed by catcalls, and that a police cordon was required to protect the French mission in Prague.[24] When Beneš phoned to inform him of the Czech mobilization, 23 September, "he was positively rejoicing. Among other things, he told me that it was he, Beneš, who had succeeded in bringing about a world coalition against the fascist offensive and that *all his calculations had proved correct*. Czechoslovakia was a victim of attack, and justice would ultimately prevail."[25]

Beneš's illusions soon mounted. By 25 September he "spoke plainly and even in a downright arrogant tone. He did not doubt in the least that aid from France and even Britain would be forthcoming. . . . *I admit . . . that I felt very uneasy because I could say nothing to Beneš, especially in reply to his 'practical questions'. He asked me how many thousand airborne troops the Red Army could rush to Czechoslovakia, what military equipment they would bring with them, what technical means would be required and in what quantity for such troops to go into action. . . . Beneš said outright that he would need an air landing the moment hostilities began, not so much in order to achieve real military results as to raise the morale of the masses, who would hail the arrival of the Russians in their splendid machines.*"[26]

---

[23] Sergei Aleksandrovskii, "Munich: Witness's Account," *International Affairs* (Moscow) (1988), No. 12: 119–32, quote from pp. 127–8.

[24] Aleksandrovskii to Commissariat of Foreign Affairs, 22 September 1938; DVP, 21: 515 (No. 364).

[25] Aleksandrovskii, "Munich: Witness's Account," 128 (my emphasis).

[26] Ibid., 129. (My emphasis.)

On 26 September, Beneš said that he was unruffled by Hitler's speech of that evening and the curses that Hitler had pronounced upon him. It was an honor to be designated as Hitler's chief antagonist. He now said that it would not come to war, "because Germany was not in a position to wage war against a mighty coalition which would include France, Britain and the Soviet Union, with the United States giving moral and possibly even material support." Hitler would now likely retreat.[27]

Obviously there was a big mood swing the next day, 27 September. "Beneš spoke quite seriously about the inevitability of war, and his tone regarding the issue of our aid was different. I had a distinct feeling that Beneš, who betrayed great nervous tension and was in an extremely serious mood, wanted us to tell him how and when we were going to help." He had received from Chamberlain a message that he represented as an expression of support, yet it was just the contrary. "It follows that Beneš simply lied to me. Why? I think because he did not want to scare us off, being anxious to get help from us at the last minute even without its being coupled with help from France and Britain. He thought that the readiness of France to make concessions to Germany stemmed from the fear of social revolution – Bolshevism – in the event of war. He said that the Slovak Agrarians had the same fear, though he himself did not. He had tried to conduct Czechoslovak foreign policy such that all the great powers interested in preserving peace and the status quo would understand that they could only be attained by the defense of Czechoslovakia."[28]

Aleksandrovskii did not see Beneš again after the 27th. They spoke by phone, however, on each of the three succeeding days, and by this time, Beneš was in despair, realizing that all the decisive questions were being settled without him.[29]

The four principals convened at Munich on the 29th. No Czechoslovaks or Soviets were present. Chamberlain carefully avoided meeting Daladier.[30] Hitler, however, had contrived to meet and coordinate plans with Mussolini, and he conceded only the gossamer fluff of compromise that actually left the whole affair at his virtually sole discretion. The Munich agreement divided the disputed Czech territory, the Sudetenland, into two parts. The first part comprised approximately half the area that Hitler had demanded in the Godesberg memorandum, and it was to be occupied in phases extending from 1 to 7 October. The remainder of the Godesberg claims were to be adjudicated by an International Commission established for the purpose. That commission consisted of the general secretary of the German

[27] Ibid., 129.
[28] Ibid., 130–1.
[29] Ibid., 132.
[30] See especially Pierre Le Goyet, *Munich, "un traquenard"?* (Paris: France-Empire, 1988).

Foreign Office, Ernst von Weizsäcker, and the British, French, Italian, and Czechoslovak ambassadors in Berlin. While the British and French Cabinets boasted in their respective parliaments that Munich limited German acquisitions to half the Godesberg demands, their representatives in the International Commission, meeting in Berlin, quickly conceded all of the previous German claims and even more. The final territorial arrangement was in fact somewhat worse than that demanded at Godesberg,[31] and it contained no provisions whatever for the protection of the civil rights, or even the lives, of the natural enemies of Nazism. The Social Democrats of the lost provinces protested: "It may be that [our] fate will also overtake those who have sacrificed us."[32] On the Czechoslovak consent to cancel their pacts with the Soviet Union and their Little Entente allies, the Anglo–French undertook to guarantee the integrity of the new, and now indefensible, frontiers – we shall see with what fortitude – although Chamberlain and Gamelin had previously regarded the far more formidable traditional frontiers as quite beyond the reach of British and French military power. Meantime, the claims of Poland and Hungary remained to be settled, to Hitler's satisfaction, of course, and conspiracies in Slovakia, goaded by him, moved toward secession and independence.

Before departing for home, Chamberlain asked William Strang of the Foreign Office to draw up an anodyne Anglo–German agreement, which he proposed to ask Hitler to sign. Slightly edited by Chamberlain himself, it said in effect that Great Britain and Germany would resort henceforth to bilateral consultations to remove from the international agenda any sources of conflict and to ensure the continuation of peace. Hitler, of course, was glad to sign such a document. As the text was evolving, Strang asked Chamberlain if it should not be communicated to Daladier. Chamberlain responded that "he saw no reason whatever for saying anything to the French."[33] Daladier was to be left out yet again.

In the sad aftermath, a truncated Czechoslovakia, formerly the proudest democracy of Eastern Europe, abandoned now and bereft of friends among the powers who were initially assumed to be the bedrock of collective security, was mercilessly ravaged. Hitler had annexed approximately as large an area of predominantly Czech population as the area of predominantly German population. His acquisitions cost the country 70–90 percent of its industries in iron and steel, coal, textiles, railway carriages, cement, porcelain, glass, chemicals, and electric power in addition to all of the celebrated spas in the Erzgebirge, especially Karlovy Vary (Karlsbad). The

[31]   Telford Taylor, *Munich: The Price of Peace* (New York: Vintage, 1980), 899–917.

[32]   J. W. Bruegel, *Czechoslovakia Before Munich: The German Minority Problem and British Appeasement Policy* (Cambridge, England: Cambridge University Press, 1973), 300.

[33]   William Strang, *Home and Abroad* (Westport, CT: Greenwood, 1983), 147.

chief armaments works of Škoda was only three miles inside the new frontier. The remainder of the state became an industrial dependent of Germany.[34]

Most important, the Erzgebirge range – the Sudeten mountains – and their fortifications had been incorporated into the Third Reich and hence had ceased to constitute a formidable barrier to German expansion to the East, and the substantial Czechoslovak military power had simply disappeared, as most of its excellent armament was transferred to the Wehrmacht, thereby immensely enhancing the striking power – especially in tanks – of the attack on France in May 1940.

---

[34] Hubert Ripka, *Munich Before and After: A Fully Documented Czechoslovak Account of the Crises of September 1938 and March 1939*, trans. Ida Sindelkova and Edgar P. Young (New York: Fertig, 1969), 492.

PART THREE

Conclusion

Chapter 7

What the Red Army Actually Did

It is pertinent here to recall the most salient features of the context of this problem. First, from 1936, annual Romanian plans of campaign foresaw the facilitation of Red Army transit: "If Russia remains allied with France and intends to support Czechoslovakia we will need to permit the Russian forces to cross Romania in order to assist the Czech army."[1] The Romanian General Staff campaign plan for 1938 addressed the "degree of probability of war on the different fronts," East, West, and South, or Russian, Hungarian, and Bulgarian. The most threatening front was clearly the Western or Hungarian. In view of Russia's treaty with France, Russian policy as enunciated at the League of Nations, and the attitude of the other powers, especially Hungary, the General Staff judged that in 1938 "war on the eastern [front] appears little likely."[2] In fact, plans for 1938 were massively and almost exclusively concerned about the "*front de vest.*" Document after document is entitled "*Front de vest.*" In the event of a large war, a war with Germany, on the Romanian West front, the assistance of the Red Army would have been desperately essential.

On the other hand, we subsequently saw that, on the firing of Titulescu, the Romanian Foreign Office and the court signaled unmistakably, not that transit rights of the Red Army would absolutely in all cases be refused, but rather their distinct disinclination, a visceral reluctance, to admit Soviet troops to the country. Finally, we must remember what is the most graphic evidence, the observation of the actual shipping across Romania

---

[1] "Dacă Rusia rămâne aliată cu Franța și înțelege a ajuta Cehoslovacia noi vom trebui să permitem forțelor ruse să treacă prin România pentru a ajuta armata cehă." Referate pentru întocmirea planului de campanie 1936; AMR. Fond Marele stat major, Secția I-a, Organizare și mobilizare. Dosar 434: Planurile de campanie 1936, pp. 65–92, quote on p. 69.

[2] Memoriu pentru revederea și punerea la curent a ipotezelor de rasboi 1938; AMR. Fond Marele stat major, Secția 3 operații. Dosar 1577: Studii în legătură cu planul de campanie 1938; Microfilm reel no. II.1.974, 93–94 ff. and passim.

of substantial quantities of Soviet military matériel as reported by the Polish consul in Kishinev 27 September 1938. On the following day, the
Romanian chief of staff, General Ionescu, told the French military attaché that the Soviets were gathering on their Western frontier a special
force, which seemed to give them increased opportunities to intervene in
Europe.[3]

So what will the decisive evidence tell us? What information were the
Romanian border guards and the intelligence section of the General Staff
picking up with their own eyes? There is abundant evidence of this kind,
but the reader must be warned. It is of the most extraordinary, the most surprising kind – so much so that merely believing it requires the presentation
of it in virtually verbatim, unvarnished, unmediated form.

In the spring the border patrol in the region of Tighina reported numerous cases of such conventional problems as illegal border crossings from
the Romanian side, of drownings in the river, of the stealing of wood from
state forest land, and the poaching of fish in the river.[4]

2 July 1938. The commandant of the border guards, General Gr.
Cornicioiu, reported (on 8 October, more than three months after the
event!) that two unauthorized persons crossed the Dniestr into the Soviet
Union. He was unable to determine the identity of one of these two people; the other was a soldier, Ion Barbu, who had been punished by ten
days of incarceration for returning late from leave.[5]

19 August 1938. A patrol in the region of Rezina observed an individual
bathing in the river. At the same time, directly opposite this individual on
the other side of the river was a Soviet citizen fishing from a boat. As the
boat approached the Romanian who was bathing, he was taken into the
boat and rowed to the Soviet bank of the river. The Romanian patrol fired
repeatedly at the boat but without result. The report concludes that the
border patrols need more riflery training.[6]

About this next report, there is something symptomatic, symbolic.

[3] Colonel Delmas to Ministry of Defense, 28 September 1938; DDF, 2nd series, 11: 684–8 (No. 457).

[4] Raport Gen. Florea Mitrănescu, I Brigada, Corpul granicelor, Tighina, 3 May 1938; AMR. Fond
    Corpul granicelor. Dosar 2348/4/a: Ordine, rapoarte, procese verbale, declaraţii şi schiţe cu privire
    la anchete şi cercetări întreprinse de corp asupra cazurilor de trecere frauduloasă a frontierei precum
    şi a unor incidente de frontieră (03.09.1938–10.11.1938), pp. 1ff.

[5] General Gr. Cornicioiu, Comandantul Corpului Granicerilor către Ministrului afacerilor interne,
    8 October 1938; AMR. Fond Corpului granicelor. Dosar 2349: Ordine, rapoarte, schiţe, procese
    verbale şi declaraţii cu privire la cercetarea cazurilor de trecere frauduloasă a frontierei de către unii
    indivizii (28.08.1938–02.11.1938), p. 31.

[6] Note of 27 August 1938 to General Staff; AMR. Fond Corpul granicelor. Dosar 2348/4/a: Or-
    dine, rapoarte, procese verbale, declaraţii şi schiţe cu privire la anchete şi cercetări întreprinse de
    corp asupra cazurilor de trecere frauduloasă a frontierei precum şi a unor incidente de frontieră
    (03.09.1938–10.11.1938), pp. 93ff.

22 August. The mare of Volea Vişman went to the river to drink and was swept by strong currents to the Soviet side of the river. Several weeks of negotiations with the Soviet side procured the return of the animal, whereupon she was submitted to the examination of a veterinarian and found to be free of any Bolshevik diseases.[7]

Same date. Two persons crossed the Dniestr from Soviet Ukraine into Romania at Nord Naslavcea. Summoned by a Romanian patrol, they surrendered without resistance. Interrogated by personnel of the intelligence section of the General Staff, they admitted having been sent by the GPU from Mogilev in a boat rowed by a fisherman. When detected and arrested, they were found to be carrying Romanian currency and a revolver with six cartridges. Their mission:

- to travel from Nord Naslavcea–Climăuţi–Staţia–Dondoşami–Satul Scăieni, then through Dăngeni and return by Voloşcova [Nord Naslavcea and Voloşcova were border points on the Ukrainian–Bessarabian frontier; Dăngeni, the farthest destination in this mission was west of the Pruth in Northeastern Moldavia];
- to study the width of the roads along this route, the strength of the bridges for artillery and tanks, to gather information on the state of public opinion;
- to gather information on military construction, military units, and to recruit informers.[8]

Night of 22–3 August. A border patrol apprehended a Soviet courier, Gheorghe Melnic, who, when challenged, hid in riverbank vegetation and attempted to escape into the interior. In the course of these events, Soviet soldiers fired at the Romanian border patrol to intimidate it and to facilitate the escape of Melnic.[9]

27 August. The border guards at Tighina apprehended Anton Sarcani, who was trying to cross the river into the Soviet Union. He and his brother had invented a motor that ran on a fuel made of a mixture of gunpowder

---

7 Referat, 18 October 1938, near village of Lublin Soroca; AMR. Fond Corpului granicelor. Dosar 2349: Ordine, rapoarte, schiţe, procese verbale şi declaraţii cu privire la cercetarea cazurilor de trecere frauduloasă a frontierei de către unii indivizii (28.08.1938–02.11.1938), pp. 69-82.

8 Comandantul Corpului granicelor General Gr. Cornicioiu către Marele stat major, Secţia II, 9 September 1938; AMR. Fond Corpul granicelor. Dosar 2348/4/a: Ordine, rapoarte, procese verbale, declaraţii şi schiţe cu privire la anchete şi cercetări întreprinse de corp asupra cazurilor de trecere frauduloasă a frontierei precum şi a unor incidente de frontieră (03.09.1938–10.11.1938), p. 192 and verso.

9 Raport Comandantului Regt. 6 Graniceri Colonel Alex. Manolescu, Chişinau, 6 Sepember 1938; AMR. Fond Corpul granicelor. Dosar 2349: Ordine, rapoarte, schiţe, procese verbale şi declaraţii cu privire la cercetarea cazurilor de trecere frauduloasă a frontierei de către unii indivizii (28.08.1938–02.11.1938), pp. 32–3.

and gasoline. Sarcani had sought and been refused a patent in Bucharest, whereupon a friend who worked as a mechanic at the Vulcan metallurgical and machine-goods factory gave the plans to the Soviet legation in Bucharest, which forwarded them to Moscow. Not having gotten a quick response, Sarcani lost patience and came to Tighina to cross into the Soviet Union. Sarcani had studied in Budapest and served in the Austro–Hungarian army in World War I.[10]

Night of 27–8 August. In the vicinity of Soroca (130 kilometers north of Kishinev) on the Dniestr, there was a strong cloud of gas identified as *creolina*[11] coming from the Soviet side of the river. It was assumed to be associated with Soviet maneuvers in which poison gas was used. It caused much sneezing and lasted all night.[12]

Night of 30–1 August. A Romanian patrol in the region of Părăul Iagorlic (location?) discovered three persons in a boat proceeding from the Soviet to the Romanian bank of the Dniestr. As the boat approached within thirty-forty meters of shore, and as the patrol prepared to fire if the three persons resisted capture, their guard dog began to bark and could not be stopped. The persons in the boat, warned thus, returned to the Soviet bank of the river. The Romanian patrol fired on the boat, apparently in vain.[13] This incident was followed by a good deal of correspondence on the acquisition and training of guard dogs. There were at about the same time a number of other incidents in which border patrols on either side of the river engaged in exchanges of gunfire, and several new cases of drownings were recorded.[14]

---

[10] Comandantul Corpului granicelor General Gr. Cornicioiu către Marele stat major, Secția 2-a, 22 September 1938; AMR. Fond Corpul granicelor. Dosar 2348/4/a: Ordine, rapoarte, procese verbale, declarații și schițe cu privire la anchete și cercetări întreprinse de corp asupra cazurilor de trecere frauduloasă a frontierei precum și a unor incidente de frontieră (03.09.1938–10.11.1938), pp. 255–6.

[11] *Creolina* is a solution obtained by the mixing of *crezol* and aromatic hydrocarbons, sodium hydroxide (?), and water. It is used chiefly as a disinfectant. *Crezol* is the name of several substances extracted from tar and charcoal, and it is used to manufacture Bakelite and antiseptics. *Dicționarul explicativ al limbii române*, 2nd ed. (Bucharest: Univers enciclopedic, 1998), 238–9.

[12] General Fl. Mitrănescu, Comandantul brigadei 1-a graniceri, către Marele stat major, Secția II-a, 23 September 1938; AMR. Fond Corpul granicelor. Dosar 2349: Ordine, rapoarte, schițe, procese verbale și declarații cu privire la cercetarea cazurilor de trecere frauduloasă a frontierei de către unii indivizii (28.08.1938–02.11.1938), pp. 12–23.

[13] Comandantul I Brigadei granicelor Gen. Fl. Mitrănescu (and accompanying documents; near village of Părăul Iagorlic-??), 17 September 1938; AMR. Fond Corpul granicelor. Dosar 2348/4/a: Ordine, rapoarte, procese verbale, declarații și schițe cu privire la anchete și cercetări întreprinse de corp asupra cazurilor de trecere frauduloasă a frontierei precum și a unor incidente de frontieră (03.09.1938–10.11.1938), pp. 205–12.

[14] Gen. Gr. Cornicioiu, Comandantul Corpului granicelor, către Ministrului afacerilor externe, 31 August 1938 (and related correspondence); AMR. Fond Corpul granicelor. Dosar 2348/4/a: Ordine, rapoarte, procese verbale, declarații și schițe cu privire la anchete și cercetări întreprinse

12 September. There was a daytime encounter of Romanian and Soviet fishing boats in the Dniestr in the region of Carolina Peninsula in the Nistru Liman. A Romanian fisherman was captured and taken to the Soviet bank. The Romanian side demanded his release.[15]

13 September 1938. The border guards were instructed to give special attention to the problem of border crossings on the Bulgarian and Soviet frontiers, being especially vigilant about foreign espionage, during the upcoming royal maneuvers, that is, during the second half of October.[16]

22 September. Here is one of the most striking and informative documents on the situation of the Soviet–Romanian frontier. It was a report on the establishment on the Soviet frontier of systematic observation and reconnoitering posts of a kind obviously not previously in place there. Each observation post was to be provided with binoculars, a map of the local vicinity, a drawing board, and an optical device known to civil engineers as a transit (Romanian *declinator*, a declination compass). Some such posts were reported completed, some under construction, and some not yet begun. The report related that Romanian efforts to pass reconnoitering patrols across the frontier into Russia had been few and were difficult in view of the strong and effective Russian border controls. It was possible only at night. Soviet countermeasures included the removal of ethnic Romanians from the frontier area. The report also complained of a deficiency of persons able to swim and thus to compose reconnoitering squads.[17]

On 28 September. As tensions mounted in all the capitals of Europe, on the day before the convening of the Munich conference, the commandant of the corps of border guards was sufficiently unconcerned about the international situation to issue instructions for the distribution of new uniforms to the corps. The new issue consisted in part of "white gloves and yellow

de corp asupra cazurilor de trecere frauduloasă a frontierei precum și a unor incidente de frontieră (03.09.1938–10.11.1938), 27 August 1938, pp. 93–108, 131, 163.

[15] Comandantul Corpului Granicelor General Gr. Cornicioiu către Marele stat major, Secția II-a (with accompanying documents), 1 October 1938; AMR. Fond Corpul granicelor. Dosar 2349: Ordine, rapoarte, schițe, procese verbale și declarații cu privire la cercetarea cazurilor de trecere frauduloasă a frontierei de către unii indivizii (28.08.1938–02.11.1938), pp. 34–44.

[16] Comandantul Regimentului I Granicelor Colonel Panaitiu Ctin către Compania 6-a Gr. Paza Giurgiu (Bulgarian frontier, Danube), 13 September 1938; AMR. Fond Corpului Granicerilor. Dosar 2361/13/a: Ordine, rapoarte, schițe, referate, procese verbale, instrucțiune și declarații cu privire la cercetarea cazurilor de trecere frauduloasă a frontierei, precum și la cazurile de pesciure clandestină în apele de pe frontiera (Nistru), efectuarea sondajelor de către vasele navigante, precum și la dotarea pichetelor cu material de clasare (18.04.1938–09.03.1939), p. 892.

[17] Memoriu asupra recunoașterilor de pe frontiera de est, 22 September 1938; AMR. Fond Marele stat major, Secția 2-a informații. Dosar 812/318/A: Memoriu asupra recunoașterilor de pe frontiera de est, 22 September 1938 (among other materials). Microfilm reel no. II.1.533, pp. 122–32.

cartridge belts," and they were to be given first to the more important border posts, which should be staffed by men tall and good-looking (*oameni înalți și chipeși*)![18]

3 October. A routine inspection carried out in the second brigade of regiment four at Chișinau (Kishinev) found everything satisfactory and attributed the exemplary good order of the unit to the competence and conscientiousness of the commander, Lieutenant Gheorghe Radu.[19]

The nature of the observations of the Romanian border guards as recorded in the archives is curious in the extreme. In the face of the most dramatic crisis of international affairs to occur since World War I, the character of their duties was casual and cavalier to a striking degree. Not only do we find the phenomena recorded to be chiefly of a trivial kind; perhaps the most striking aspect of these records is the lapse of time between the occurrence of an event and the reporting of it to headquarters. The reader can easily observe this feature of the correspondence by referring to the documentation in the footnotes.

There are other elements of the records of the border guards and the General Staff intelligence section that are worth our attention.

The first is the fact that there are absolutely no reports of Red Army mobilization, movement, and activity inside the Soviet frontier of the kind that the Poles were simultaneously recording.

The second is the fact that the contemporary military activity inside the Czechoslovak and Hungarian frontiers was carefully observed and recorded, as exemplified in a number of reports.

18 August. General Jan Syrový arrived at Rahău, a Czech town approximately twenty-five kilometers from the Romanian border town of Valea Vișeului, in the company of two other generals, one of whom was from the air force. The purpose of the visit was the inspection of fortifications and the observation of antiaircraft exercises.[20]

---

[18] Instrucțiuni Comandantului Corpului Granicelor General Gr. Cornicioiu, 28 September 1938; AMR. Fond Corpului Granicerilor. Dosar 2361/13/a: Ordine, rapoarte, schițe, referate, procese verbale, instrucțiune și declarații cu privire la cercetarea cazurilor de trecere frauduloasă a frontierei, precum și la cazurile de pescuire clandestină în apele de pe frontiera (Nistru), efectuarea sondajelor de către vasele navigante, precum și la dotarea pichetelor cu material de clasare (18.04.1938–09.03.1939), pp. 945–46.

[19] Raport Lt. Gheorghe Radu, Brigada 2 Regt. 4, Chișinau, 3 October 1938; AMR. Fond Corpul granicerilor. Dosar nr. 2364/15/b/1: Ordine, rapoarte și dări de seama referitoare la inspecțiile efectuate de către unii ofițerii din cadrul unităților subordonate la pichetele de graniceri, precum și la asigurarea pazei frontierei de către aceste unități (07.04.1938–21.03.1939). Microfilm reel no. II.2.2330, pp. 410–16.

[20] Prefectură județului Maramureș către Corpul 6 Armata din Cluj, 20 August 1938; AMR. Fond Corpul 6 Armata, Statul Major, Biroul 2. Dosar Special Nr. 6b: Informațiuni asupra partidelor politice, manifeste și diferite informațiuni externe primite de la Chestura Pol. și Reg. de Poliție Cluj, Insp. Reg. Jand. Cluj și Prefecturile de județe 11 martii 1938–31 martii 1939, p. 214.

8 September. The prefect of Satu-Mare reported the call-up of two classes of Hungarian reservists for maneuvers. These troops were concentrated in the region of Budapest–Seghedin and had been moving for several days toward the Czechoslovak frontier.[21]

24 September. The mobilization of the Czechoslovak army was reported in considerable detail, including the requisitioning of private vehicles capable of assisting transport to frontiers and the evacuation of industry along German–Hungarian frontiers. The local population was said to be taking refuge in the Tatra Mountains. Train traffic through Valeu Vişelui was interrupted, border guards were confiscating radios, and some frontier units were being transferred to the Polish frontier.[22]

24–6 September. The Czechs were observed to begin closing the frontier posts of Valea Vişeului and Lunca la Tisa. They were evacuating part of the population from the Hungarian and German frontiers and interrupting train traffic along these frontiers as well as along the Polish frontier and confiscating radios in the border districts.[23]

27 September. A repetition of the observations of the previous note on both Czechoslovakia and Hungary.[24]

There is one analogous bit of evidence in Romanian foreign-ministry records. On 29 September, Comnen queried his Prague legation about reports of Soviet troops in Czechoslovakia. "According to some reports there are said to be in Czechoslovakia a sufficiently significant number of Soviet soldiers and officers who have crossed recently the frontier regions between Romania and Poland by plane at great altitudes. Please verify this [report] discreetly and transmit to us all the information that you are able to obtain."[25] There is in the archives no apparent response to this request.

[21] Prefectură judeţului Satu-Mare către Corpul VI. Armata, Bir. 2, Cluj, 8 September 1938; AMR. Fond Corpul 6 Armata, Statul Major, Biroul 2. Dosar Special Nr. 6b: Informaţiuni asupra partidelor politice, manifeste şi diferite informaţiuni externe primite de la Chestura Pol. şi Reg. de Poliţie Cluj, Insp. Reg. Jand. Cluj şi Prefecturile de judeţe 11 martii 1938–31 martii 1939, p. 289.

[22] Notă Inspectorului de Poliţie, Cluj, 27 September 1938; AMR. Fond Corpul 6 Armata, Statul Major, Biroul 2. Dosar Special Nr. 6b: Informaţiuni asupra partidelor politice, manifeste şi diferite informaţiuni externe primite de la Chestura Pol. şi Reg. de Poliţie Cluj, Insp. Reg. Jand. Cluj şi Prefecturile de judeţe 11 martii 1938–31 martii 1939, pp. 314–15.

[23] Comandantul Jandarmilor, Maramureş, Notă informativă nr. 47, 21 September 1938; AMR. Fond Corpul 6 Armata, Statul Major, Biroul 2. Dosar Special Nr. 6b: Informaţiuni asupra partidelor politice, manifeste şi diferite informaţiuni externe primite de la Chestura Pol. şi Reg. de Poliţie Cluj, Insp. Reg. Jand. Cluj şi Prefecturile de judeţe 11 martii 1938–31 martii 1939, pp. 313–14.

[24] Prefectură judeţului Satu-Mare către Comandantul VI Corpul Armata, II Biroul, Cluj, 27 September 1938; AMR. Fond Corpul 6 Armata, Statul Major, Biroul 2. Dosar Special Nr. 6b: Informaţiuni asupra partidelor politice, manifeste şi diferite informaţiuni externe primite de la Chestura Pol. şi Reg. de Poliţie Cluj, Insp. Reg. Jand. Cluj şi Prefecturile de judeţe 11 martii 1938–31 martii 1939, p. 32.

[25] Comnen to Prague Legation, 29 September 1938; RMAE. Fond 71/Romînia. Vol. 103, p. 345.

These reports on the Hungarian and the Czechoslovak military dispositions are found in the archival records of the Sixth Romanian Army Corps.
There are no comparable reports in the records of the Fourth Army Corps,
the one stationed along the Dniestr border of the Ukraine. So the Romanians made the kind of observations inside Hungary and Czechoslovakia
that the Poles were at the same time making inside the Soviet Union,
whereas the Romanians appear to have ignored Soviet military developments entirely.[26]

Two additional pieces of evidence are perhaps decisive on the likelihood
of Red Army movement into Romania. First, if such movement took
place, or if it was planned, it would certainly have been reflected in train
traffic, but in September 1938 the preplanned schedule of military supply
trains shows no sign of interruptions, of changes of schedule, or of the
intrusion of any dramatic events at all.[27]

Second, during the fateful week before the meeting in Munich, 29
September, the Soviet telephone and telegraph office in Odessa requested
the establishment of a telephone link from Odessa to Bucharest through
Tighina. The request initiated a spate of correspondence between Romanian Telephone and Telegraph and the General Staff. The Soviet request
was prompted by the consideration how to maintain telephone and telegraph contact with Prague in the event that such communication was
interrupted across Poland. Romanian Telephone and Telegraph approved
the request on the grounds that it would put Romania in a position to mon-
itor developments in the region more completely and give it better control
of information and communications in general. As it observed, in present
conditions, a Moscow-to-Prague line was considered indispensable. Of
course, there were some political obstacles to overcome, as acceding to the
request was apparently regarded as having legal implications for the question of territorial claims in Bessarabia, the same considerations that had
previously spoiled the negotiations on establishing regular airline service
between Moscow and Prague. Eventually, during the first week of October, the intelligence section of the General Staff advised against it, and the
operations section advised the Directorate of Telephone and Telegraph that
it was a question for the Foreign Ministry to decide, because, as the General
Staff explained, *there were no relations or communications between the Romanian
and Soviet armies at all*.[28] Given the nature of Stalinism, perhaps this lack of

---

[26] AMR. Fond Corpul 4 Armata, Statul Major, Biroul 2. Dosar 4339: Comandantul Corpului 4
Armata.

[27] AMR. Marele stat major, Secția 3 operații. Dosar 1578: Ceruri de transport pe frontul de est a
diferitelor unități militare.

[28] Marele stat major către Ministrul apărării naționale, 5 October 1938; AMR. Fond Marele stat
major, Secția 3 operații. Dosar 1602: Documente privind legăturile de ordin militar între România
și U.R.S.S. (1938–1939). Microfilm reel no. II.1.116, pp. 655–6.

communication was not so surprising, but it makes any thought of a Red Army move into Romania, on any basis other than outright hostilities, which Litvinov had repeatedly repudiated, unthinkable.

There is, however, in this otherwise relatively uniformly and coherently documented account one dissonant note. In a meeting with Litvinov on 20 June 1938, the Romanian minister in Moscow, Nicolae Dianu, was listening to a litany of the usual Soviet complaints, including the problem of establishing the commercial airline, the visit of General Ionescu to Warsaw, and other matters. Dianu's response was surprising and intriguing. "I said that I appreciated the open manner in which he spoke his mind, however instead of these secondary questions, it surprises me that he doesn't sufficiently appreciate [*preţui*] our attitude, by which we have allowed the transit of Russian and Czechoslovak planes and materials *in the air and on the ground*, which might have caused us great difficulties." Litvinov responded, "Yes, it seems that Poland has protested to you."[29]

Now, what are we to make of this observation? I can only refer to Churchill's characterization of Soviet affairs, "a riddle wrapped in a mystery inside an enigma."[30]

In any event, the accumulation of evidence adduced here drives us to one unavoidable conclusion: We are forced to doubt the authenticity of the many observations made in the Polish consular report of 27 September. We can only speculate on the sources of the misrepresentation or misunderstanding, whatever it was, but it seems clear that the Red Army was not moving into Romania. Whether military matériel was moving, given both the consul's observations and Nicolae Dianu's reference to the movement of "materials both in the air and on the ground," is perhaps an open question. The absence of any such observations on the part of the Romanian border guards and General Staff intelligence section is, however, extremely curious; but, then, so is the incredibly insubstantial – trivial and gossamer – quality of those observations more generally. In fact, it is more than curious; it is suspicious, and it is therefore a question to which we shall have to return.

---

[29] Dianu to Ministry of Foreign Affairs, 20 June 1938; RMAE. Fond 71/URSS. Vol. 135, 246–7ff. Duplicate in RMAE. Fond 71/Romînia. Vol. 102, pp. 170–1. The Romanian original of this important text here is "totuşi in local acestor chestiuni secondare mă miră că ne preţueşti destul atitudinea noastră care am lăsat să treacă avioane şi materiale ruseşti şi cehoslovace în aer şi pe uscat, ceeace ne-ar putea produce mari dificultăţi."

[30] BBC radio broadcast, 1 October 1939.

Chapter 8

What the Red Army Might Feasibly Have Done

Our first order of business here is to dispose of two problems in the documentary record that constitute obstacles to an authentic account of the story, one problem of evidentiary contamination and one of void of evidence.

First, we must dispose of a misleading story nearly omnipresent in the recent historiography, a story that has obscured the reality of Soviet–Romanian military relations in September 1938. Jiri Hochman published a document in which Romanian Foreign Minister N. P. Comnen allegedly furnished Soviet Foreign Minister Maksim Litvinov, just a week before the meeting at Munich, formal permission for the transit of the Red Army across Romania on its way to Czechoslovakia. There was, Hochman says, no response, and he emphasizes the point to show that the Czechs were betrayed by their Soviet as well as by their French allies.[1] This document is now regarded as one of the staples of traditional Western and Czech émigré historiography and the arguments and conclusions that it serves. The original of this document, however, has never been produced, and its authenticity is open to serious question on several grounds. The reasons for skepticism are multiple.

One dubious feature of the document is immediately apparent: the massive and multiple mistakes in French grammar and spelling, around fifty such in seven printed pages: *"au côtés de," "au conditions," "aprés," "cella," "pour de telle raisons," "la population civil," "tout l'opération," "tout l'Europe," "par voi de terre," "tout garantie," "plusiers," "en aucune cas," "une durrée de 6 jours," "autorités compententes," "la demand expressé,"* and so forth, many of which are conspicuously Anglophone, for example, *"member," "l'armament," "l'equipment," "un assault des forces," "response," "conflict."*

---

[1] Romanian Foreign Minister Comnen to Soviet Foreign Minister Litvinov, 24 September 1938; Jiri Hochman, *The Soviet Union and the Failure of Collective Security* (Ithaca, NY: Cornell University Press, 1984), Appendix C, 194–201.

Not one of these gaffes is acknowledged, and it simply begs belief that a Romanian government whose native language was Romance and whose experienced diplomats were Francophile as well as Francophone could massacre a French text in this fashion.

In addition to questions of style are two jarringly implausible elements of content. First, although Comnen allegedly (p. 196) limited the size of the Soviet force permitted to proceed overland to 100,000 men, yet later (p. 200) he allegedly *encouraged* the Soviets to dispatch *"par une voie combinée de terre et aérienne"* 250,000–350,000 men. That is to say, he envisioned the transport of up to 250,000 troops *by air* while stipulating that the entire transfer of Soviet armed forces, those by land and those by air, must be completed in six days, "144 hours." We are asked to believe that the Soviet air force possessed the capacity to airlift in six days a quarter of a million troops onto Czech airfields that were as yet unprepared to receive them.

The second problem of the document's content is that it assures its recipient that it would also be communicated to the minister of foreign affairs and the president of Czechoslovakia; yet in all of the brouhaha surrounding this disputed subject, we have never heard so much as a word about the document from the personnel of the Czech government. President Beneš's memoirs relate in detail his persistent inquiries of Soviet Ambassador Aleksandrovskii whether the Czechs could count on Soviet assistance, but they contain not a hint of Comnen's assurance of free Red Army passage.[2] Of course, the fact that we have heard nothing about it from the Soviet side simply enhances the thrust of the argument of Soviet betrayal.

An equally difficult problem of plausibility is that the alleged author of the document, Romanian Foreign Minister Nicolae Petrescu-Comnen, published after the war three volumes of memoirs, and none of them mentions the controversial item.[3]

The document is rendered more suspect by the story of its provenance. Its source, as Hochman frankly acknowledged, is the Czech émigré historian Ivan Pfaff, who has worked for some years now in Germany. Pfaff's work is considered tendentious and unreliable, both at home (i.e., in the Czech Republic) and abroad, and with good reason, as we shall see. The thesis of his most recent work, *Die Sowjetunion und die Verteidigung der Tschechoslowakei, 1934–1938: Versuch der Revision einer Legende*, a development of his earlier work, *Sovětská zrada 1938 (Soviet Betrayal 1938)* (Prague, 1993), is apparent in the subtitle. It is a massive attack on the orthodox

---

[2] See, e.g., Edvard Beneš, *Mnichovské dny: pameti* (Prague: Svoboda, 1968), Chapter 6: "Sovětský svaz a Československo," 310–24.

[3] Nicolae Petrescu-Comnen, *Preludi del grande dramma: ricordi i documenti di un diplomatico* (Rome: Edizioni Leonardo, 1947); idem, *I responsabili* (Milan: Mondadori, 1949); idem., *Luci e ombre sull'Europa* (Milan: Bompiani, 1957).

Soviet position that the Red Army would have come to the defense of Czechoslovakia, and naturally it cites the document that the author had previously furnished to Hochman.

This work is open to serious reservations. Most conspicuously, Pfaff makes *no use* of the most significant Soviet collection of documents on the subject, although it was published simultaneously in a *Czech edition*.[4] This omission, however, is only one of many such problems. He cites perfectly credulously Litvinov's notoriously spurious memoirs (pp. 311, 412); he describes Louis Fischer as a French Communist journalist (p. 353); he cites, wrongly, documents from *Foreign Relations of the United States* (p. 393); he makes no reference to Igor Lukes's authoritative account of Beneš's foreign policy[5] or to the indispensable memoirs of Soviet Marshal M.V. Zakharov.[6] Moreover, he takes no account of the really authoritative studies of Romanian foreign policy by Dov B. Lungu, Viorica Moisuc, and Ioan Talpeş,[7] and none of these authors has found in the Romanian foreign-affairs archives any sign of the document that Comnen allegedly provided to Litvinov.

One crucial example of Pfaff's use of evidence is especially symptomatic of the problems of the work. According to the published French diplomatic documents, Soviet Commissar of Defense K. E. Voroshilov informed French Chief of Staff Maurice Gamelin that the Soviets had mobilized and posted to the frontier thirty divisions in preparation for a joint defense of Czechoslovakia.[8] Pfaff characterizes this report as "pure invention" (p. 422). In fact, we have already reviewed an imposing assembly of evidence to show that the mobilization of an even larger force on the frontier was almost unavoidably obvious.[9]

I suggest that the evidence adduced here is sufficient to discredit the authenticity of Comnen's alleged approval of Soviet rights of passage.

---

[4]   *Dokumenty i materialy po istorii sovetsko–chekhoslovatskikh otnoshenii*, 5 vols. (Moscow: Nauka, 1973–1988); and its Czech edition, *Dokumenty a materialy k dějinam československo-sovětských vztahů*, Čestmír Amort, ed., 5 vols. (Prague: Academia, 1975–1984).

[5]   Igor Lukes, *Czechoslovakia Between Stalin and Hitler: The Diplomacy of Edvard Beneš in the 1930s* (New York: Oxford University Press, 1996).

[6]   *General'nyi shtab v predvoennye gody* (Moscow: Voenizdat, 1989). Zakharov was at the time of Munich assistant to Soviet Chief of Staff B. M. Shaposhnikov. At the time of the writing of his memoirs, he was himself Soviet chief of staff, although publication was delayed twenty years.

[7]   Dov B. Lungu, *Romania and the Great Powers, 1933–1940* (Durham, NC: Duke University Press, 1989); Viorica Moisuc, *Diplomaţia României şi problema apărării suveranităţii şi independenţei naţionale in perioda martie 1938–mai 1940* (Bucharest: Editură Academiei, 1971); idem, ed., *Probleme de politică externă a României* (Bucharest: Editură militară, 1971); Ioan Talpeş, *Diplomaţie şi apărare: coordonate ale politicii externe româneşti, 1933–1939* (Bucharest: Editură ştiinţifică şi enciclopedică, 1988).

[8]   Note du Directeur politique, Démarche de l'attaché militaire soviétique, 26 September 1938; *DDF, 1932–1939*, 2nd series, 11: 581.

[9]   See Chapter 5 of this book, "The Red Army Mobilizes."

The second serious problem of evidence bedeviling the recovery of the authentic story of the Soviets at Munich is a lack of evidence on one crucial point. It would tell us a great deal about Soviet intentions if we had the Red Army's strategic operational plans for 1938. Most of the miniscule amount that we know about this intriguing subject comes from the controversy generated by a work now generally considered discredited, Viktor Suvorov, *Icebreaker: Who Started the Second World War?* (London, 1990).[10] Unfortunately, the response of Russian military historians has done little to clarify the matter of Soviet operational plans. In fact, their work suggests a gaping deficit of pertinent information in the military archives, a deficit so suspicious as itself to suggest, even if a trifle incredibly, *the absence of any such plans* before the spring of 1941.[11]

Now, if we set aside the garbled issue of Romanian permission for Red Army passage and the regrettable absence of Soviet operational plans, where does it leave us in the question of Soviet intentions? What was the Red Army in a position to do if the outbreak of war and its treaty obligations had called on it to intervene?

The first issue to consider here is what kind of capacity Czechoslovakia had to defend itself. Was it strong enough to hold out until such time as outside support could reach it? Although there is no very precise way to know what might have happened but did not, there have been some serious studies of the question, not least by the German generals whose assignment was to attack and destroy it.

One authoritative opinion was left by the British military attaché, Lieutenant-Colonel H. C. T. Stronge, who had privileged access to whatever he wanted to see of the Czechoslovak fortifications. He was received, on reaching his post in the spring of 1938, by the chief of the General Staff, General Ludvík Krejčí, who gave him full access to the frontier fortifications for three days in the company of a General Staff officer to answer his questions on the condition that he inform no one but Minister Newton and the authorities in London and that he travel only in civilian clothes.

---

[10] For an authoritative assessment, see Teddy J. Uldricks, "The Icebreaker Controversy: Did Stalin Plan to Attack Hitler?" *Slavic Review* 59 (1999): 626–43.

[11] See, in particular, *Gotovil li Stalin nastupatel'nuiu voinu protiv Gitlera?* (Moscow: AIRO–XX, 1995); Iu. A. Gor'kov, "Gotovil li Stalin uprezhdaiushchii udar protiv Gitlera v 1941 g.?" *Novaia i noveishaia istoriia,* 1993, No. 3: 29–45; idem, *Kreml'. Stavka. Genshtab.* (Tver': TOO TK ANTEK, 1995); idem, "22. June 1941: Verteidigung oder Angriff? Recherchen in russischen Zentralarchiven," in Bianca Pietow-Ennker, ed., *Präventivkrieg? Der deutsche Angriff auf die Sowjetunion* (Frankfurt am Main: Fischer Taschenbuch Verlag, 2000), 190–207, a decisive summary of the most aggressive Russian research (with references). A most helpful piece of work in the controversy is Cynthia A. Roberts, "Planning for War: The Red Army and the Catastrophe of 1941," *Europe–Asia Studies* 47 (1995): 1293–1326.

Stronge was very favorably impressed with the strength and placement of the defenses that he reviewed. They were at the time of his visit yet incomplete and scheduled to be completed in six months, that is, in the fall of 1938. The sector of the front that he saw was the oldest and best defended, and he made the point, otherwise well known, that the newest part of the front, the Austrian frontier, was necessarily less well prepared. As Stronge continued at his post and grew increasingly well informed about the Czechoslovak army, he reported that "here was a force capable of defending its frontiers and willing to so so [sic, do so] at any cost," that "the assumption of Germany's ability to invade, conquer and retain control of the Czech Republic in the autumn of 1938 is unrealistic." He cited as particular reasons for his opinion the strength of the frontier works and the loss of German surprise in the mounting atmosphere of crisis. He estimated that the Czechoslovak army could hold out against a German attack unassisted by allies for three months.[12]

General Eugène Faucher of the French military mission in Czechoslovakia was a considerably more seasoned observer, speaking as he did fluent Czech and having been on that station since 1921 and its chief since 1926. His opinion of the Czechoslovak capacity to hold out alone in the face of a German attack was given in an interview in December 1938. He made the point that the Czech fortifications on the newest − weakest − part of the frontier, the Austrian, while far from complete, were advancing remarkably well. In spite of the weakness of the Czech air force relative to the German Luftwaffe, he suggested that Soviet assistance in the air would be exceptionally effective, as the Czech airports were well placed and would facilitate bombardment of such targets as Vienna, Dresden, and Breslau, the principal industrial centers of Eastern Germany, all within a few minutes flying time. In summary, he thought, as Colonel Stronge did, that the Czechoslovak army could hold the Germans for several months.[13]

We have a variety of other contemporary opinions. The Czechoslovak chief of the General Staff, General Ludvík Krejčí, thought that the participation of Poland in the attack would limit the Czech capacity to hold out to three weeks.[14] The official military history of Czechoslovakia estimated that the Czechs could hold out for a month without the assistance

[12] Brigadier H. C. T. Stronge, "The Czechoslovak Army and the Munich Crisis: A Personal Memorandum," *War and Society: A Yearbook of Military History* 1 (1975): 162–77.
[13] Interview published in *'Époque*, 24 December 1938, cited in Hubert Ripka, *Munich: Before and After*, trans. Ida Sindelková and Edgar P. Young (New York: Howard Fertig, 1969), 296–97; also Pierre Le Goyet, *Munich, "un traquenard"?* (Paris: France-Empire, 1988), 374.
[14] Telford Taylor, *Munich: The Price of Peace* (New York: Vintage, 1980), 790.

of their allies. When mobilization was complete, Czechoslovakia would have a million and a half men under arms, 10 percent of the population.[15] The German generals contradicted each other and themselves both in their memoirs and their testimony at Nuremberg, and hence their reliability is suspect.[16] Hitler's able minister of munitions, Albert Speer, quoted Hitler himself, obviously impressed, after the occupation and inspection of the defenses: "Given a resolute defense, taking them would have been very difficult and would have cost a great many lives."[17] Probably the most considered and credible opinion, however, is to be found in two more recent professional studies, the particulars of which are cited here.[18]

The comparative strengths of the military forces of the two sides were not utterly discrepant[19]:

	Czechoslovak	German
Divisions	42	47
Artillery pieces	2,250	3,000
Tanks	418	2,100
Combat aviation	600	1,230

Of course, it makes sense to take into account that the German advantage in aircraft and tanks may well have been substantially offset by the chief Czech asset, not represented in the preceding table, the frontier fortifications. In addition, we know that the Czechoslovak armaments industry was world renowned. It played a significant – and ironic – role in the German offensive against France in 1940.

For perspective, it is useful to remember that the French frontier with Germany was less than 400 kilometers long, whereas the Czechoslovak frontier with Germany (including Austria), on the other hand, was over 2,000 kilometers long. If we consider those parts of the French and Czechoslovak frontiers exposed to enemies other than Germany, France had an Italian frontier of 455 kilometers, whereas Czechoslovakia had a Polish frontier of 984 kilometers and a Hungarian frontier of 832

[15] Zdeněk Procházka, ed., *Vojenské dějiny Československa*, 5 vols. (Prague: Naše vojsko, 1986–1989), 3: 501, 516–17.

[16] See the citations in Jonathan Zorach, "Czechoslovakia's Fortifications: Their Development and Role in the 1938 Munich Crisis," *Militärgeschichtliche Mitteilungen* 2 (1976): 82.

[17] Albert Speer, *Inside the Third Reich*, trans. Richard and Clara Winston (New York: Macmillan, 1970), 111.

[18] Zorach, "Czechoslovakia's Fortifications," 81–94; Milan Hauner, "La Tchécoslovaquie en tant que facteur militaire," in *Munich 1938: mythes et réalités* (Paris Institut national d'études slaves, 1979), 179–92.

[19] Hauner, "La Tschécoslovaquie en tant que facteur militaire," 183.

kilometers. (When the crisis climaxed, it was the Germans and the Poles who were prepared to go onto the offensive militarily.) If we consider the German part of these two frontiers alone, then Czechoslovakia had five times the exposure of France and one quarter of the population of France. If we consider a Czechoslovak army of 1.5 million men, to cover the frontier against all enemies would have allotted approximately 393 soldiers per kilometer. To make matters worse, a number of places of strategic significance in Czechoslovakia were located close to the frontier: Prague, eighty kilometers; Pilsen (Škoda works), sixty kilometers; Brno (metallurgy and armaments, e.g., Bren gun), forty kilometers. The scant ratio of manpower to frontier exposure and the need to defend these strategic points necessarily required the deployment of the bulk of the army on the frontier and left the country largely without the opportunity to concentrate a strategic reserve.

As 22 percent of the population of Czechoslovakia was Sudeten German, so was a significant proportion of the army, including one officer in ten. In the mobilization of 23 September, some of the Sudetens responded to call-up, some did not – between 20 percent and 60 percent in different regions. Of the vehicles requisitioned in Sudeten areas, 45 percent were reported "*en panne.*"

The fortifications on the mountain frontier, the Erzgebirge, formed the chief Czechoslovak military asset, the Czechoslovak "Maginot Line." They were not, of course, so formidable as the genuine French counterpart. They were in the first place much lighter and thinner, but they were naturally considerably enhanced by the mountain terrain. The Maginot Line had been started in 1930, the Czechoslovak counterpart only in 1935, but the Czechoslovaks had been able to abbreviate their planning and engineering work considerably as a consequence of being able to exploit the French plans and designs.

If we assume a like per capita capacity of defensibility in Czechoslovakia and in France, factor in the population ratio of 1:4 and the ratio of hostile frontiers between the two allies at 1:7.5 (less than 400 kilometers in France as against nearly 3,000 kilometers in Czechoslovakia, including here the Polish but not the Hungarian frontier with Czechoslovakia), then what we might call the crude coefficient of defensibility of the two countries was 1:30.

From the viewpoint of the tactical challenge of overcoming the frontier defenses, perhaps the most authoritative summary opinion derives from the experimental bombardments conducted by the Wehrmacht against them after Munich. These tests showed that heavy artillery (15-centimeter howitzers) and the fabled 88-millimeter guns were effective against all but the heaviest fortifications. The military reports of these bombardments "clearly argued that Czechoslovak defenses were inadequate and that

Czechoslovak resistance would have been short-lived, a few weeks at most."[20]

There were, however, larger strategic issues in the panorama of the military challenges of Munich. As Basil H. Liddell–Hart told Winston Churchill, in spite of the inferior preparation of the Anglo–French armed forces, it was better to fight in 1938 *with* the forty-two Czechoslovak divisions than in 1939 *without* them! In addition, Milan Hauner makes the interesting point that the Czechs made a mistake in hiding their really quite robust military preparations so thoroughly as they did. If their preparedness had been better appreciated in Germany, the German generals would have been even more reluctant to undertake a campaign; if it had been better known in the Anglo–French camp, the challenge would not have seemed so awesome as it did.[21]

Perhaps the most comprehensive geostrategic conceptions of this problem were those of President Beneš and his chief of the General Staff, General Krejčí. As they both explained to Aleksandrovskii, Czechoslovakia could be saved from its neighbors/enemies – Germans, Poles, Hungarians – only if its friends understood what they themselves ardently believed: that Czechoslovakia was the cornerstone of collective security and that Europe itself was not safe without it.[22] In other words, Munich was an all-European issue, and Europe would fail itself if it failed Czechoslovakia. The events that followed ratified this judgment explicitly.

In sum, although authoritative opinion maintains that the Czechoslovaks could not have held out indefinitely on their own, it is generally agreed that they would have given a fierce account of themselves and that, in tandem with reasonable support, they would have been formidable indeed.

So what was the prospect of reasonable support, in particular, support of the Red Army? In fact, the prospects were not very bright. There were several obstacles. The most obvious was the antagonism of Poland and the reluctance of Romania to cooperate with the Red Army. Another familiar obstacle to an effective Soviet intervention, a notorious one, is the decimation of the officer corps that the purges had accomplished. The unseasoned replacements for the seasoned cadres purged simply lacked the experience necessary to command something so technically complex as modern war – the loss, for example, of 51 of 57 corps commanders

---

[20] Zorach, "Czechoslovakia's Fortifications," 88, 91 (quote). Zorach has used to good advantage the *Denkschrift über die tschecho-slowakische Landesbefestigung* (Berlin: Reichsdruckerei, 1941).

[21] Hauner, "La Tschécoslovaquie en tant que facteur militaire," 189.

[22] Sergei Aleksandrovskii, "Munich: Witness's Account," *International Affairs* (Moscow) (1988), No. 12: 121, 129–30.

and 140 of 186 divisional commanders.[23] It was largely for this reason, as we have seen, that the French allegedly held the Red Army in such low esteem – allegedly, because the French are subject to the suspicion of exaggerating all of their own liabilities and belittling their assets. Most of the military attachés in Moscow believed that the purges had deprived the Red Army of an offensive capacity. The British attaché, Colonel R. C. W. G. Firebrace, may be cited as typical: In the wake of the Tukhachevskii purge, in particular, he thought the Red Army incapable of advancing to the assistance of its French and Czechoslovak allies.[24] The German military attaché, General Ernst Köstring, judged the Red Army more critically yet. He thought it incapable in the wake of the purges of conducting any kind of war.[25] Of course, we have now the later experience of the Red Army in the Winter War against Finland to assist us in assessing it, and that experience was not encouraging.

Another influential factor often mentioned but insufficiently probed is the system of railroad logistics available to the Red Army in 1938. The rail and the road systems over a route of some 500 miles of Romania between the Soviet Union and Czechoslovakia were inadequate to transport a modern army. Comnen himself made this point "map in hand" on several occasions to the French, the British, and the Germans.[26] The most authoritative account of this problem came from French Minister Thierry in Bucharest: "In regard to the technical aspect of the problem, . . . there is not yet any direct communication by rail between Russia and Czechoslovakia over Romanian territory. The lines under construction will not be complete before next year at the earliest, and they will in any case permit only a limited traffic, around a dozen small trains a day. . . . As for the road network, it is far from being adequate to transport significant forces, especially motorized [forces]. If the situation is more favorable in Bessarabia,

---

[23] The basic facts are in Robert C. Tucker, *Stalin in Power: The Revolution from Above, 1928–1941* (New York: Norton, 1992), 434–40, 514–15 and Robert Conquest, *The Great Terror: A Reassessment* (New York: Oxford University Press, 1990), Chapter 7, "Assault on the Army," 182–213. Especially for military purges, see John Erickson, *The Soviet High Command: A Military–Political History, 1918–1941* (New York: St. Martin's, 1962), 449–73.

[24] Firebrace to Chilston, 18 April 1938; DBFP, 3rd series, 1: 162–5 (No. 148).

[25] Letters of 8 August 1938; Hermann Teske, *General Ernst Köstring: der militärische Mittler zwischen dem deutschen Reich und der Sowjetunion 1921–1941* (Frankfurt am Main: Mittler, 1965), 202–3.

[26] Comnen (Geneva) to Ministry, 12 September 1938; RMAE. Fond 71/Romînia. Volume 103, p. 70; Chargé d'Affaires Stelzer (Bucharest) to Auswärtiges Amt, 6 September 1938; DGFP, Series D, 2: 701 (No. 434); Lord de la Warr to Viscount Halifax, 15 September 1938; DBFP, 3rd series, 2: 355 (No. 898); N. P. Comnen, *Preludi del grande dramma: ricordi i documenti di un diplomatico* (Rome: Edizioni Leonardo, 1947), 84; Georges Bonnet, *Défense de la paix*, 2 vols. (Paris: Éditions du cheval ailé, 1946–1948), 1: 202; Note du ministre, 11 Septembre 1938; DDF, 2nd series, 11: 161 (No. 96).

where, during the summer dry season, one could easily drive off the roads, which are few and poor, it is not so in the Carpathians, where the progress of convoys is necessarily confined to the roads." There were only three useful roads, and they would accommodate only three divisions at a time, in Thierry's opinion.[27]

The French General Staff concurred. When the question was raised (by Premier Léon Blum) in the Permanent Committee of National Defense, General Gamelin "respond[ed] that he does not see what effective aid Russia might initially provide." In fact, Russian mobilization might divert the Polish and Romanian armies to the east. "The transport of the Russian army by the sole poor railroad is not to be envisaged." The only real possibility was the dispatch of motorized troops, but even so the roads were far from promising.[28] The Soviets were obviously aware of the problems of military transport across Romania. Just two weeks before the Munich conference, Litvinov explained the matter to Louis Fischer: "The Rumanian railroads are poor and our heavy tanks would have difficulty on their poor bridges and highways. But we could help in the air."[29]

This generally pessimistic assessment of the poor prospect of rail transfer is confirmed by contemporary maps. All major Romanian rail lines connected with Poland and Hungary. No major lines crossed the frontier of Slovakia. The Romanian railroad net was distinctly centrifugal, as it had been built largely in the prewar Austrian, Hungarian, and Russian peripheries of the postwar Romanian state.[30] No rail line of any kind provided a direct connection between the Soviet Ukraine and Czechoslovakia, and all lines in the area were single track. There were in fact only approximately 360 kilometers of double tracking in the Romanian railway system, and all of that was in the far southern part of the country, extending only a little way above Bucharest and Ploieşti, thus useless for transport between the Ukraine and Slovakia. At the end of 1942, the United States Office of Strategic Services did a survey of railroads and rail stations in

---

[27] Thierry to Bonnet, 9 July 1938; ibid., 10: 338.

[28] Procès–verbal de la séance du Comité permanent de la défense nationale, 15 March 1938; Maurice Gustave Gamelin, *Servir*, 2: *Le prologue du drame (1930–août 1939)* (Paris: Plon, 1946), 324. This same meeting concluded that the Germans could attack Czechoslovakia and cover Poland while still leaving fifty divisions facing the French frontier. Ibid., 347. In fact, they left five divisions. Williamson Murray, *The Change in the European Balance of Power, 1938–1939: The Path to Ruin* (Princeton, NJ: Princeton University Press, 1984), 218–19, 221. It was not France's finest hour. The frightened French were searching frantically for excuses to surrender.

[29] Louis Fischer, *Men and Politics: An Autobiography* (New York: Duell, Sloan, and Pearce, 1941), 561.

[30] Joseph Rothschild, *East Central Europe Between the Two World Wars* (Seattle, WA: University of Washington Press, 1974), 287.

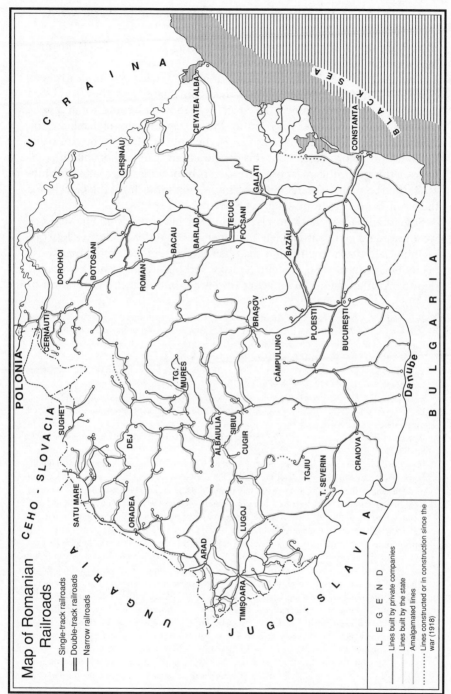

Map of Romanian Railroads

― Single-track railroads
≡ Double-track railroads
― Narrow railroads

U C R A I N A

POLONIA

CEHO - SLOVACIA

U N G A R I A

JUGO - SLAVIA

BULGARIA

BLACK SEA

Danube

CHIŞINĂU
CEYATEA ALBA
CONSTANTA
GALATI
TECUCI
FOCSANI
BACAU
BARLAD
BAZĂU
DOROHOI
BOTOSANI
ROMAN
CERNAUTI
SUGHET
BRAŞOV
PLOESTI
BUCUREŞTI
CÂMPULUNG
TG. MUREŞ
DEJ
ALBAIULIA
SIBIU
CUGIR
TGJIU
T. SEVERIN
CRAIOVA
SATU MARE
ORADEA
ARAD
LUGOJ
TIMIŞOARA

L E G E N D

―― Lines built by private companies
―― Lines built by the state
⋯⋯ Amalgamated lines
⋯⋯⋯ Lines constructed or in construction since the
    war (1918)

Map 2. Romanian railroads, 1930s.

159

Eastern Europe to identify appropriate targets for bombing. No Romanian sites were found to be among them.[31]

This unsatisfactory state of military transport facilities was clearly recognized by the Czechoslovaks and the Romanians, and they addressed themselves to overcoming it. In April 1936 they had come to an agreement to build a rail line, financed by Prague, specifically to facilitate the transfer of the Red Army to Slovakia. At the time of Munich the construction was still incomplete,[32] but this development – and others like it – tell us something significant about Romanian intentions.[33] In June and July 1938, the Romanians were continuing to solicit funds from the Czechs for the completion of this new railway system.[34]

Soviet railroads were themselves in unenviable condition. The strain of world war and civil war had left a comparatively underdeveloped network of Imperial Russian railroads a shambles, a near derelict, reducing its capacity by as much as 80 percent. Trotsky and his *udarniki* (shock workers) then performed their storm tactics of revival, but even the restoration of

---

[31] *Enciclopedia României*, 4 vols. (Bucharest: Imprimeria naţionala, 1936–1943), 1: 50; Ion Ardeleanu *Atlas pentru istoria României* (Bucharest: Editură Didactică şi pedagogică, 1983), map 66, "Economia României între 1919–1938"; New York Public Library Map Division (Repository of U.S. Office of Strategic Services materials from World War II): *Europe: Selected Railroad Objectives*, Map No. 51, 9 January 1943, Branch of Research and Analysis, OSS; *Romania and Bulgaria: Major Railroads*, Lithograph No. 3840, OSS, 31 August 1944.

[32] Boris Celovsky, *Das Münchener Abkommen 1938* (Stuttgart: Deutsche Verlags-Anstalt, 1958), 204–5; Larry L. Watts, Jr., "Romania and the Czechoslovak Crisis: The Military Perspective," unpublished paper presented 22 November 1997 on panel "The Czechs at Munich: Friends and Enemies in Eastern Europe" at Seattle meeting of the American Association for the Advancement of Slavic Studies.

[33] In fact, we have the rarest kind of account of travel from Moscow to Prague during the final month of the crisis from what is perhaps not the likeliest kind of source. A small Soviet military delegation made the trip in the last days of August (as indicated, 8/29 and presumably following) and reported that it required four changes of train – Tiraspol, Tighina, Ploieşti–West, and Ploieşti–Ziud (sic; presumably Ploieşti–South; the term Ziud here is my transliteration from Russian of Russian transliteration from Romanian; Romanian south = *sud*) – and four days. The delegation was scheduled to remain for three months. Its assignment was not indicated. After Munich, it was no longer welcome and was in fact asked to return ahead of schedule. Unaccountably, it reported that its trip home was longer and more complicated as a consequence of the redrawn frontiers. Czechoslovakian Situation Reports, Rossiiskii gosudarstvennyi voennyi arkhiv, Otdel vneshnikh snoshenii, R[azvedyvatel'noe] U[pravlenie] R[aboche]-K[restianskaia] K[rasnaia] A[rmiia], undated; U.S. Library of Congress. Volkogonov Papers, Box 16, Folder 2, Microfilm Reel 10. If we allow for a simple clerical error in the numerical designation of the month, it may be that this was the delegation for which Moscow requested on urgent basis 28 *September* and got the following day visas and couriers' papers for three people to travel by rail from *Kiev* – not Moscow, as they were to travel Moscow to Kiev by plane – to Prague. The mission of these people was not indicated. Dianu to Ministry, 28 September 1938 and Crutzescu (Prague) to Ministry, 29 September 1938; RMAE. Fond 71/România. Vol. 103, pp. 287–8, 354.

[34] Gheorghe Paraschivescu (of the foreign ministry) to Prague Legation, 18 June and 2 July 1938; RMAE. Fond 71/România. Vol. 102, pp. 145, 252.

old capacity left Soviet railroads, like most of Soviet industrial technology, even farther than previously behind the ever innovating achievements of contemporary Western European countries.

In March 1935, Soviet Chief of Staff Marshal Tukhachevskii had told U.S. Ambassador William Bullitt that "at the present moment the Soviet Union would be unable to bring any military aid to Czechoslovakia in case of German attack."[35] Shortly thereafter Bullitt explained why. The Red Army "can not undertake offensive operations due to the fact that the railroads are still inadequate for the peacetime needs of the country and to the equally important fact that there are literally no modern highways in the entire Soviet Union."[36]

The Five-Year Plans (FYPs) did not have the same dramatic impact on rail transport that they had in Soviet industry. The first FYP increased double or multiple tracking from 15,609 to 19,006 kilometers, and the second one added another 3,380 kilometers of a planned 11,000.[37] The bulk of the new building of track in all three plans, however, was devoted to improving the communications of the major economic centers located in widely separated parts of the vast country, that is, bringing the Ukraine, Central Asia, the Donbass, the Urals, the Far East, Leningrad, and Murmansk into better contact with the center (Moscow).[38] In the meantime, both the principle of *shturmovshchina* (storm tactics) and the impact of the purges took a considerable toll on railway construction and efficiency. In 1935, A. A. Andreev was replaced as commissar of communications by L. M. Kaganovich, who applied the method that one authoritative history calls, perhaps inappropriately, "*knut i prianik*" (carrot and stick) – there was more stick than carrot. The same history characterizes the massive repressions of 1937–1938 as "*neveroiatnye nadumannye obvineniia*" (improbably far-fetched accusations). "Mass arrests and liquidations" destroyed "the best technical-engineering cadres of the railroads."[39] At the same time, the railroads were plagued by problems of fuel supply (coal), which delayed transport and caused shortfalls in the plans.[40] Seasonal factors were also

[35] Bullitt to Secretary of State, 7 March 1936; *Foreign Relations of the United States: Diplomatic Papers, 1936*, 5 vols. (Washington, DC: Government Printing Office, 1953), 1: 213.

[36] Bullitt to Secretary of State, 30 April 1936; Orville H. Bullitt, ed., *For the President, Personal and Secret: Correspondence between Franklin D. Roosevelt and William C. Bullitt* (Boston: Houghton Mifflin, 1972), 155.

[37] G. M. Fadeev, E. Ia. Kraskovskii, and M. M. Uzdin, *Istoriia zheleznodorozhnogo transporta Rossii*, 2 vols. (Moscow/St. Peterburg: Ivan Fedorov, 1994–1999), 2: 49, 75.

[38] Ibid., 73, 112; J. N. Westwood, *A History of Russian Railways* (London: Allen & Unwin, 1964), 231.

[39] Fadeev et al., *Istoriia zheleznodorozhnogo transporta Rossii*, 2: 79–82; Bruce W. Menning, "Soviet Railroads and War Planning, 1927–1939," American Association for the Advancement of Slavic Studies presentation, Boston, November 1997.

[40] Fadeev et al., *Istoriia zheleznodorozhnogo transporta Rossii*, 2: 115.

a larger problem in the Russian environment than elsewhere. There was the *shturmovshchina* of seed, fertilizer, and machinery in the spring planting and a similar extravaganza in the fall harvest. Construction work was thus practicable only in the summer, as the primary wintertime challenge was to keep the system functional at all.[41] Several conditions constituted a whole series, a virtual plague, of Achilles's heels: the quality of the track, the quality of the roadbed (often sand rather than gravel), and the shortage of freight cars, among others.[42]

The FYPs did not address strategic railroad logistics systematically. The first FYPs did little to improve strategic railways, actually reducing expenditure on military routes. In spite of the growing evidence of an external threat, Stalin allowed only one sixth to one seventh of the sum requested by the General Staff in 1938–1939.[43] This apparent blindness suggests that Stalin was as excessively confident of his capacity to manage foreign affairs satisfactorily as was the unfortunate Edvard Beneš, that Stalin insisted stubbornly on the subordination of foreign to domestic concerns.[44] In any event, Bruce Menning's conclusion, based on careful archival study, is that "the strategic railroad net of the Soviet Union in 1941 was in poor condition and was consequently not prepared for reliable support of large-scale offensive operations on the potential Western theater of operations."[45]

Insofar as available statistics enable us to make coherent comparisons in 1938 of the preparedness for war of the railways of the Soviet Union and those of its neighbors and enemies, this pessimistic judgment is borne out. We need figures on the density and efficiency of railroad operations.[46]

---

[41] E. A. Rees, *Stalinism and Soviet Rail Transport, 1928–41* (New York: St. Martin's 1995), 8–9. Rees specifically abjures dealing with the military railway network, but the problems mentioned here could hardly be avoided.

[42] Westwood, *History of Soviet Railways*, 229, 247–8.

[43] Menning, "Soviet Railroads and War Planning, 1927–1939," 1, 9–10, 26–7.

[44] An impression that is hard to avoid, e.g., in Lennart Samuelson, *Plans for Stalin's War Machine: Tukhachevskii and Military–Economic Planning, 1925–1941* (Basingstoke, England: Macmillan, 2000).

[45] B. W. Menning, "Sovetskie zheleznye dorogi i planirovanie voennykh deistvii: 1941 god," in N. O. Chubarian, *Voina i politika, 1938–1941* (Moscow: Nauka, 1999), 359.

[46] Fadeev et al., *Istoriia zheleznodorozhnogo transporta Rossii*, 2: passim; Westwood, *History of Russian Railways*; Menning, "Soviet Railroads and War Planning"; idem, "Sovetskie zheleznye dorogi i planirovanie voennykh deistvii: 1941 god"; *Statistique internationale des chemins de fer, 1938* (Paris: Union internationale des chemins de fer, 1939); Berthold Stumpf, *Kleine Geschichte der deutschen Eisenbahnen* (Mainz: Hüthig und Dreyer, 1955); *Hundert Jahre deutschen Eisenbahnen: Jubilaümschrift*, 2nd ed. (Berlin: Reichsverkehrministerium, 1938); Reichsverkehrministerium, *Die Reichsbahn: amtliches Nachrichtenblatt der deutschen Reichsbahn und der Gesellschaft "Reichsautobahnen"* (Berlin: Otto Eisner, 1937); Rees, *Stalinism and Soviet Rail Transport, 1928–1941*; A. A. Grigorev, ed., *Kratkaia geograficheskaia entsiklopediia*, 5 vols. (Moscow: Sovetskaia entsiklopediia, 1960–66); P. E. Garbutt, *The Russian Railways* (London: Sampson, Law, Marston, 1949); Ministère de l'économie nationale (France), *Les chemins de fer en U.R.S.S.* (Paris: Presses universitaires de France, 1946); *Der neue Brockhaus*, 4 vols. (Leipzig: Brockhaus, 1938); *Columbia Gazetteer of the World*, ed. Saul B. Cohen,

	Annual Ton-km/km^2 National Surface Area	Freight Cars/km^2 National Surface Area	Double Track/km^2 National Surface Area[47]
Germany	196,000	1.25	0.051
UK	109,000	2.43	0.066
Czechoslovakia	64,632	0.50	0.0085
Poland	37,064	0.38	0.012
Romania	19,644	0.18	0.0012

Now, the pertinent task is to present Soviet figures on railroads by comparable criteria of categories. It is not easy, and it requires extrapolating, adding and subtracting, and surmising a bit. Within reasonable limits of precision, it is possible. There are two features of the USSR that make the country as a whole intrinsically incomparable with the other countries of Europe listed in the preceding table: (1) its size in general and (2) the size of Siberia in particular (ca. 70 percent of the surface area of the country), especially given the fact that Siberia has little to do, in terms of short-term military logistics, with the problem of mounting a campaign on the Western frontier of the country. Given those factors, it seems to make little sense to compare numbers of freight cars per unit of surface area or kilometer-tons of freight hauled annually per unit of surface area, because there is no way to know what proportion of either of the two quantities was allotted to the European area of the Soviet Union. The one figure of meaningful comparability is length of double tracking per unit of surface area in the *European part* of the USSR (interpreted here to include the European part of the RSFSR and the Ukraine), and that figure is 0.0042. In other words, the European part of the USSR had three and a half times the efficiency of carrying capacity of Romania, approximately one third that of Poland, and one twelfth that of Germany.

A few additional facts help to put matters a bit more fully into focus. Railroad transport accounted for more than 85 percent of Soviet freight transport at the end of the 1930s; sea transport, 5 percent; river transport, 7.3 percent; and trucks, 1.8 percent.[48] When the territories of the Baltic countries, Eastern Poland, and Bessarabia were incorporated into the USSR in the wake of the Nazi–Soviet Pact, the Soviet railroad administration discovered that it was no small task to integrate the operation of

3 vols. (New York: Columbia University Press, 1998); Richard Widdow, ed., *Encyclopedic World Atlas*, 4th ed. (New York: Oxford University Press, 1997).

[47] Measuring national standard gauge of track only, differing as it did in the Soviet Union and elsewhere.

[48] Fadeev et al., *Istoriia zheleznodorozhnogo transporta Rossii*, 2: 313.

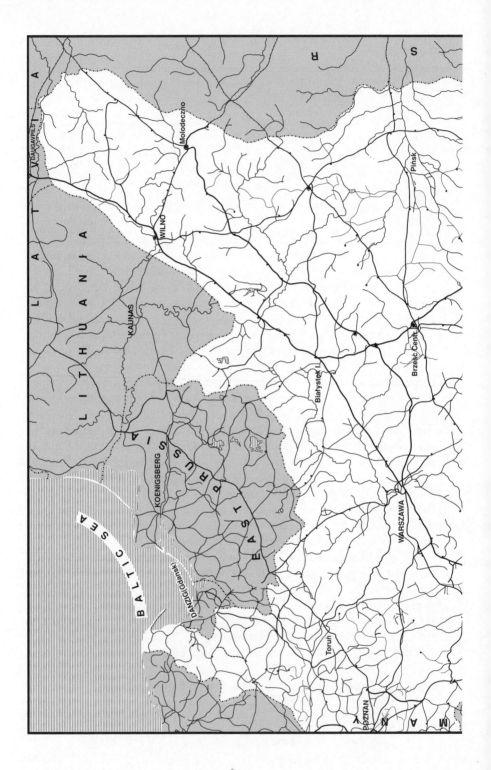

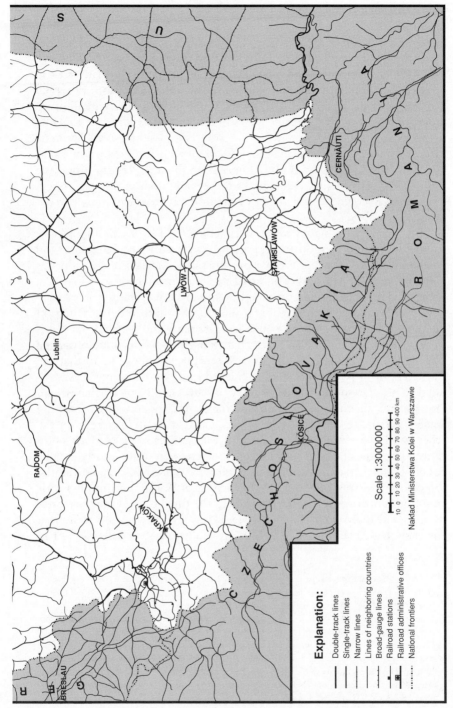

Map 3. Polish railroads, 1930s.

Explanation:

Double-track lines
Single-track lines
Narrow lines
Lines of neighboring countries
Broad-gauge lines
Railroad stations
Railroad administrative offices
National frontiers

Scale 1:3000000

10 0 10 20 30 40 50 60 70 80 90 400 km

Nakład Ministerstwa Kolei w Warszawie

railroads of foreign construction and foreign specifications – most importantly the smaller rail gauge that was standard west of the Soviet frontier – and, in fact, this task was only partially completed on the German invasion of 1941.[49] It would, then, have been a seriously inhibiting factor of supply and transport in September 1938. Finally, the Winter War with Finland provided a test case of the challenge of military logistics almost entirely by rail in an atmosphere of urgency, and Soviet rails failed the test. Approximately 160 trains a day arrived at Leningrad carrying supplies for the front, but there were 100,000 rail cars lying idle in the area, constituting little more than a gargantuan roadblock. In these circumstances, only thirty-six trains per day could be dispatched to the front, approximately 23 percent of those available.[50]

There were two obvious routes over which the Red Army might have attempted an intervention in support of Czechoslovakia, Romania, and Poland. We have seen the Romanian situation. The Polish situation was quite different. The feasibility of the Polish route, from the strictly logistical point of view, is easily demonstrated by the preceding statistical comparisons.[51] If Poland falls expectedly far short of the railroad development of the most advanced European countries, Germany and Great Britain, it is clear nevertheless that Poland was far better equipped in double-tracked rails – by a factor of ten – than was Romania, the more so in that the entire length of Romanian double-tracked rails (360 kilometers) was located in the far south of the country, in the vicinity of Bucharest and Ploieşti, and was thus nearly useless to transport a modern army from the Soviet Ukraine to Slovakia. The advantages that Poland offered, on the other hand, were not only a greater density and capacity of track but a vastly more advantageous location of it. There were three nearly parallel double-tracked systems running through what Voroshilov would call the Vilno corridor (west of Minsk) to the vicinity of Warsaw and another running from northwest Ukraine and joining the three parallel tracks at Brest (Brześć) and Białystok.[52] Furthermore, it was precisely on this route that Soviet strategic planning – G. S. Isserson and M. N. Tukhachevskii – had

---

[49] Menning, "Sovetskie zheleznye dorogi i planirovanie voennykh deistvii: 1941 god," 363; Fadeev et al., *Istoriia zheleznodorozhnogo transporta Rossii*, 2: 119.

[50] Fadeev et al., *Istoriia zheleznodorozhnogo transporta Rossii*, 2: 314.

[51] *Statistique internationale des chemins de fer, 1938*, passim. Soviet statistics are generally missing from this collection, and, although it is possible nowadays to find some comparable Soviet rail statistics, I have considered that the peculiarity of Soviet – or Russian – geography relative to that of the countries of modest size in Central and Western Europe, would make a mockery of the analysis.

[52] Uncatalogued maps, Library of Congress Geography and Map Room: Koleje Rzeczpospolitej Polskiej, Władysław Groszek, ed. (Bydgoszcz: Biblijoteka Polska, 1932); Mapa sieci kolejowej Rzeczypospolitej Polskiej (N.P.: T-wo Ruch S.A., 1938); Eisenbahnkarte von Polen. Reichskriegsministerium. Nur für Dienstgebrauch bestimmt. Nachdruck und Vervielfältigung verboten.

centered attention since the early 1930s.[53] Here were logistical opportunities altogether dwarfing those of Romania.

In the spring of 1936, the French General Staff had asked the Soviet military attaché in Paris how the Soviet Union would render aid to France if Germany attacked France. His reply was blunt and infinitely intriguing: "*en attaquant la Pologne.*"[54] At the end of the summer of 1936, a political journalist in Prague had asked Aleksandrovskii what Moscow would do if Hitler attacked Czechoslovakia. Aleksandrovskii said that if such an attack provoked only a local conflict, Moscow could not do much, but if it provoked a world war, "the Soviets would disregard everything and march to [Czechoslovakia's assistance] through Romania as well as through Poland."[55]

Of the five Soviet army groups mobilized and posted to the frontier in September 1938, four were stationed on the Polish border, one on the Romanian border.[56]

---

[53] Bruce W. Menning, "Soviet Railroads and War Planning, 1927–1939," paper given at American Association for the Advancement of Slavic Studies meeting in Boston, November 1997.

[54] Testimony of Léon Noël, French ambassador to Poland, 1935–1940, 27 April 1948; Commission d'enquête parlementaire, *Les événements survenus en France de 1933 à 1945: témoignages et documents*, 9 vols. (Paris: Presses universitaires de France, 1951–1952), 4: 861; Yvon Lacaze, *La France et Munich: étude d'un processus décisionnel en matière de relations internationales* (Bern, Switzerland: Peter Lang, 1992), 307.

[55] Igor Lukes, *Czechoslovakia Between Stalin and Hitler: The Diplomacy of Edvard Beneš in the 1930s* (New York: Oxford University Press, 1996), 76.

[56] See preceding map.

Chapter 9

Epilogue

There were other consequences of the decisions taken at Munich, multiple consequences for the whole of Europe. Having been rendered defenseless by the surrender of border fortifications, Czechoslovakia was unable to offer any resistance when the German army moved beyond the demarcation line of Munich and into the purely Czech territory of Bohemia and Moravia in March 1939. At the same time, Hitler sponsored the independence of Slovakia before turning it into a satellite regime. Meanwhile, Poland, having blindly assisted in the mutilation of Czechoslovakia, thus destroyed a potential ally against the aggressor and became thereby the next virtually defenseless victim. When Poland fell, the French were left without any continental ally to divert a part of the strength of the German army from their own frontier. To make matters worse, the Wehrmacht capitalized on the excellent military hardware of the former Czechoslovak army to train and equip ten new divisions at once. Half of the tanks deployed by General Erwin Rommel's Panzer division in France in 1940 – the most rapidly advancing German division in the campaign – were of Czechoslovak manufacture. The French, like the Poles, had contributed in the sacrifice of Czechoslovakia to their own undoing.

Just as Foreign Minister Nicolae Petrescu-Comnen had foreseen, the Munich tragedy engulfed his own Romania as well. Its Little Entente security pact disappeared along with Czechoslovakia, and the new Soviet–German comity following the Nazi–Soviet Pact of August 1939 portended no good for Romania. In June 1940, the Soviet Union annexed Bessarabia. In the Vienna Award of August–September 1940, Hitler did his own partition of Romania, giving Southern Dobrudja to Bulgaria and approximately 40 percent of Transylvania to Hungary. Immediately afterwards, King Carol II was forced to abdicate in favor of his son Michael, and Marshall Ion Antonescu, assuming dictatorial powers, in November joined the Tripartite Pact for a catastrophic war on the Soviet Union.

On the morrow of Munich, the French were too deluded to recognize the portents of their own disaster. Chamberlain suddenly became very popular in France. A new name was adopted for the French parasol/ *parapluie*: "un Chamberlain." The crowds that greeted Daladier's return at the Bourget airport were ecstatic. Daladier himself was not. He was quite apprehensive about his reception there and had gulped several glasses of champagne before facing the confrontation. Surprised, relieved, and in some paradoxical sense simultaneously disappointed at the joyful scene, he turned to Alexis Léger and opined, "*Les gens sont fous.*"[1]

In Eastern Europe, there was a chorus of despair. As the Bulgarian ambassador in Moscow, hearing the news of Munich, said to his French counterpart, "If it is really so, we and all the little peoples of Europe, could only seek the protection of Germany and submit ourselves to its wishes in order to escape the fate that awaits Czechoslovakia." Having had the news confirmed, he was nearly incredulous: "It is true then, France has abandoned Czechoslovakia and all of us with it, and with us its traditional policy. You must know then that in all the little countries of Europe this 30th September will be a day of distress and mourning. For my part, in destroying a faith that I acquired from youth at the desks in the classroom, one of the great sorrows of my life."[2] In response to the Anglo–French diplomats who brought him the bitter news, Czechoslovak Foreign Minister Kamil Krofta kept his temper but issued a clear warning: "This is for us a disaster which we have not merited. . . . I do not know whether your countries will benefit by these decisions which have been made at Munich, but we are certainly not the last [to be assaulted]; after us, there [will be] others."[3] Beneš' was more plainspoken: "It's a betrayal which will be its own punishment. It is incredible. They think that they will save themselves from war and revolution at our expense. They are wrong."[4]

Not everyone in the Anglo–French camp found the compromise of Munich promising for the peace of Europe. The French ambassador in Berlin, André François-Poncet, was overheard to say, "See how France treats the only allies who remained faithful to her."[5] Churchill spoke his own characteristic idiom in Commons: "The government had to choose

---

[1] Élisabeth du Réau, *Édouard Daladier, 1884–1970,* (Paris: Fayard, 1993), 285; Pierre Le Goyet, *Munich, "un traquenard"?* (Paris: France-Empire, 1988), 365.

[2] Robert Coulondre, *De Staline à Hitler: Souvenirs de deux ambassades, 1936–1939* (Paris: Hachette, 1950), 161, 163.

[3] Hubert Ripka, *Munich Before and After* (New York: Fertig, 1969), 231.

[4] Z. A. B. Zeman with Antonín Klimek, *The Life of Edvard Beneš, 1884–1948: Czechoslovakia in Peace and War* (Oxford, England: Clarendon, 1997), 134.

[5] Telford Taylor, *Munich: The Price of Peace* (New York: Vintage, 1980), 48.

between war and shame. They chose shame, and they will get war, too."[6]
Far away in the relative safety of the United States, Franklin Roosevelt,
seeing clearly the directions in which European affairs were trending, had
urged the powers to convoke the conference that Munich turned out to be,
and he later had the most serious doubts about it. "I am not sure now that
I am proud of what I wrote to Hitler in urging that he sit down around the
table and make peace. That may have saved many, many lives now, but that
may ultimately result in the loss of many times that number of lives later."[7]

Perhaps the most poignant commentary on the tragedy that the complacency and cowardice of Anglo–French policy inflicted on the continent
is the letter of resignation of the chief of the French military mission in
Prague. General Faucher's letter was addressed to Daladier as premier and
minister of defense. He had previously communicated the appalling shock
that the retreat of France from its obligations during the weeks preceding
Munich had inflicted on Czechoslovak society. There was some rebound
of faith and confidence, he said, on Anglo–French approval of mobilization in Prague. Yet the results of the Munich conference were followed by
a redoubling of indignation:

> Anti–French demonstrations have taken place again in Prague. M. le Ministre
> de France [Victor de Lacroix] told me that he is sent [French] decorations
> every day. The director of the Institut français announces the dissolution of
> several of its sections; he awaits the disappearance of all of them. French
> diplomas are returned to the Institut. We envisage the transformation of the
> French lycée into a Czechoslovak gymnasium; parents are withdrawing their
> children.
>
> Czechs qualified to speak for the sentiments of the population tell me [that
> one idea dominates]: they have been betrayed. The minister of railroads wrote
> to me on 24 September: "I have seen many men cry. I asked them: why
> are you crying, men of little faith? We have arms and we are not cowards.
> They answered: 'We are crying because of the betrayal of France, which we
> loved.'"
>
> The judgments of the press . . . are more categorical: . . . "[French] betrayal
> is without historical precedent."
>
> Czech officers are saying to me . . . you have assumed the duties of Hitler's
> executioners.
>
> If for any reason whatever you did not think [yourselves] able to support
> your engagements, why did you not say so frankly?

---

[6]   Michael J. Carley, *1939: The Alliance that Never Was and the Coming of World War II* (Chicago: Ivan
      R. Dee, 1999), 71.
[7]   Henry Morgenthau, *From the Morgenthau Diaries*, ed. John Morton Blum, 3 vols. (Boston:
      Houghton-Mifflin, 1959–1967), 2: 49.

What remains today of the moral prestige of France ... ? France will participate ... in the guarantee of the new frontiers. What confidence can one have that it will keep its word ... especially in circumstances much worse than those of yesterday?

I seek in vain for a decisive argument to oppose to [that question].

I cannot forget, moreover, that you yourself at one time, M. le Président, charged me to carry to President Beneš the assurance that an attack directed at Czechoslovakia would activate an immediate entry of French forces into combat. The memory of this mission has contributed no little to my decision to ask you to relieve me of my duties.

People say to me, "We will survive. There have been more difficult moments in our history. To yield in our present circumstances is cruel but not dishonorable. The essential thing is not to lose [one's] honor. But, France. ... "

In your telegram ... of September 28, you appeal to me to continue to fulfill the duties of a French general. Among those duties, there is one to which I have always been attentive: that of telling you the truth without succumbing to the temptation of embellishing it when I suppose that it may be disagreeable to recognize.[8]

There were few Frenchmen indeed who had the intelligent realism to understand the import of what had been done and fewer yet who had the courage of Faucher to say so. Most of France was euphoric, or at least soporific. Across the Channel, criticism, prompted by Churchill and his sympathizers and an increasingly skeptical press, was growing. The *Manchester Guardian* offered a stinging definition of appeasement: "A clever plan of selling off your friends in order to buy off your enemies."[9] Chamberlain was, however, unmoved by the criticism. He was convinced that Munich had opened the way to an enduring peace. "A lot of people seem to me to be losing their heads," he said, " and talking and thinking as though Munich had made war more instead of less imminent."[10] Hence he was less, rather than more, concerned to advance the pace of rearmament.

Chamberlain's complacency received quite a jolt when, in the second week of March 1939, Hitler engineered the secession of Slovakia from

---

[8] Faucher to Daladier, 6 October 1938; DDF, 2nd series, 12: 93–6 (No. 49). Faucher went home to France, joined the resistance, and was arrested and sent to a concentration camp in January 1944. In May 1945, he was liberated by the U.S. army. He died in 1964 in his ninetieth year. Richard Francis Crane, *A French Conscience in Prague: Louis Eugène Faucher and the Abandonment of Czechoslovakia* (Boulder, CO: East European Monographs, 1996).

[9] 25 February 1939, as quoted in Frank McDonough, *Neville Chamberlain, Appeasement and the British Road to War* (Manchester, England: Manchester University Press, 1998), 2.

[10] Keith Middlemas, *The Diplomacy of Illusion: The British Government and Germany, 1937–1939* (Aldershot, England: Gregg Revivals, 1991), 414–15.

Czechoslovakia and sent his army into Prague. The British and the French had issued formal guarantees of the new German–Czechoslovak frontier of their own design at Munich, yet neither of them moved a soldier in response to Hitler's bold scrapping of his solemn promise that the Sudeten territory was his last such claim in Europe. There can be no more pathetic record of British inadequacy than Halifax's gentle admonition to Berlin: "His Majesty's Government had no desire to interfere unnecessarily [!] . . . They are, however . . . deeply concerned for the success of all efforts to restore confidence and a relaxation of tension in Europe. . . . From that point of view they would deplore any action in Central Europe which would cause a setback to the growth of this general confidence on which all improvement in the economic situation depends and to which such improvement might in its turn contribute."[11]

Chamberlain naturally had to make a statement in Commons as these events were unfolding. He was asked in particular about the guarantee that Britain had given to Czechoslovakia. He responded awkwardly and inconsistently. He said, as the new Czech government was summoned to Berlin to learn its fate, that his government had guaranteed Czechoslovakia against "unprovoked aggression" and that "no such aggression has yet taken place." The following day, when such aggression had clearly taken place, he said that his government would not respond to it because the state to which the guarantee had been issued no longer existed, the secession of Slovakia being an internal affair. Mr. Chamberlain could give lessons in the arts of casuistry. Finally, he said that he "bitterly regrett[ed] what has now occurred. But do not let us on that account be deflected from our course."[12] The course of paying tribute to aggressors in the coin of other nations at the peril of one's own.

In the immediate aftermath of the German occupation of Prague, a series of new factors entered the diplomatic equation to accelerate the pace of events and to open up new paths of development. First, Hitler set his sights on his next objective, as numbers of Cassandras in Eastern Europe had foreseen that he would – on Poland. On 21 March, with the conquest of Prague only a week old, he demanded of Poland the cession of Danzig and an extraterritorial rail route across the Polish corridor to East Prussia. The Poles declined. Second, the Chamberlain cabinet, embarrassed by the failure of appeasement and under considerable pressure from public opinion as national elections loomed in the fall, issued on 31 March a unilateral, nonreciprocal guarantee of Polish territorial integrity. Third, the British joint chiefs, having done an inventory of British commitments and compared it with the lackluster inventory of British armaments and military

[11] Halifax to Henderson, 14 March 1939; DBFP, 3rd series, 4: 250 (No. 247).
[12] Hansard, *Parliamentary Debates, Commons* 345, 5th session, columns 438–40.

preparation, advised on 27 March the formation of a triple alliance of Britain, France, and the Soviet Union against Hitler. Fourth, on 3 May, Stalin fired his foreign commissar, Maksim Litvinov, the most celebrated champion of collective security, and thus suggested to the diplomatic world that he was open to alternative policies – of which Litvinov himself, incidentally, had long since warned.

Many observers thought, frivolously as it turned out, that bridging the divide between Nazism and Bolshevism was out of the question. More insightful voices warned that it was not so. Robert Coulondre's warnings grew almost monotonous.[13] The French military attaché in Moscow, Colonel Auguste-Antoine Palasse, wrote home in midsummer: "I consider it possible at any time [toujours], if we do not begin to negotiate quickly, to see the USSR at first go into isolation in a neutrality of anticipation in order thereafter to work out an understanding with Germany on the basis of a partition of Poland and the Baltic states."[14]

If the British and the French were suspicious of Moscow, Moscow had reason enough to be suspicious of them in turn. The publicly announced policy of appeasement in Britain had since the Rhineland crisis of 1936 facilitated Hitler's movement in one distinct direction, after all, the direction toward the border of the USSR. The failure to enforce Versailles at the time of *Anschluss* did not speak well of Western resolve; French desertion of her faithful ally in Prague was worse; failing to honor their own guarantee of the new Munich frontier of Czechoslovakia seemed somehow climactic and irredeemable. Yet more was to follow. As Litvinov had said to American Ambassador Davies, there was no reciprocal trust between Moscow and Paris. As a British diplomat in Warsaw admonished the Foreign Office in midsummer 1939, "May I whisper to you that from the Polish point of view our record in protecting victims of aggression has not recently been impressive?"[15] Yet the British and French seemed disposed, after bargaining away all of the military advantages of Southeast Europe, to take their stand in an infinitely weaker position alongside Poland.

At this point, both the plans of Hitler and the resources of his enemies – the diplomatic machinations of the powers – began to depend heavily on the mysterious intentions of the Kremlin. The next major move on the continental chessboard would have to take the Soviet position into account. At the same time, Moscow had to consider, first, how sturdy and valuable diplomatically and militarily a genuine military alliance with the Anglo–French would be and, second, how feasible such an arrangement

---

[13] See, e.g., Coulondre, *De Staline à Hitler: souvenirs de deux ambassades, 1936–1939*, 270–2.

[14] Pierre Le Goyet, *Le mystère Gamelin* (Paris: Presses de la Cité, 1976), 215.

[15] Clifford Norton to Cadogan, 10 July 1939; DBFP, 3rd series, 6: 319 (No. 289).

was – or whether the German alternative, superficially so little plausible, was the better one.

While Churchill warned that containing Hitler would require an arrangement with Moscow, British policy continued to vacillate. On the one hand, the policy of appeasement had foundered so conspicuously as to become such an embarrassment that the word was by tacit consent banned from official usage. Yet even after the British had taken their stand alongside the French in defense of Poland, there continued nevertheless to be a variety of little publicized but real liaisons, sometimes with established diplomats, sometimes with shadowy itinerants, running between London and Berlin.

Herr Helmuth Wohlthat, commisioner of the German Four-Year Plan, came to London on 26 July to discuss commercial issues with Sir Horace Wilson of the treasury and R. S. Hudson of the department of overseas trade. Wilson declared that the substance of what he had to say was approved by Chamberlain. He wished to discuss a spheres-of-influence agreement. In addition, Wilson "told Herr Wohlthat that the conclusion of a non-aggression pact [with Germany] would enable Britain to rid herself of her commitments *vis-à-vis* Poland" – whose territorial integrity had been guaranteed by the Anglo–French the preceding March. Herr Wohlthat asked whether Germany could add other questions to the agenda of negotiations between the two powers, colonial questions in particular. "Wilson answered in the affirmative; he said that the Führer had only to take a sheet of paper and jot down his points; the British Government would be prepared to discuss them. . . . The decisive thing here was that the Führer should authorize some person to discuss the above-mentioned program."[16]

Wohlthat's own memorandum on these conversations was given to Göring in Berlin a few days later. He listed a variety of items that he had been led in London to believe would constitute a willing agenda of British negotiations: a joint Anglo–German declaration of nonaggression, which would render superfluous, according to Wilson, the British guarantee to Poland (and Romania); mutual declarations of noninterference of Germany in the British Commonwealth or of Britain in "Greater Germany," clearly implying here a withdrawal of British interest in the question of Danzig; revision of the Treaty of Versailles as it applied to colonial and mandates questions; disarmament; common assurances of the supply of raw materials and cooperation in commercial relations in the Commonwealth, China, and Russia; and "loans for the German Reichsbank."[17] It was in great part the German program of rapid rearmament

---

[16] Memorandum of the German ambassador (Dirksen) in Britain, 21 July 1939; *Soviet Peace Efforts on the Eve of World War II (September 1938–August 1939)*, V. Falin, ed., 2 vols. (Moscow: Novosti, 1973), 2: 144–7 (No. 379).

[17] Wohlthat memorandum, 24 July 1939; DGFP, D, 6: 977–83 (No. 716).

that accounted for the deficit of both raw materials and foreign exchange in Germany and hence required an early choice between slowing the pace of armaments or using them to conquer new resources abroad. Wohlthat must have been incredulous to hear the British offering to relieve the Germans of this dilemma.

Ambassador Dirksen reported a similar conversation on 3 August with Sir Horace Wilson. Wilson proposed to negotiate a nonaggression treaty, after which Britain would give up its guarantee to Poland; improvement of their reciprocal foreign trade; deliveries of raw materials; colonial questions; a nonintervention agreement "which would embrace the Danzig question"; and limitations of armaments. Wilson was explicit that such negotiation must take place in the greatest secrecy, as the British public had grown antagonistic to any further measures in the nature of appeasement.[18]

In spite of these ongoing feelers between London and Berlin, the British public was by this time unwilling to countenance any further Nazi aggression. The British cabinet, then, evidently considering its own unilateral guarantee of Polish territory insufficient, proceeded to a remarkably detailed written alliance of mutual defense that specifically stipulated Germany as the likely aggressor and Danzig as the likely target of German designs.[19] It was a very specific and binding engagement. Still, however, Birger Dahlerus, a Swedish businessman and petrel of peace continued to carry messages between London and Berlin.[20] On 26 August, the day after the signing of the British pact with Poland, Dahlerus brought Hitler a letter from Halifax full of the usual platitudes: Britain wanted a peaceful solution; the atmosphere must be allowed to calm down; the British were urging the Poles to exercise restraint – it was always the Czechs and the Poles on whom the British urged self-control, while they said no such thing to Hitler, although they lived in constant fear of some "mad-dog act" on his part.[21]

These maneuverings did not go unnoticed in Moscow. Ambassador Maiskii reported 26 August that he was observing continuing contacts between Chamberlain and Hitler: "Munich-like sentiments can be

---

[18] Memorandum of Dirksen, 3 August 1939; *Documents and Materials Relating to the Eve of the Second World War*, 2 vols. (New York: International Publishers, 1948), 2: 116–25 (No. 24).

[19] Text of Anglo–Polish Agreement of Mutual Assistance, and Secret Protocol, 25 August 1939; *Documents on International Affairs, 1939*, ed. Arnold J. Toynbee, 2 vols. (New York: Oxford University Press, 1951–1954), 1: 469–71.

[20] Various notes of F. K. Roberts, 26–27 August; DBFP, 3rd series, 7: 281–6 (No. 349); D. C. Watt, *How War Came: The Immediate Origins of the Second World War* (New York: Pantheon, 1989), 503–5.

[21] Hitler told Karl Burckhardt, the League high commissioner of Danzig, about this time, that "if the slightest incident happened now, I shall crush the Poles without warning in such a way that no trace of Poland can be found afterwards." Roger Makim's minutes, 14 August 1939; DBFP, 3rd series, 6: 692 (No. 659).

unmistakably felt in the air since yesterday. . . . The British Ambassador in Berlin, Henderson, arrived in London today by plane and gave the Cabinet some kind of communication from Hitler the contents of which are kept secret so far. A meeting of the British Government has just ended; it discussed the communication but so far the Cabinet has taken no decision on it. Another government meeting is scheduled for tomorrow morning."[22] If Moscow had little reason for confidence in Anglo–French resolve before Munich, it had as little thereafter.

In fact, Hitler was proposing a pact with Britain: Germany to get Danzig and the Corridor; Poland a free port in Danzig; a corridor to Gdynia; a guarantee for Poland's frontiers; an agreement about Germany's colonies; guarantees for the German minority; and a German pledge to defend the British Empire.[23] Dahlerus was literally shuttling between Göring/Hitler and Halifax/Chamberlain, and Henderson in Berlin still believed that the Polish problem derived chiefly from the stubbornness of the Poles, that Danzig should belong to Germany by right of self-determination. In addition, the British government was resorting again to Mussolini to act as intermediary for it in Berlin. It suggested to Mussolini, for example, that he ask Hitler to accept a corps of neutral observers to police the German–Polish frontier.[24]

At the same time, as the tension generated by Hitler's threat to Poland mounted, it became obvious to both sides that the position of the Soviet Union in the question mattered a great deal. Already in the spring, the British joint chiefs had recommended a triple alliance of Britain, France, and the Soviet Union. There was little enthusiasm for it in the British Cabinet, yet the logic of it was compelling. At length, a joint Anglo–French delegation was sent to Moscow to negotiate a genuine military convention.

By this time, German diplomacy was already beginning to drop hints of an arrangement between Moscow and Berlin. On 4 August, in the course of a long interview with Molotov, Count von der Schulenburg assured him that if war broke out between Germany and Poland, "we were prepared to protect all Soviet interests and come to an understanding with the Soviet Government on this matter." Molotov, he said, "showed evident interest." Finally, he reported, "from Molotov's whole attitude it was evident that the Soviet Government are, admittedly, increasingly prepared for improvement in German–Soviet relations, although the old

---

[22] Maiskii to Commissariat of Foreign Affairs, 26 August 1938; *Soviet Peace Efforts* 2: 267–8 (No. 444).
[23] Watt, *How War Came*, 505. See DBFP, 3rd series, 7: 281–83 (No. 349). The really important thing here was that Dahlerus was playing up his own importance and that it was Göring's rivalry with Ribbentrop that allowed him to do so. Ribbentrop had failed to get an alliance with Britain, and he was determined to be revenged. Göring, in competition, facilitated any British access to Hitler.
[24] Halifax to Sir P. Loraine, 25 August 1938; DBFP, 3rd series, 7: 240–1 (No. 296).

mistrust of Germany persists. My general impression is that the Soviet Government are at present determined to conclude an agreement with Britain and France, if they fulfil all Soviet wishes."[25]

The Anglo–French negotiations of a military alliance with Moscow were opened on 12 August. Here was the grand opportunity to realize a genuine collective security better late than never. As a matter of convention, the Soviet negotiator, Marshall Kliment Voroshilov, exhibited his own diplomatic powers, which authorized him, quite simply, both to negotiate and to sign a military convention with the visitors.[26] He then asked for an exhibit of the presumably similar powers of the Anglo–French delegation. The French negotiator, General Joseph Doumenc, duly presented his powers. British Admiral Reginald Drax, on the other hand, demurred, saying that he had no written powers, that he had been authorized to negotiate but had no powers to sign. It was agreed that such powers were necessary and would be requested. Marshall Voroshilov then asked for a presentation of the military plans that the visiting delegations had in mind. Admiral Drax said that he had no precise plan. General Doumenc said that France planned to use all its forces against Germany and that he thought that the USSR should do the same. Marshal Voroshilov, however, wanted something more specific, and they agreed to adjourn in order to prepare the military plans that they would present on the following day.[27]

At the next meeting, General Doumenc gave a rather detailed account of the French armed forces and their planned deployment in the event of war. Voroshilov posed a variety of questions – British military cooperation, contingency plans for the Italian front, expectations of the Polish alliance, and so forth – most of which were answered to his satisfaction. Then he posed the capital question that had loomed so large since long before Munich: what kind of cooperation did the French General Staff expect of Soviet forces? He drew attention to the fact that the USSR had no common border with Germany. "We can, therefore, only take part in the war on the territory of neighbouring states, particularly Poland and Rumania."[28] General Doumenc promised to answer the question the following day.

Marshal Voroshilov opened discussions at the next meeting by stating the question more specifically: "What part do the present Missions, or the General Staffs of France and Britain, consider the Soviet Union should play in the war against an aggressor if he attacks France and Britain [or] if he attacks Poland or Rumania . . . ?" General Doumenc replied with a great deal of diplomatic fencing and equivocal generalizations. Marshal Voroshilov persisted: "I want a clear answer to my very clear question. . . . Do the

[25] Schulenburg to Foreign Ministry, 4 August 1939; DGFP, Series D, 6: 1059–62 (No. 766).
[26] *Soviet Peace Efforts*, 2: 177–8 (No. 400).
[27] Ibid., 185–90 (No. 411).
[28] Ibid., 191–201 (Nos. 412–413).

French and British General Staffs think that the Soviet land forces will be admitted to Polish territory in order to make direct contact with the enemy in case Poland is attacked . . . ? And one more thing: Is it proposed to allow Soviet troops across Rumanian territory if the aggressor attacks Rumania?" General Doumenc and Admiral Drax conferred and surmised that Poland and Romania would certainly ask for assistance. Marshal Voroshilov then came unmistakably to the point at which he had been driving: "Passage of our troops onto Polish territory . . . , and through Rumanian territory, is a preliminary condition. It is a preliminary condition of our negotiations and of a joint Treaty between the three states [i.e., Britain, France, Soviet Union]. If that is not granted, if the question is not solved favourably, I doubt the usefulness of our conversations. . . . Without an exact and unequivocal answer to these questions further conversations will not have any real meaning. Upon receipt of an answer to these . . . questions we shall at once present our plan and our proposals. . . . Without a positive solution of this question the whole recent attempt to conclude a Military Convention between France, Britain and the Soviet Union is . . . doomed to fail."[29]

At this point, the French and British missions turned to their governments and requested an answer to Marshal Voroshilov's question from Poland and Romania. In the meantime, Soviet Chief of Staff B. M. Shaposhnikov detailed Soviet war plans. He boasted a force of 120 divisions of 19,000 men each, and he described three variants of operational plans.

I. If Germany attacked France and Britain, the Soviet Union would at once field 70 percent of the combined strength of France and Britain. In this case, Moscow expected the Poles to attack Germany in a force of forty to forty-five divisions and to admit Soviet troops across Poland. The Soviet Union would expect the combined navies of Britain and France to enter the Baltic, take possession of the Åland Islands, the Möön (Muhu) Archipelago (Estonia), the port of Hangö, and other Baltic ports and islands in order to interrupt the flow of iron ore from Sweden to Germany; to blockade the North Sea coast of Germany; to control the Mediterranean and close the Suez Canal and the Dardanelles; and to patrol the water routes along the coast of Norway to Murmansk and Archangel in order to suppress the operation of German submarines and surface vessels.

II. If Germany attacked Poland and Romania, Moscow assumed Hungarian cooperation with Germany and Polish assistance to Romania. In this case, France and Britain must attack Germany at once. Equally important, they must procure approval for the entry of Soviet forces into Poland and Romania. In this event, the USSR would field at once 100 percent of

[29] Ibid., 202–10 (No. 415).

the forces of Britain and France, and the tasks of the British and French navies should be the same as in the case of variant I.

III. If Germany attacked the USSR through Finland, Estonia, and Latvia, then Britain and France must enter the war at once and procure rights of passage for the Red Army through Poland and Romania. In this case, Britain and France must field 70 percent of the strength of Soviet forces, and the actions of the British and French navies should be the same as in the case of variants I and II. Poland would also be expected to deploy all its forces against the aggressor.

In exchange for these rather explicit plans, the French presented a "Draft Franco–Anglo–Soviet Military Agreement" containing two articles. First, the three powers should agree on an active Eastern as well as Western front. Second, they agree to deploy all their forces "on all enemy fronts on which they can fight effectively" according to the judgment of their respective Supreme Commands.[30]

Marshal Voroshilov objected that the principles of the French draft were "too universal, abstract and immaterial, and do not bind anyone to anything. . . . we have not gathered here to adopt some general declaration, but rather to work out a concrete military convention fixing the number of divisions, guns, tanks, aircraft, naval squadrons, etc., to act jointly in the defence of the contracting Powers. . . . the meetings of the Military Missions of Britain, France and the USSR, if they seriously wish to arrive at a concrete decision for common action against aggression, should not waste time on meaningless declarations, and should decide this basic question as quickly as possible." Furthermore, he observed that there had been no satisfactory Anglo–French response to what he described as "the cardinal question," the right of Soviet forces to operate on Polish and Romanian territory. Only after the resolution of that question would it be possible to proceed to discussion of reciprocal obligations of common military plans. Without a resolution of that question, all particulars of military planning consisted, he said, of useless preliminaries.[31] On the following day, 17 August, Voroshilov threatened to break off the talks until such time as the Soviet side received a clear answer to this "cardinal question." Upon the appeal of the visiting delegation, however, he consented to meet again on 21 August.[32] When no reply to his question had arrived by that date, Marshal Voroshilov adjourned further meetings indefinitely.[33]

By that time, the Soviet press had announced the arrival of German Foreign Minister Joachim von Ribbentrop for the negotiation of a

[30] Ibid., 201–2 (No. 413).
[31] Ibid., 233–6 (No. 426).
[32] Ibid., 240–8 (No. 429).
[33] Ibid., 254–9 (No. 437).

nonaggression pact, which was consummated late in the evening of 23 August, leaving Anglo–French diplomacy in tattered disarray and the strategic security of France and Britain only a little less shaken than that of Poland. The German invasion of Poland ensued on 1 September.

The Anglo–French response to this brutal challenge to their commitment is not the least remarkable – frightful – part of the story of their supine posture vis-à-vis the aggressor. Chamberlain dithered. He demanded the withdrawal of the German army from Poland. Messages continued between London and Berlin. Commons was scheduled to meet for a declaration of the prime minister on 2 September, the second day of the war, but it was postponed over and over while the cabinet worked for coordination with the French. Finally, at 7:45 P.M., Chamberlain spoke of negotiating with Berlin, with France, with Mussolini, who was calling for another meeting in the style of Munich, of the withdrawal of the German army from Poland. He spoke weakly and made a poor impression, a miserable impression. Leo Amery, fed up with vacillation, shouted "Speak for England." Arthur Greenwood (Labor) said "I am greatly disturbed. An act of aggression took place thirty-eight hours ago. The moment that act of aggression took place one of the most important treaties of modern times automatically came into operation. . . . I wonder how long we are prepared to vacillate at a time when Britain, and all that Britain stands for, and human civilization are in peril." As an observer noted, "A puff of smoke would have brought the Government down." Chamberlain had plainly betrayed the consensual intent of his cabinet meeting of that very afternoon. The cabinet was angry, as he sensed that the entire Commons was.[34] On the following day – late on the following day, with Chamberlain still hesitating – war was declared.

Yet more surprising things were in the works. In the course of the negotiations of the Western military delegations in Moscow, the Anglo–French mission had raised one pointed question of more interest subsequently than at the time: If Poland could be persuaded to admit Soviet troops in the event of war, "is the Soviet Union agreeable to participate in providing supplies, armaments, raw materials and other industrial material for Poland?"[35] In an interview granted the newspaper *Izvestiia* on 27 August, Marshal Voroshilov hinted, admittedly vaguely and equivocally but intriguingly, *four days now after the conclusion of the Nazi–Soviet pact for a joint attack on and partition of Poland*, that the Soviet Union might be willing to grant Poland military supplies in the event of war.[36] More interestingly

---

[34] Watt, *How War Came*, 575, 579.
[35] Military Questions to the Soviet Military Mission, 16 August 1938; *Soviet Peace Efforts* 2: 236 (No. 426).
[36] Interview with the Head of the Soviet Military Mission, K. Y. Voroshilov, on the Negotiations with the Military Missions of Britain and France, 27 August, 1939; ibid.: 270–2 (No. 446).

yet, the Soviet minister in Warsaw, Nikolai Sharonov paid a call on Foreign Minister Beck on 2 September and raised an intriguing question. On the second day of the war, he asked, in Beck's words, "why we were not negotiating with the Soviets regarding supplies, as the 'Voroshilov interview' has opened up the possibility of getting them. I have instructed Moscow to investigate the situation."[37]

Beck sent these instructions to Moscow by special courier, but the disorder and destruction that the German air attack had inflicted on Polish communications delayed his arrival until 6 September. When Ambassador Wacław Grzybowski raised the question with the Soviet foreign commissariat, Molotov's negative response was explained in a rather convoluted fashion. As he reported to Colonel Beck,[38]

> M. Sharonov's suggestions are no longer opportune. M. Molotov has informed me that the intervention of Great Britain and France has created an entirely new situation, which Marshal Voroshilov . . . could not take into consideration when giving the interview. At present the Soviets are compelled to safeguard first and foremost their own interests, remaining outside the conflict. For us Poland, said M. Molotov, is now synonymous with England. In regard to the practical question which I raised of supply of raw materials and the eventual supply of war materials, he maintains the position of a strict observance of the agreements existing between us. In consequence the Soviets are prepared to supply us only with those raw materials which are provided for in the quotas for the current year. As to war materials, in face of the changed situation, he does not consider that the Soviet Government could supply them at present. On the transit question he informed me that all transit of a military character might be in contradiction with the Pact concluded with Germany, and so he does not consider that the Soviet Government could allow it.

The mere thought of "remaining outside the conflict" was itself a direct violation of the terms of their treaty, then a few days old, with Germany! Was Moscow still considering collective security? In any event, the Soviets waited seventeen days before entering Poland on the side of Germany. Was Moscow waiting for an offer enabling it to enter on the side of the angels?

[37] Telegram from Minister Beck to the Polish Embassy in London concerning his conversation with Ambassador Sharonov on prospective Soviet supplies to Poland, 2 September 1939; *Documents on Polish-Soviet Relations, 1939–1945*, 2 vols. (London: Heinemann, 1961–1967), 1: 42 (No. 36).

[38] Grzybowski to Beck, 8 September 1938; ibid., 43 (No. 39).

Chapter 10

Assessment of Soviet Intentions

Now, what is most significant in this story for the assessment of Soviet intentions?

First there is the serious evidence of Litvinov's working – and *thinking how* – to avoid war altogether, explaining that war was not in the Soviet interest. We have *not* found him trying to provoke Lenin's conception of an imperialist war among the capitalist powers. Thus he told William Bullitt on the remilitarization of the Rhineland that he hoped that France would not march troops into the Rhineland, because it would mean immediate war. He wrote home from Geneva on 23 September 1938 to suggest that Soviet mobilization – he was presumably ignorant of the substantial but unannounced partial mobilization of the preceding two days – might even then deflect Hitler from starting a war. His consistently avowed objective, in private communications such as these, not to speak of his public speeches, was to save the peace. He had earlier informed Aleksandrovskii that Moscow was willing to countenance any reasonable measures of compromise in the Sudeten conflict that would both *save the peace* and leave Czechoslovakia *free and independent*.

What was the nature of Moscow's commitment to Czechoslovakia? In early August 1938, Litvinov instructed Aleksandrovskii that Moscow's interest in Czechoslovakia consisted in blocking Hitler's drive to the southeast. A couple of weeks later, he told the German ambassador, Count von der Schulenburg, that the Sudeten issue was for Moscow strictly a question of power politics, of balance of power, that, as he had also told the French correspondent of *Le Temps*, Moscow had no interest in defending Versailles, to which it was not a party: It had always favored self-determination of peoples, and its attitude to the Sudeten issue would have been quite different if the democratic Weimar regime still governed Germany.

We have two indications that the Red Army was actively prepared to intervene in Romania: the Romanian minister's reminder to Litvinov that Romania had allowed the transit of Czechoslovak and Soviet planes and materials both "in the air and on the ground" and the Polish consular report of 27 September. On the other hand, we have many indications of the lack of observations of such intervention (with the single exception of the overflights of Soviet planes purchased pursuant to an agreement made even before Anschluss). Disregarding the multiple public Soviet assurances of assistance to Czechoslovakia, all of which have long since been recorded and, in the main, skeptically – perhaps justifiably – dismissed, we must remember the agitprop meeting of Soviet soldiers (25 September 1938) who were expecting to march to Czechoslovakia. In this instance, of course, *no route of approach* was specified.

As long ago as March 1935, Chief of Staff Tukhachevskii had told U.S. Ambassador Bullitt that the Soviet Union would be unable at that time to bring any assistance to Czechoslovakia. Bullitt explained that it was because of the lack of adequate rail and road logistics. This situation had not changed by 1938. At that time, both Romanian Foreign Minister Comnen and the French minister in Bucharest, Thierry, had repeatedly declared that Romanian transport facilities were not sufficient to make a timely transit of the Red Army over Romania feasible. Litvinov himself had told Louis Fischer in mid-September 1938 that Moscow could help only in the air. He had written to Aleksandrovskii that it was doubtful whether Moscow could do anything serious for Czechoslovakia without the cooperation of the Western powers, and he despaired of that cooperation.

Why, then, did Litvinov continue to proclaim that Moscow would fulfill its commitments? Unfortunately, we do not have access to Stalin's mind, and we do not have access to the Russian Presidential Archive. We have only hints and surmises to guide us. In the spring of 1936, both the Soviet military attaché in Paris and Minister Aleksandrovskii in Prague, in response to the question how the Red Army would come to the assistance of Czechoslovakia, stated plainly that it would come through Poland, where we have seen that the rail network was considerably more advantageous than that of Romania. The simultaneity of the Soviet mobilization of 21–3 September and the warning to Poland that its intervention in Czechoslovakia would abrogate the Polish–Soviet treaty of nonaggression, 23 September, is a factor deserving consideration, as is perhaps the crude analogy between Soviet posture vis-à-vis Poland in September 1938 and in September 1939.

Even after Munich, even after the Anglo–French issuance of the guarantee to Poland, Ambassador Maiskii suspected the continuation of efforts in the British cabinet to make a deal with Berlin. We have seen the Wohlthat–Wilson exchanges, British offers of a nonaggression agreement and of the extension of loans to Germany, all at the expense of both the unilateral guarantee of 31 March 1939 to Poland and the Anglo–Polish treaty of mutual defense of 25 August 1939. Given what we now know of Kim

Philby and his friends, Moscow must have known much more about these negotiations than Maiskii did. How reliable could Moscow believe the commitments of London to be?

Yet even so, Moscow accepted willingly the offer that it had been actively soliciting since 1936 to engage in General Staff talks. In the spring of 1937 and again in the face of the Munich crisis, Litvinov proposed a military convention with France and Czechoslovakia. In the summer of 1939, Molotov and Voroshilov proposed a military convention with France and Great Britain. In 1937, Potemkin suggested to the French some relatively tangible outlines of the obligations that Moscow was willing to assume. In the summer of 1938, these proposals were simply ignored, and hence we do not know what kind of stipulations Moscow had in mind. In 1939, Moscow was impressively explicit on what the Soviets planned to do, spelling out in considerable detail the quantity and quality of forces to be committed to a campaign and the theaters of deployment in the event of the outbreak of war. What is especially intriguing here is the question why Moscow would have bound itself to treaty stipulations of force levels and areas of deployment in the event of developments perhaps only weeks away if it did not intend to honor them. The Soviet government was especially eager to confront the Wehrmacht west of the Soviet frontier.

Most intriguing – however gossamer – is a pair of analogous Soviet initiatives in September 1938 and September 1939. When Fierlinger informed Potemkin in Moscow of the terms of the Anglo–French virtual ultimatum of 19 September 1938 and Prague's acceptance of them, Potemkin asked why the Czechoslovaks had not asked Moscow for assistance. Moreover, although the acceptance of that document in Prague, stipulating as it did the abrogation of the Czech alliance with Moscow, provided the Soviet government the perfect opportunity to suspend its obligations to Czechoslovakia – obligations that were, without the prospect of French military cooperation, onerous – Litvinov stated explicitly and publicly at the League that Moscow did not seek to escape its obligations, that it regarded the treaty as still valid. In a similarly curious fashion, when Hitler invaded Poland in September 1939, Moscow asked the Poles – to whom it had no obligation whatever and in spite of its fresh obligations to the Germans! – why they had not asked for Soviet assistance.

Finally, the quality of these tentative conclusions depends on the integrity of the evidence in the archives – or, more precisely, it rests upon the integrity of the *accessible* archival evidence. I was fortunate to be able to see some important evidence on the issues examined here in the archives of Moscow, but I was denied, as usual, access to vastly larger quantities of material. Access to historical evidence in Moscow remains such a serious problem as to make it quite impossible to have full faith in the authenticity of the research experience there. Do the Russians – Imperial, Soviet, or post-Soviet – not want us to know their history, or do they not want to know it themselves?

When I worked in the Romanian Military Archive, I found the evidence of observations on the Soviet frontier strikingly, even suspiciously, spare and trivial. Hence I raised the question, Was the archive still in possession of all original Romanian documents? I was given a confident answer.

1. Moscow requisitioned and continues to hold the entire archive of wartime dictator Ion Antonescu.
2. The Germans never went over the head of Antonescu about anything, hence did not requisition any archives there.
3. The Romanian Securitate sometimes requisitioned and kept particular materials, but the materials of interest to me were not among them.

So, in sum, everything of interest to me remained there.

In the Romanian Archive of the Ministry of Foreign Affairs, I was shown great gaps in the personnel files of Romanian diplomats stationed in Moscow. The archivists there were convinced that significant items were removed at some time early after World War II by visiting Soviet authorities. The leading specialist in Bucharest on Soviet–Romanian relations has worked extensively in former Soviet archives and found in them substantial amounts of Romanian documentation, especially in the former Osobyi arkhiv.[1] At the Foreign Affairs Archive, it is suspected that Soviet authorities took any items of interest to them from any or all archive(s) in Romania. My own inquiries at the Osobyi arkhiv elicited the response that it contained no Romanian materials, presumably including the Antonescu papers, which are widely believed to be there.

In sum, for Russian reasons, the search for historical validity in Eastern Europe remains, as always, dicey and uncertain.

Finally, the evidence adduced in my research suggests a far-from-certain conclusion. Although Stalin still wished in the face of Munich to postpone the outbreak of a war that he must have foreseen as inevitable in the long run, before the League's abrogation of Article 16 during the last week of September 1938, he would have resorted to some contrived mandate bestowed by the League Covenant to intervene in the war through the territory of Poland. His aim would have been the containment of Nazi imperialism and the protection of Soviet security. More precise and confident conclusions must await access to the records of the Commissariat of Defense, the Commissariat of Foreign Affairs, and the Presidential Archive.

---

[1] The Osobyi arkhiv is the depository for documents captured abroad. It is apparently currently being amalgamated with the Rossiiskii gosudarstvennyi voennyi arkhiv.

The argument here is that Stalin was pursuing a conventional game of national-security strategy. Yet Igor Lukes and Ivan Pfaff have argued in a number of places[2] that Stalin planned to exploit the potential outbreak of war over the Sudetenland in 1938 to extend the Bolshevik Revolution over a substantial part of Eastern Europe after the fashion that he actually used in the period 1944–1948.[3] The evidence for this view comes chiefly from a document giving the text of a speech that Stalin's lieutenant Andrei A. Zhdanov allegedly gave to the Central Committee of the Czechoslovak Communist Party on the evening of 20–21 August 1938. Zhdanov is said to have urged the Czechoslovak Party to encourage the working class to regard a German attack on Czechoslovakia and the world war that would naturally ensue as the opportunity to initiate a new wave of proletarian revolutions, assisted, Zhdanov is said to have observed, by the Soviet Red Army's marching side by side with the Czechoslovak working class, first against Nazi Germany and subsequently against the entire capitalist world order. The occasion was said to be adorned by the presence of Harry Pollitt, general secretary of the Communist Party of Great Britain, and Marcel Cachin, editor of the French Communist daily paper, *L'Humanité*.[4]

Milan Hauner has raised the question of the authenticity of this document and the tale told in it. He argues that neither Pollitt nor Cachin can be shown by evidence from British or French sources to have been in Prague at the time, that no Czechoslovak Central Committee members ever recalled this meeting, and that there was no other evidence of it, either photographic or stenographic. In addition, he points out that the Moscow daily newspapers, *Pravda* and *Izvestiia*, carried a large photograph of Zhdanov among the Supreme Soviet delegates in the Kremlin on the same day when he was supposed to have been in Prague. Moreover, Pfaff, in his version of the story, has placed the Comintern boss, Georgi Dimitrov, in Prague in mid-September, although Dimitrov's diary records that he was on vacation in the Caucasus at the time.[5]

[2]   To be fair to Lukes, it must be recognized that he is not generally respectful of Pfaff's work; he simply shares Pfaff's view of this particular issue.

[3]   Igor Lukes, "Stalin and Czechoslovakia in 1938–39: An Autopsy of a Myth," in idem. and Erik Goldstein, eds., *The Munich Crisis, 1938: Prelude to World War II* (London/Portland, OR: Cass, 1999), 13–47; idem., *Czechoslovakia Between Stalin and Hitler: The Diplomacy of Edvard Beneš in the 1930s* (New York: Oxford University Press, 1996); idem., "Did Stalin Desire War in 1938? A New Look at Soviet Behavior during the May and September Crises," *Diplomacy and Statecraft* 2 (1991): 3–53; idem., "Stalin and Beneš at the end of September 1938: New Evidence from the Prague Archives," *Slavic Review* 52 (1993): 28–48; Ivan Pfaff, *Die Sowjetunion und die Verteidigung der Tschechoslowakei 1934–1938: Versuch der Revision einer Legende* (Cologne: Böhlau, 1996), 320–1.

[4]   Lukes, *Czechoslovakia Between Hitler and Stalin*, 198–99; Pfaff, *Die Sowjetunion und die Verteidigung der Tschechoslowakei*, 320–1.

[5]   Milan Hauner, "Zrada, sovětizace, nebo historický lapsus? Ke kritice dvou dokumentů k československo-sovětským vztahům z roku 1938," *Soudobé dějiny* 4 (1999): 545–71; on Dimitrov's

Lukes naturally responded to this criticism. He now suggests that the Zhdanov who allegedly appeared to speak in Prague in August 1938 may not have been Stalin's lieutenant, A. A. Zhdanov. This point seems to me unlikely, as it is hard to imagine that there was more than one Soviet Zhdanov authorized by so severe a taskmaster as Stalin to speak so boldly of such momentous subjects as the author of the speech in question is alleged to have done. Lukes further supposes that the meeting at which the speech was given took place not in 1938, as the dating of the document was written in later – perhaps in the 1950s – and that it may have occurred not in Prague but in Moscow. This point is also problematical, as there is clear reference in the text to the crisis posed by the "Henlein party."[6] Lukes remains convinced, however, that the text of the speech embodied the real intentions of Soviet policy in Czechoslovakia and in Europe more generally on the eve of Munich.[7]

Apart from the critical observations of Hauner, there is another major consideration that calls into question the authenticity of this document and the argument to which it naturally gives rise. The content of the speech is simply at variance with the Popular Front line of the Comintern enunciated at the Seventh Comintern Congress of August 1935 and pursued by the Communist Parties of the world from that date until the Nazi–Soviet pact of August 1939. The two most conspicuous examples of Soviet intervention in potentially revolutionary situations in world affairs of that time are Spain and China, and it makes no sense to ignore them and the obvious evidence that they provide for the nature of Soviet foreign policy in other areas of potential Soviet intervention.

The basic Comintern line on Spain throughout the 1920s and 1930s was that it was a country of "uncompleted bourgeois–democratic revolution." Hence it was a country suitable for proletarian–socialist leadership of a bourgeois–democratic revolution. The Spanish Communist Party stood in classic Marxist–Leninist fashion for rights of secession of national-minority areas – just as in Czechoslovakia – such as Catalonia, Biscay, and Galicia.[8] Republican participants in the civil war do not tell us of revolutionary aims. Thus Franz Borkenau: "The basic ideas of Communist military policy were: No revolution during the war; strict discipline . . . within the ranks; strict political control of the army . . . with the aim of creating an ideology adapted to this policy, an ideology, that is, mainly based on

presence in Prague 14 September 1938, see Pfaff, *Die Sowjetunion und die Verteidigung der Tschechoslowakei*, 363.

[6] Hauner, "Zrada, sovětizace, nebo historický lapsus? Ke kritice dvou dokumentů," 549.

[7] Igor Lukes, "Dva dokumenty na věčné téma: československo-sovětské vztahy ve třicátých letech," *Soudobé dějiny* 7 (2000): 364.

[8] Kermit E. McKenzie, *Comintern and World Revolution, 1928–1943: The Shaping of Doctrine* (New York: Columbia University Press, 1963), 73, 78, 80, 106, 251–3.

nationalism."[9] In the opinion of David Cattell, "Numbers of the middle class joined the [Communist] party because they saw it as the most stable and conservative element of the Left."[10] In fact, E. H. Carr insists, that "Stalin discounted [world revolution] from the first. By the 1930s he regarded it as a positive nuisance and as an obstacle to a prudent policy designed to protect the interests of the USSR." In the late 1930s, he was preoccupied with internal affairs and probably had little time for foreign policy. "The issue of the subordination of Comintern to the interests of Soviet foreign policy was ever present in Spain.... It represented a subordination of communist principles to considerations of a policy which merely used communists to achieve its ends. It was a system which found wider application in eastern Europe after the liquidation of Comintern and the end of the Second World War."[11]

Specialists who approach the subject from the vantage point of Madrid rather than that of Moscow are of the same opinion. Thus Stanley Payne: "Stalin's goal was to brace the Republican war effort . . . and through the struggle in Spain hold at bay Germany and Italy while winning support from France for the new Russian policy of collective security.... The aim was not to set up an outright Communist regime, which would have been difficult and would have alienated the western powers."[12] Pierre Broué and Émile Témime agree: In 1936, "the USSR had ceased to be the driving force of the world revolutionary movement. It was the era when Stalin undertook the liquidation of the old guard of Bolsheviks [and] decapitated the international communist movement in a series of trials and purges.... The Spanish affair, in the eyes of Moscow, must not at all costs furnish the occasion for isolating the USSR and separating it from the western democracies."[13]

Of course, the entire historiography of the Spanish Civil War – and especially the memoir literature supporting it – is a hotbed of impassioned controversy, and the relative generosity of revelations from Soviet archives characteristic of the early 1990s gave us important new evidence on the disputed issues. We now have the correspondence of Stalin and Georgi Dimitrov, president of the Comintern at the time, and it is entirely

9   Franz Borkenau, "Introduction," in José Martín Blasquez, *I Helped to Build an Army: Civil War Memoirs of a Spanish Staff Officer* (London: Secker and Warburg, 1939), xi.
10 David Cattell, *Communism and the Spanish Civil War* (Berkeley, CA: University of California Press, 1955), 95–6.
11 E. H. Carr, *The Comintern and the Spanish Civil War*, ed. Tamara Deutscher (London: Macmillan, 1984), 84–5.
12 Stanley G. Payne, *A History of Spain and Portugal*, 2 vols. (Madison, WI: University of Wisconsin Press, 1973), 2: 660.
13 Pierre Broué and Émile Témime, *La révolution et la guerre d'Espagne* (Paris: Éditions du minuit, 1961), 170–2.

consonant with the evidence already adduced. Thus Dimitrov forwarded to Stalin, 23 July 1936, a directive that he had just sent to the Spanish Central Committee: "We strongly recommend: 1. To concentrate everything on the most important task of the moment, i.e., on the prompt suppression and the definitive liquidation of the fascist rebellion, rather than being carried away by plans to be realized after victory; 2. To avoid any activities which might undermine the unity of the popular front in the struggle against the rebels; . . . 4. Not to run ahead, not to depart from the positions of a democratic regime, and not to go beyond the struggle for a genuine democratic republic; 5. As long as it is possible to avoid the direct participation of Communists in the government, . . . since it is easier thereby to retain the unity of the popular front."[14]

Equally important is Gerald Howson's work in Soviet military records. He has shown how Moscow subjected the Republican war effort to merciless exploitation in the discriminatory pricing of arms.[15] A new volume of documents from Soviet military records comes down on the side of Broué and Témime, Carr, and Payne, citing "hard evidence that proves what many had suspected since the beginning of the Spanish Civil War: that Stalin sought from the very beginning to control events in Spain and to manage or prevent the spread of actual social revolution."[16] The long-term plan was presumably to halt the spread of Fascism, to illustrate the wisdom of collective security to the Western powers, and to build a prototype of the people's democracy to establish a country friendly to the USSR, like those of Eastern Europe in 1945 and following.

In China, as in Spain, there was civil war between left and right and a foreign presence, thus the same general pattern of three-way conflict, although the Chinese analogy with the wartime Balkans is much closer.[17] As in Spain, Moscow gave aid, relatively large quantities, but chiefly or

---

[14] Dimitrov to Luis Diaz [sic], copy to Stalin, 23 July 1936; *Dimitrov and Stalin, 1934–1943: Letters from the Soviet Archives*, ed. Alexander Dallin and F. I. Firsov, trans. V. A. Staklo (New Haven, CT: Yale University Press, 2000), 107–08.

[15] Gerald Howson, *Arms for Spain: The Untold Story of the Spanish Civil War* (London: John Albemarle, 1998).

[16] Ronald Radosh, Mary R. Habeck, and Grigory Sevostianov, eds., *Spain Betrayed: The Soviet Union in the Spanish Civil War* (New Haven, CT: Yale University Press, 2001), xviii. See also Stéphane Courtois and Jean-Louis Panne, "The Shadow of the NKVD in Spain," in Stéphane Courtois, ed., *The Black Book of Communism: Crimes, Terror, Repression* (Cambridge, MA: Harvard University Press, 1999), 333–52; and François Furet, *The Passing of an Illusion: The Idea of Communism in the Twentieth Century* (Chicago: University of Chicago Press, 1999), 245–65.

[17] The literature here, both memoirs and monographs, is quite large. Probably the best-known memoir is Fitzroy Maclean, *Eastern Approaches* (London: Jonathan Cape, 1949); an authoritative monograph is Walter Roberts, *Tito, Mihailovic, and the Allies, 1941–1945* (New Brunswick, NJ: Rutgers University Press, 1974). Both illustrate the analogy, as do similar memoirs and studies of Albania and Greece.

exclusively to the Kuomintang, not to the Communists.[18] From the Seventh Comintern Congress of 1935, the Chinese party formally followed the Popular Front line, although often reluctantly and not consistently loyally. Mao and company were remote, communications were not good, and Mao had ideas of his own, which are most graphically described in Edgar Snow's classic *Red Star over China*: "the first day of the anti-Japanese war will be the beginning of the end of Chiang Kai-shek."[19] When the Communists' new-found ally, displaced Manchurian warlord Chang Hsueh-liang, took advantage of a visit of Chiang to take him captive, Mao was eager to put him on trial and eliminate him. When contrary instructions arrived from Moscow, instructions obviously more consonant with the goal of the Popular Front, Mao went into a rage.[20] Still, he complied. When the "returned student clique," also known as the "twenty-eight Bolsheviks," arrived in Yenan from their Soviet training in Moscow, Mao had a real fight on his hands to retain control of the Chinese party, to "make Marxism Chinese," as he put it, but he prevailed. In sum, there was an early version of the Sino–Soviet conflict here. Mao appears to have thought, as Chiang Kai-shek did as well, that the United States would eventually do what it would be too costly for either the Kuomintang or the Communist forces to do, to defeat the Japanese. Hence it was the native enemy who was the more dangerous. As Chiang is alleged to have said, "the Japanese are a disease of the skin, but the communists are a disease of the heart," and Mao would undoubtedly have agreed if the name Nationalists were substituted for the name Communists. Thus while Mao was committed chiefly to seizing power in China, Moscow was dedicated chiefly to using all native forces in China, at whatever cost to them, to keep the Japanese army away from the Soviet frontier. And therefore, as in Spain, Moscow sought to form as broad a coalition as possible against Fascism – or the invader – and that policy most distinctly required putting all notions of revolution on the shelf.[21]

---

[18] This aid consisted of 904 aircraft, 2,118 motor vehicles, 1,140 artillery pieces, and quantities of small arms and ammunition. John W. Garver, *Chinese-Soviet Relations, 1937–1945: The Diplomacy of Chinese Nationalism* (New York: Oxford University Press, 1988), 38.

[19] First edition 1937. Mao appeared, like Chiang, to think that the Americans would eventually dispose of the Japanese threat; hence the primary task was the elimination of the native enemy.

[20] *Dimitrov and Stalin, 1934–1943*, 107–8; Edgar Snow, *Random Notes on Red China, 1936–1945* (Cambridge, MA: Harvard University Press, 1957), 2–3.

[21] The literature easily allows the *plausible* conclusion that Stalin preferred the victory of Chiang to the victory of Mao. Tetsuya Kataoka, *Resistance and Revolution in China: The Communists and the Second United Front* (Berkeley, CA: University of California Press, 1974); Charles B. McLane, *Soviet Policy and the Chinese Communists, 1931–1946* (New York: Columbia University Press, 1958); Chalmers Johnson, *Peasant Nationalism and Communist Power: The Emergence of Revolutionary China, 1937–1945*

Of course, Czechoslovakia was not a perfect analog of Spain and China. Spain was far away with no common Soviet frontier. China was far away from the heart of Russia but had a common Asian frontier. Czechoslovakia was proximate but lacked a common frontier. In Spain and China there were active military conflicts involving forces identified in both cases by the Comintern as Fascist. In China, the Japanese Fascists were a principal protagonist. In Spain the German and Italian Fascists were an important auxiliary. Soviet aid in both cases was significant but not decisive. Czechoslovakia was without active military conflict but was promised Soviet aid if and when it began.

The Czechoslovak Communist Party had supported in the 1920s and early 1930s whatever separatist and secessionist sentiment there was among the minority nationalities, but in reaction to the Soviet–Czechoslovak alliance of 16 May 1935, the Party hurriedly reversed its position and struck a conspicuously patriotic posture for the national general election only three days later. From the Seventh Comintern Congress of July–August 1935, it followed the Popular Front line, as did the other Communist Parties of Europe.[22]

In sum, in the face of the growing evidence of the threat of German aggression, Soviet policy in the Comintern was everywhere governed by the thrust of the Popular Front. Nowhere did imminent communist revolution appear to be on the agenda. Hence it is unlikely that Stalin was following such a policy in Czechoslovakia. Rather Stalin sought to postpone war and upheaval in Europe until the Soviet Union had recovered from the purge process and his recent innovations in military weaponry were in abundant supply – probably 1942. In the meantime, he was convinced that a solid coalition of great powers in support of the concept of collective security would suffice to halt the march of the Nazi menace. As he said to Anthony Eden in 1935, "the only way to meet the present situation was by some scheme of pacts. Germany must be made to realize that if she attacked any other nation she would have Europe against her."[23] In formulating the military conventions necessary to dissuade Hitler from further adventures,

---

(Stanford, CA: Stanford University Press, 1962); Mark Selden, *The Yenan Way in Revolutionary China* (Cambridge, MA: Harvard University Press, 1971); Edward E. Rice, *Mao's Way* (Berkeley, CA: University of California Press, 1972); Chang Kuo-t'ao, *Autobiography: The Rise of the Chinese Communist Party, 1921–1938*, 2 vols. (Lawrence, KS: University of Kansas Press, 1971–1972).

[22] Jacques Rupnik, *Histoire du parti communiste tchécoslovaque: des origines à la prise du pouvoir* (Paris: Presses de la Fondation nationale des sciences politiques, 1981), 110–19; Paul Zinner, *Communist Strategy and Tactics in Czechoslovakia, 1918–1948* (Westport, CT: Greenwood Press, 1975), 54–8.

[23] Anthony Eden, *Facing the Dictators* (Boston: Houghton Mifflin, 1962), 173.

Stalin was determined to send his military forces into Poland with or without Polish consent, as it was only the *platzdarm* of Poland that offered the large forces of the Red Army a feasible field of operations.

If there is any prospect of the refinement and improvement of conclusions such as these, it awaits the capricious impulses of the furtive Neanderthals who are keepers of the secrets of the Russian archives.

Appendices

Appendix 1: Pertinent Paragraphs of the League of Nations Covenant

Article 5

Except where otherwise expressly provided in this Covenant or by the terms of the present Treaty, decisions at any meeting of the Assembly or of the Council shall require the agreement of all the Members of the League represented at the meeting.

All matters of procedure at meetings of the Assembly or of the Council, including the appointment of Committees to investigate particular matters, shall be regulated by the Assembly or by the Council and may be decided by a majority of the Members of the League represented at the meeting.

Article 10

The Members of the League undertake to respect and preserve as against external aggression the territorial integrity and existing political independence of all Members of the League. In case of any such aggression or in case of any threat or danger of such aggression the Council shall advise upon the means by which this obligation shall be fulfilled.

Article 11

Any war or threat of war, whether immediately affecting any of the Members of the League or not, is hereby declared a matter of concern to the whole League, and the League shall take any action that may be deemed wise and effectual to safeguard the peace of nations. In case any such emergency should arise the Secretary General shall on the request of any Member of the League forthwith summon a meeting of the Council.

It is also declared to be the friendly right of each Member of the League to bring to the attention of the Assembly or of the Council any circumstance whatever affecting international relations which threatens to disturb international peace or the good understanding between nations upon which peace depends.

Article 12
[The signatories consent to submit disputes among themselves to arbitration.]

Article 13
[Alternatively, signatories may submit such disputes to the Permanent Court of International Justice.]

Article 15
[Or, alternatively, to the Council of the League.]

Article 16
Should any Member of the League resort to war in disregard of its covenants under Articles 12, 13, or 15, it shall *ipso facto* be deemed to have committed an act of war against all other Members of the League, which hereby undertake immediately to subject it to the severance of all trade or financial relations, the prohibition of all intercourse between their nationals and the nationals of the covenant-breaking State, and the prevention of all financial, commercial or personal intercourse between the nationals of the covenant-breaking State and the nationals of any other State, whether a Member of the League or not.

It shall be the duty of the Council in such case to recommend to the several Governments concerned what effective military, naval or air force the Members of the League shall severally contribute to the armed forces to be used to protect the covenants of the League.

The Members of the League agree, further, that they will mutually support one another in the financial and economic measures which are taken under this Article, in order to minimise the loss and inconvenience resulting from the above measures, and that they will mutually support one another in resisting any special measures aimed at one of their number by the covenant-breaking State, and that they will take the necessary steps to afford passage through their territory to the forces of any of the Members of the League which are co-operating to protect the covenants of the League.

Any Member of the League which has violated any covenant of the League may be declared to be no longer a Member of the League by a vote of the Council concurred in by the Representatives of all the other Members of the League represented thereon.

Article 17
In the event of a dispute between a Member of the League and a State which is not a Member of the League, or between States not Members of the League, the State or States not Members of the League shall be invited to accept the obligations of membership in the League for the purposes of such dispute, upon such conditions as the Council may deem just. If such invitation is accepted, the provisions of Articles 12 to 16 inclusive shall be applied with such modifications as may be deemed necessary by the Council.... If a State so invited shall refuse to accept the obligations of membership in the League for the purposes of such dispute, and shall resort to war against a Member of the League, the provisions of Article 16 shall be applicable as against the State taking such action.

Appendix 2: Franco-Soviet and Czechoslovak-Soviet Pacts: Excerpts[1]

The Franco-Soviet Treaty of Mutual Assistance, 2 May 1935
Article I. In the event that France or the U.S.S.R. are subjected to the threat or the danger of aggression on the part of a European state, the U.S.S.R. and France engage themselves reciprocally to proceed to an immediate mutual consultation on measures to take in order to observe the provisions of Article 10 of the League of Nations Pact.

Article 2. In the event that, in the circumstances described in Article 15, paragraph 7, of the League of Nations Pact, France or the U.S.S.R. may be, in spite of the genuinely pacific intentions of the two countries, the subject of unprovoked aggression on the part of a European state, the U.S.S.R. and France will immediately lend each other reciprocal aid and assistance.

Article 3. Taking into consideration the fact that, according to Article 16 of the League of Nations Pact, every member of the League that resorts to war contrary to the engagements assumed in Articles 12, 13 or 15 of the Pact is *ipso facto* considered as having committed an act of war against all the other members of the League, France and the U.S.S.R. engage themselves reciprocally, [should either of them be the object of unprovoked aggression], to lend immediate aid and assistance in activating the application of Article 16 of the Pact.

The same obligation is assumed in the event that either France or the U.S.S.R. is the object of aggression on the part of a European state in the

[1] Translated from the French text in *Documents on International Affairs, 1935*, ed. John W. Wheeler-Bennett and Stephen Heald, 2 vols. (New York: Oxford University Press, 1936), 1: 116–19 and 138–9.

circumstances described in Article 17, paragraphs 1 and 3, of the League of Nations Pact.

Protocole de Signature

Article 1. It is understood that the effect of Article 3 is to oblige each Contracting Party to lend immediate assistance to the other in conforming immediately to the recommendations of the Council of the League of Nations as soon as they are annnounced under Article 16 of the Pact. It is equally understood that the two Contracting Parties will act in concert to elicit the recommendations of the Council with all the celerity that circumstances require and that, if nevertheless, the Council, for any reason whatever, does not make any recommendation or does not arrive at a unanimous decision, the obligation of assistance will nonetheless be implemented. . . .

The Czechoslovak-Soviet Treaty of Mutual Assistance, 16 May 1935

The two treaties are nearly identical. The major difference is cited here.

Protocole de Signature

Article 2. [The treaty may be activated only after the Franco–Soviet treaty is activated.]

Selected Source Materials and Literature

Let us consider here what are probably the most productive future avenues of inquiry into the mysteries of Soviet policy at Munich.

My surmise is that my research and that of Dov B. Lungu, Viorica Moisuc, and Ioan Talpeş (see the listings in the literature section) have very nearly exhausted the prospects in Romanian archives unless new groups of documents are discovered, perhaps captured documents currently housed in Russia.

In the Czech Republic I found to my great disappointment at the Vojenský historický archív that nearly all of the pertinent military records had been destroyed by the Czechs on the movement of the Wehrmacht into Prague in March 1939. My occasional disagreement with his interpretation notwithstanding, much the most authoritative research into the Czech diplomatic records is that of Igor Lukes. See also, however, the comments of Milan Hauner (both given in the literature section).

The most promising place to look for elucidation and elaboration of the questions treated here is in Russian archival depositories closed to me. My own work in the Rossiiskii gosudarstvennyi voennyi arkhiv, as subsequently cited, was, although limited, of enormous significance for the findings related in this book. If we are to make new discoveries, we must count heavily on the Ministry of Defense archive (Tsentral'nyi arkhiv Ministerstva oborony) and the foreign-affairs archive (Arkhiv vneshnei politiki Rossiiskoi federatsii), most probably the former. Perhaps the publication of a serious, deliberate, and impartial inquiry into Soviet policy, such as I presume to think this present one is, will prompt our Russian colleagues, that is, historians, to prompt their archivists, to be more forthcoming than is their usual habit. It is conceivable that the most significant materials are to be found in Politbiuro records in the old party archive, known at the time of my research as the Rossiiskii tsentr khraneniia i izucheniia dokumentov noveishei istorii (since renamed Rossiiskii gosudarstvennyi arkhiv sotsial'no–politicheskoi istorii). I was admitted to work there, but I discovered that the particular materials relating to defense policy remain closed for the period after 1934. It is also conceivable that Romanian materials in the archive of captured documents, the Osobyi arkhiv, are significant. In short, so far as I can tell, we Western researchers have advanced the inquiry as far as possible without the assistance of our Russian colleagues. The ball is in their court.

I. UNPUBLISHED SOURCES

Rossiiskii gosudarstvennyi voennyi arkhiv

F. 25880, op. 5, d. 5. Protokoly zasedanii Voennogo soveta Kievskogo osobogo voennogo okruga za 1938 g. 20 marta 1938 g.–31 dekabria 1938 g.

F. 33987, op. 3s, d. 1145. Zapis' besedy Potemkina s frantsuzskim poslom Kulondrom i pis'ma Litvinova o nalazhivanii diplomaticheskikh otnosheniiakh s Rumyniei. (copies)

———, ———, d. 1146. Zapisi besed V. P. Potemkina s frantsuzskim poslom Kulondrom, frantsuzskim poverennym v delakh Paiiarom i chekhoslovatskim poslannikom Firlingerom o podgotovke Germanieu okupatsii Chekhoslovakii, o pozitsii Anglii i Frantsii v chekhoslovatskom voprose i chesko-pol'skikh otnosheniiakh; Pis'ma M. M. Litvinova v TsK VKP (b) i polpreda SSSR vo Frantsii M. M. Litvinovu o voennykh prigotovleniiakh Germanii, okypatsii eiu Chekhoslovakii i vnutripoliticheskom polozhenii vo Frantsii; Spetssoobshcheniia Razvedyvatel'nogo upravleniia RKKA o polozhenii v Ispanii i Frantsii i drugie materialy. (copies)

F. 37977, op. 4s, d. 279. Obshchie voprosy po podgotovke teatrov voennykh deistvii v protivovozdushnoi otnoshenii/AZO, MO, VNOS/po zapadnomu teatru voennykh deistvii/ direktivy G Sh doklady Narkoma oborony pravitel'stvu, Upravleniia PVO RKKA i komanduiushchego KVO po PVO Moskvy, Leningrada, Kieva i Baku/11.5.1937– 10.5.1938.

———, ———, d. 293. Otchety po boevoi podgotovke okrugov/SibVO, URVO, ZabVO, BVO, SKVO, SAVO, PriVO, LVO, MVO/22.10.1937–31.12.1938.

———, ———, d. 295. Otchety po operativnoi podgotovke okrugov, armii, akademii i TsU/SibVO, URVO, MVO, SAVO, ORVO, KalVO, PriVO i UBP/RKKA 1.1.– 31.12.1938.

———, ———, d. 296. Otchety po operativnoi podgotovke okrugov, armii, akademii i TsU/BOVO, KOVO/1 ianvaria 1938 g.–31 dekabria 1938 g.

———, op. 5s, d. 479. Ucheniia v KOVO sentiabr'/oktiabr' 1938 goda.

———, ———, dd. 486–487. Operativnye dokumenty po BOVO/sbory/23.9.– 31.12.1938.

Arhivele militare române

Fond Marele stat major. Secția I-a, Organizare și mobilizare. Dosar 434: Planurile de campanie 1936.

———. Secția 2-a informații. Dosar 464: "Frontul de est." Ipoteza. Informații asupra marilor unitați sovietice, organizare, dislocare. Lucrări de fortificație semnalate pe Nistre. Ipoteze probabile de război etc. (23.06.1937–14.07.1939).

———. ———. Dosar 812/318/A: Memoriu asupra recunoașterilor de pe frontiera de est, 22 septembrie 1938.

———.———. Dosar 813/10: Notă cu privire la atitudinea Uniunii Sovietice faţă de evenimentele din Europa centrală.

———. Secţia 3 operaţii. Dosar 1577: Studii în legătură cu planul de campanie 1938.

———.———. Dosar 1578: Ceruri de transport pe frontul de est a diferitelor unitaţi militare.

———.———. Dosar 1602: Documente privind legăturile de ordin militar între România şi U.R.S.S. (1938–1939).

Fond Corpul granicelor. Dosar 2348/4/a: Ordine, rapoarte, procese verbale, declaraţii şi schiţe cu privire la anchete şi cercetări întreprinse de corp asupra cazurilor de trecere frauduloasă a frontierei precum şi a unor incidente de frontieră (03.09.1938–10.11.1938).

———. Dosar 2349: Ordine, rapoarte, schiţe, procese verbale şi declaraţii cu privire la cercetarea cazurilor de trecere frauduloasă a frontierei de către unii indivizii (28.08.1938–02.11.1938).

———. Dosar 2361/13/a: Ordine, rapoarţe, schite, referate, procese verbale, instrucţiune şi declaraţii cu privire la cercetarea cazurilor de trecere frauduloasă a frontierei, precum şi la cazurile de pesciure clandestină în apele de pe frontiera (Nistru), efectuarea sondajelor de către vasele navigante, precum şi la dotarea pichetelor cu material de lasare (18.04.1938–09.03.1939).

———. Dosar nr. 2364/15/b/1: Ordine, rapoarte şi dări de seama referitoare la inspecţiile efectuate de către unii ofiţerii din cadrul unitaţilor subordonate la pichetele de graniceri, precum şi la asigurarea pazei frontierei de către aceste unitaţi (07.04.1938–21.03.1939).

Fond Corpul 6 Armata, Statul Major, Biroul 2. Dosar Special Nr. 6b: Informaţiuni asupra partidelor politice, manifeste şi diferite informaţiuni externe primite de la Chestura Pol. şi Reg. de Poliţie Cluj, Insp. Reg. Jand. Cluj şi Prefecturile de judeţe 11 martii 1938–31 martii 1939.

Fond Cabinetul Ministrului. Dosar 80: Livret Chestinunea Sudeţi.

Ministerul Afacerilor externe

Fond 71/U.R.S.S., 1920–1944. Vol. 1: Telegrame Moscova, 1935–1939.

———,———. Vol. 52: Relaţii cu Cehoslovacia, 1920–1944.

———,———. Vols. 84–85: Relaţii cu Romînia, 1937–1938.

———,———. Vol. 135. Culegere de documente privind relaţii romîno-sovietic, 1933–1940.

Fond 71/Romînia. Vols. 101–103: Copii după telegramele trimise şi primite de la oficiile din exterior. Aprilie–15 octombrie 1938.

———. Vols. 252–259: Copii după rapoartele primite de la oficiile dîn exterior şi copii după note verbale, referate şi texte de acorduri şi tratate, martie-octombrie 1938.

II. PUBLISHED SOURCES

A. Official Documents

Das Abkommen von München 1938. Václav Král, ed. Prague: Academia, 1968.

Allianz Hitler-Horthy-Mussolini: Dokumente zur ungarischen Aussenpolitik (1933–1944). Magda Ádám, Gyula Jukász, and Lajos Kerekes, eds. Budapest: Akadémiai Kiadó, 1966.

Dimitrov and Stalin, 1934–1943: Letters from the Soviet Archives. Alexander Dallin and F. I. Firsov, eds. V. A. Staklo, trans. New Haven, CT: Yale University Press, 2000.

Documents and Materials Relating to the Eve of the Second World War. New York: International Publishers, 1948. 2 vols.

Documents diplomatiques français, 1932–1939. 2nd series: *1936–1939.* Paris: Imprimerie nationale, 1963–1986. 19 vols.

Documents on British Foreign Policy, 1919–1939. 2nd series: *1929–1938.* London: H. M. Stationery Office, 1946–1984. 21 vols.; 3rd series: *1938–1939.* London: H. M. Stationery Office, 1949–1961. 9 vols.

Documents on German Foreign Policy, 1918–1945. Series D: *1937–1945 [1941].* Washington, DC: U.S. Government Printing Office, 1949–1964. 13 vols.

Documents on Polish-Soviet Relations, 1939–1945. London: Heinemann for Sikorski Institute, 1961–1967. 2 vols.

"Documents relatifs à la politique étrangère de la Hongrie dans la période de la crise Tschécoslovaque (1938–1939)." Magda Ádám, ed. *Acta historica Academiae scientiarum Hungaricae* 10 (Nos. 3–4, 1964).

Dokumenty po istorii Miunkhenskogo sgovora, 1937–1939. Moscow: Politizdat, 1979.

Dokumenty i materialy po istorii sovetsko-chekhoslovatskikh otnoshenii. Moscow: Nauka, 1973–1988. 5 vols.

Dokumenty i materialy po istorii sovetsko-pol'skikh otnoshenii. Moscow: Nauka, 1963–1986. 12 vols.

Dokumenty vneshnei politiki SSSR. Moscow: Politizdat, 1959–1977. 21 vols.

Les événements survenus en France de 1933 à 1945: témoignages. Paris: Presses universitaires de France, 1951–1952. 9 vols.

God krizisa, 1938–1939: dokumenty i materialy. Moscow: Politizdat, 1990.

For the President, Personal and Secret: Correspondence Between Franklin D. Roosevelt and William C. Bullitt. Orville H. Bullitt, ed. Boston: Houghton Mifflin, 1972.

Monachium 1938: polskie dokumenty diplomatyczne. Zbigniew Landau and Jerzy Tomaszewski, eds. Warsaw: Panstwowe wydawnictwo naukowe, 1985.

Na pomoc Československému lidu: dokumenty o československo-sovětském přátelství z let 1938–1945. Čestmír Amort, ed. Prague: Academia, 1960.

New Documents on the History of Munich. Prague: Orbis, 1958.

"Polska korespondencja dyplomatyczna na temat wojskowej pomocy ZSRR dla Czechoslowacji w 1938 r. przez terytorjum Rumunii." Jerzy Tomaszewski, ed. *Z dziejów rozwoju pánstw socjalistycznych* 1 (1983): 159–84.

Soviet Peace Efforts on the Eve of World War II (September 1938–August 1939). Moscow: Novosti, 1973. 2 vols.

The Speeches of Adolf Hitler, April 1922–August 1939. New York: Oxford University Press, 1942. 2 vols.

Statistique internationale des chemins de fer: année 1938. Paris: Union internationale des chemins de fer, 1939.

B. MEMOIRS AND DIARIES

Aleksandrovskii, S. "Munich: Witness's Account." *International Affairs* 1988, No. 12: 119–32.

Beck, Józef. *Dernier rapport: politique polonaise, 1926–1939.* Neuchâtel: La Baconnière, 1951.

Beneš, Edvard. *Mnichovské dny: paměti.* Prague: Svoboda, 1968.

Bonnet, Georges. *Défense de la paix.* Paris: Editions du cheval ailé, 1946–1948. 2 vols.

Ciano, Galeazzo. *Diary, 1937–1938*. Andreas Mayor, trans. London: Methuen, 1952.

Cooper, Alfred Duff. *Old Men Forget*. New York: Dutton, 1954.

Coulondre, Robert. *De Staline à Hitler: souvenirs de deux ambassades, 1936–1939*. Paris: Hachette, 1950.

Fischer, Louis. *Men and Politics: An Autobiography*. New York: Duell, Sloan and Pearce, 1941.

François-Poncet, André. *The Fateful Years: Memoirs of a French Ambassador in Berlin, 1931–1938*. Jacques Leclercq, trans. New York: Harcourt, Brace, 1949.

Gamelin, Maurice Gustave. *Servir*. Paris: Plon, 1946–1947. 3 vols.

Gottwald, Klement. *O československé zahraniční politice*. Prague: SNPL, 1950.

Harvey, Oliver. *Diplomatic Diaries, 1937–1940*. John Harvey, ed. London: Collins, 1970.

Herwarth von Bittenfeld, Hans-Heinrich. *Against Two Evils: Memoirs of a Diplomat–Soldier During the Third Reich*. New York: Rawson, Wade, 1981.

Lipski, Józef. *Diplomat in Berlin, 1933–1939*. Wacław Jedrzejewicz, ed. New York: Columbia University Press, 1968.

Lukasiewicz, Juliusz. *Diplomat in Paris: Papers and Memoirs*. Wacław Jedrzejewicz, ed. New York: Columbia University Press, 1970.

Maiskii, Ivan. *Memoirs of a Soviet Ambassador: The War, 1939–1943*. Andrew Rothstein, trans. New York: Scribner, 1968.

———. *The Munich Drama*. Moscow: Novosti, 1972.

Martín Blazquez, José. *I Helped to Build an Army: Civil War Memoirs of a Spanish Staff Officer*. London: Secker and Warburg, 1939.

Morgenthau, Henry. *Diaries*. John Morton Blum, ed. Boston: Houghton Mifflin, 1959–1967. 3 vols.

Paul-Boncour, Joseph. *Entre deux guerres: souvenirs sur la troisième république*. Paris: Plon, 1945. 3 vols.

Petrescu-Comnen, Nicolae. *Luci i ombre sull'Europa, 1914–1950*. Milan: Bompiani, 1957.

———. *Preludi del grande dramma: ricordi i documenti di un diplomatico*. Rome: Edizioni Leonardo, 1947.

———. *I responsabili*. Verona: Mondadari, 1949.

Ripka, Hubert. *Munich Before and After: A Fully Documented Czechoslovak Account of the Crises of September 1938 and March 1939*. Ida Sindelková and Edgar P. Young, eds. New York: Fertig, 1969.

Szembek, Jan. *Diariusz i teki*. Tytus Komarnicki, ed. London: Orbis, 1964–1972. 4 vols.

———. *Journal, 1933–1939*. J. Rzewuska and T. Zaleski, trans. Paris: Plon, 1952.

Zakharov, Matvei Vasil'evich. *General'nyi shtab v predvoennye gody*. Moscow: Voenizdat, 1989.

II. LITERATURE

Ádám, Magda. *Richtung, Selbstvernichtung: die Kleine Entente, 1920–1938*. Brigitte Engel, trans. [Vienna?]: Österreichische Bundesverlag, [1988].

Adamthwaite, Anthony. *France and the Coming of the Second World War, 1936–1939*. London: Frank Cass, 1977.

Alexander, Martin S. *The Republic in Danger: General Maurice Gamelin and the Politics of French Defence, 1933–1940*. Cambridge, England: Cambridge University Press, 1992.

Andrew, Christopher and Jeremy Noakes, eds. *Intelligence and International Relations, 1900–1945.* Exeter, England: Exeter University Press, 1987.

Batowski, Henryk. *Rok 1938: dwie agresje hitlerowskie.* Poznan: Wydawnictwo poznańskie, 1985.

———. *Zdrada monachijska: sprawa Czechoslowacji i dyplomacja euroejska w roku 1938.* Poznan: Wydawnictwo poznańskie, 1973.

Beloff, Max. *The Foreign Policy of Soviet Russia, 1929–1941.* London: Oxford University Press, 1947–1949. 2 vols.

Boldt, Frank, ed. *München 1938: Das Ende des alten Europa.* Essen: Reiner Hobbing, 1990.

Boyce, Robert, ed. *French Foreign and Defence Policy, 1918–1940.* London: Routledge, 1998.

Broué, Pierre and Émile Témime. *The Revolution and the Civil War in Spain.* Tony White, trans. Cambridge, MA: MIT Press, 1972.

Bruegel, J. W. *Czechoslovakia Before Munich: The German Minority Problem and British Appeasement Policy.* Cambridge, England: Cambridge University Press, 1973.

———. *Tschechen und Deutsche, 1918–1938.* Munich: Nymphenburger Verlagshandlung, 1974.

Carley, Michael Jabara. *1939: The Alliance that Never Was and the Coming of World War II.* Chicago: Ivan Dee, 1999.

Celovsky, Boris. *Das Münchener Abkommen 1938.* Stuttgart: Deutsche Verlags-Anstalt, 1958.

Cienciala, Anna. *Poland and the Western Powers, 1938–1939: A Study in the Interdependence of Eastern and Western Europe.* Toronto: University of Toronto Press, 1968.

Coox, Alvin D. *The Anatomy of a Small War: The Soviet–Japanese Struggle for Changkufeng/Khasan, 1938.* Westport, CT: Greenwood, 1977.

Crane, Richard Francis. *A French Conscience in Prague: Louis Eugène Faucher and the Abandonment of Czechoslovakia.* Boulder, CO: East European Monographs, 1996.

Du Réau, Elizabeth. *Édouard Daladier, 1884–1970.* Paris: Fayard, 1993.

Duroselle, Jean-Baptiste. *La décadence, 1932–1939.* Paris: Imprimerie nationale, 1985.

Dutailly, Henry. *Les problèmes de l'armée de terre française: 1935–1939.* Paris: Imprimerie nationale, 1980.

Emmerson, James Thomas. *The Rhineland Crisis, 7 March 1936: A Study in Multilateral Diplomacy.* Ames, IA: Iowa State University Press, 1977.

Erickson, John. *The Soviet High Command: A Military–Political History, 1918–1941.* London: Macmillan, 1962.

Eubank, Keith. *Munich.* Norman, OK: University of Oklahoma Press, 1963.

Fadeev, G. M., E. Ia. Kraskovskii, and M. M. Uzdin. *Istoriia zheleznodorozhnogo transporta Rossii.* Moscow: Ivan Fedorov, 1994–1999. 2 vols.

Farnham, Barbara Rearden. *Roosevelt and the Munich Crisis: A Study of Political Decision-Making.* Princeton, NJ: Princeton University Press, 1997.

Fest, Joachim. *Plotting Hitler's Death: The German Resistance to Hitler, 1933–1945.* Bruce Little, trans. New York: Metropolitan Books, 1996.

Gilbert, Martin and Richard Gott. *The Appeasers.* Boston: Houghton Mifflin, 1963.

Gor'kov, Iurii Aleksandrovich. "Gotovil li Stalin uprezhdaiushchii udar protiv Gitlera v 1941 g.?" *Novaia i noveishaia istoriia,* 1993, No. 3: 29–45.

———. *Kreml'. Stavka. Genshtab.* Tver': TOO TK ANTEK, 1995.

Gorodetsky, Gabriel. *Grand Delusion: Stalin and the German Invasion of Russia.* New Haven, CT: Yale University Press, 1999.

————, ed. *Soviet Foreign Policy 1917–1991: A Retrospective*. Portland, OR: Frank Cass, 1994.

Gotovil li Stalin nastu pateľ nuin Voinu protiv Gitlera? Moscow: AIRO-XX, 1995.

Grechko, A. A. *et al. Istoriia vtoroi mirovoi voiny, 1939–1945*. Moscow: Voenizdat, 1973–1982. 12 vols.

Haslam, Jonathan. *The Soviet Union and the Search for Collective Security in Europe, 1933–1939*. London: Macmillan, 1984.

Hauner, Milan. "Zaři 1938: kapitulovat či bojovat?" *Svědectví* 49 (1975): 151–68.

————. "Zrada, sovětizace, nebo historický lapsus? Ke kritice dvou dokumentů k československo-sovětským vztahům z roku 1938," *Soudobé dějiny* 4 (1999): 545–71.

Haynes, Rebecca. *Romanian Policy Towards Germany, 1936–1940*. Basingstoke, England: Macmillan, 2000.

Herman, John. *The Paris Embassy of Sir Eric Phipps: Anglo-French Relations and the Foreign Office, 1937–1939*. Brighton, England: Sussex Academic Press, 1998.

Hillgruber, Andreas. *Hitler, König Carol und Marschall Antonescu: die deutsch–rumänischen Beziehungen 1938–1944*. 2nd ed. Wiesbaden: Franz Steiner, 1965.

Hitchins, Keith. *Rumania 1866–1947*. Oxford, England: Clarendon, 1994.

Hochman, Jiri. *The Soviet Union and the Failure of Collective Security, 1934–1938*. Ithaca, NY: Cornell University Press, 1984.

Hoffmann, Peter. *The History of the German Resistance, 1933–1945*. Richard Barry, trans. Cambridge, MA: MIT Press, 1977.

Hoptner, J. B. *Yugoslavia in Crisis, 1934–1941*. New York: Columbia University Press, 1962.

Howson, Gerald. *Arms for Spain: The Untold Story of the Spanish Civil War*. London: Murray, 1998.

Jackson, Peter. *France and the Nazi Menace: Intelligence and Policy-Making, 1933–1939*. New York: Oxford University Press, 2000.

————. "French Military Intelligence and Czechoslovakia, 1938." *Diplomacy and Statecraft* 5 (1994): 81–106.

John, Miloslav. *Československé letectvo v roce 1938*. Beroun: Barako and Fox, 1996.

Jordan, Nicole. *The Popular Front and Central Europe: The Dilemma of French Impotence, 1918–1940*. New York: Cambridge University Press, 1992.

Jukes, G. "The Red Army and the Munich Crisis." *Journal of Contemporary History* 26 (1991): 195–214.

Kaufmann, J. E. and H. W. Kaufmann. *The Maginot Line: None Shall Pass*. Westport, CT: Praeger, 1997.

Kiesling, Eugenia. *Arming Against Hitler: France and the Limits of Military Planning*. Lawrence, KS: University of Kansas Press, 1996.

Kural, Václav. *Československo roku 1938*. Prague: Ústav mezinárodních vztahů, 1993.

Lacaze, Yvon. *La France et Munich: étude d'un processus décisionnel en matière de relations internationales*. Berne: Peter Lang, 1992.

Latynski, Maya, ed. *Reappraising the Munich Pact: Continental Perspectives*. Washington, DC: Wilson Center and Johns Hopkins University Press, 1992.

Le Goyet, Pierre. *France-Pologne, 1919–1939: de l'amitié romantique à la méfiance réciproque*. Paris: France-Empire, 1991.

————. *Munich, "un traquenard"?* Paris: France-Empire, 1988.

————. *Le mystère Gamelin*. Paris: Presses de la Cité, 1976.

Lukes, Igor. *Czechoslovakia Between Stalin and Hitler: The Diplomacy of Edvard Beneš in the 1930s.* New York: Oxford University Press, 1996.

————. "Did Stalin Desire War in 1938? A New Look at Soviet Behavior during the May and September Crises." *Diplomacy and Statecraft* 2 (1991): 3–53.

————. "Stalin and Beneš at the End of September 1938: New Evidence from the Prague Archives." *Slavic Review* 52 (1993): 28–48.

———— and Eric Goldstein, eds. *The Munich Crisis 1938: Prelude to World War II.* London/Portland, OR: Frank Cass, 1999.

Lungu, Dov B. *Romania and the Great Powers, 1933–1940.* Durham, NC: Duke University Press, 1989.

Luža, Radomír. *The Transfer of the Sudeten Germans: A Study of Czech–German Relations, 1933–1939.* New York: New York University Press, 1964.

Macartney, C. A. and A. W. Palmer. *Independent Eastern Europe: A History.* London: Macmillan, 1962.

Mamatey, Victor S. and Radomír Luža, eds. *A History of the Czechoslovak Republic, 1918–1948.* Princeton, NJ: Princeton University Press, 1973.

Martel, Gordon, ed. *The Origins of the Second World War Reconsidered.* 2nd ed. New York: Routledge, 1999.

May, Ernest R., ed. *Knowing One's Enemies: Intelligence Assessment Before the Two World Wars.* Princeton, NJ: Princeton University Press, 1984.

McDonough, Frank. *Neville Chamberlain, Appeasement and the British Road to War.* Manchester, England: Manchester University Press, 1998.

McKenzie, Kermit. *Comintern and World Revolution, 1928–1943: The Shaping of Doctrine.* New York: Columbia University Press, 1963.

Menning, Bruce. "Soviet Railroads and War Planning, 1927–1939." Paper presented at the American Association for Advancement of Slavic Studies, Boston, 1997.

Middlemas, Keith. *Diplomacy of Illusion: The British Government and Germany, 1937–1939.* Aldershot: Gregg Revivals, 1991.

Moisuc, Viorica. *Diplomația României și problema apărarii suveranității și independenței naționale in perioada martie 1938–mai 1940.* Bucharest: Editură Academiei, 1971.

————, ed. *Probleme de politică externă a României.* Bucharest: Editură militară, 1971.

Munich 1938: mythes et réalités. Paris: Institut national d'études slaves, 1979.

Murray, Williamson. *The Change in the European Balance of Power, 1938–1939: The Path to Ruin.* Princeton, NJ: Princeton University Press, 1984.

Pagel, Jürgen. *Polen und die Sowjetunion 1938–1939: die polnisch–sowjetischen Beziehungen in den Krisen der europäischen Politik am Vorabend des Zweiten Weltkrieges.* Stuttgart: Franz Steiner Verlag, 1992.

Parker, R. A. C. *Chamberlain and Appeasement: British Policy and the Coming of the Second World War.* New York: St. Martin's, 1993.

Pfaff, Ivan. *Sovětská zrada 1938.* Prague: BEA, 1993.

————. *Die Sowjetunion und die Verteidigung der Tschechoslowakei, 1934–1938: Versuch der Revision einer Legende.* Cologne: Böhlau, 1996.

Phillips, Hugh. *Between the Revolution and the West: A Political Biography of Maxim M. Litvinov.* Boulder, CO: Westview, 1992.

Prasolov, S. I., ed. *Sovetsko–chekhoslovatskie otnosheniia mezhdu dvumia voinami 1918–1939.* Moscow: Nauka, 1968.

Procházka, Zdeněk ed., *Vojenské dějiny Československa, 1918–1939*. Prague: Naše vojsko, 1985–1989. 5 vols.

Raack, Richard C. *Stalin's Drive to the West, 1938–1945: The Origins of the Cold War*. Stanford, CA: Stanford University Press, 1995.

Radosh, Ronald, Mary Habeck, and Grigory Sevostianov. *Spain Betrayed: The Soviet Union in the Spanish Civil War*. New Haven, CT: Yale University Press, 2001.

Rees, E. A. *Stalinism and Soviet Rail Transport, 1928–41*. New York: St. Martin's, 1995.

Reichert, Günter. *Das Scheitern der Kleinen Entente: Internationale Beziehungen in Donauraum von 1933 bis 1938*. Munich: Fides, 1971.

Roberts, Cynthia. "Planning for War: The Red Army and the Catastrophe of 1941." *Europe–Asia Studies* 47 (1995): 1293–1326.

Roberts, Geoffrey. *The Soviet Union and the Origins of the Second World War: Russo–German Relations and the Road to War, 1933–1941*. New York: St. Martin's, 1995.

———. *The Unholy Alliance: Stalin's Pact with Hitler*. Bloomington, IN: Indiana University Press, 1989.

Rothschild, Joseph. *East Central Europe Between the Two World Wars*. Seattle, WA: University of Washington Press, 1974.

Rothstein, Robert L. *Alliances and Small Powers*. New York: Columbia University Press, 1968.

Rzheshevskii, Oleg. *Europe 1939: Was War Inevitable?* Moscow: Progress Publishers, 1989.

Sakmyster, Thomas L. *Hungary, the Great Powers, and the Danubian Crisis, 1936–1939*. Athens, GA: University of Georgia Press, 1980.

Samuelson, Lennart. *Plans for Stalin's War Machine: Tukhachevskii and Military–Economic Planning, 1925–1941*. Basingstoke, England: Macmillan, 2000.

Savu, Alexandru Gh. *Dictatură regală (1938–1940)*. Bucharest: Editură politică, 1970.

Schuker, Stephen A. "France and the Remilitarization of the Rhineland, 1936." *French Historical Studies* 14 (1986): 299–338.

Seton-Watson, Hugh. *Eastern Europe Between the Wars, 1918–1941*. 3rd ed. New York: Harper, 1962.

Sheviakov, A. A. *Sovetsko–rumynskie otnosheniia i problema evropeiskoi bezopastnosti 1932–1939*. Moscow: Nauka, 1977.

Speer, Albert. *Inside the Third Reich*. Richard and Clara Wilson, trans. New York: Avon, 1971.

Steiner, Zara. "The Soviet Commissariat of Foreign Affairs and the Czechoslovakian Crisis in 1938: New Materials from the Soviet Archives." *The Historical Journal* 42 (1999): 751–79.

Stoecker, Sally. *Forging Stalin's Army: Tukhachevsky and the Politics of Military Innovation*. Boulder, CO: Westview, 1998.

Stone, David R. *Hammer and Rifle: The Militarization of the Soviet Union, 1926–1933*. Lawrence, KS: University of Kansas Press, 2000.

Stone, Norman and Eduard Stroubal, eds. *Czechoslovakia: Crossroads and Crises, 1918–1988*. Basingstoke, England: Macmillan, 1989.

Streinu, Vladimir [Nicolae Iordache]. *La Petite Entente et l'Europe*. Geneva: Institut universitaire de hautes études internationales, 1977.

Stronge, H. C. T. "The Czechoslovak Army and the Munich Crisis: A Personal Memorandum." *War and Society: A Yearbook of Military History* 1 (1975): 162–77.

Taborsky, Edward. *President Edvard Beneš Between East and West, 1938–1948*. Stanford, CA: Stanford University Press, 1981.

Talpeş, Ioan. "Date noi privind poziţia Romaniei in contextul contradicţulor internationale din vara anului 1938." *Revista de istorie* 28 (1975): 1649–70.

―――. "Măsuri şi acţiuni diplomatici şi militare in vederea întăririi capacitatii de apărare a ţării în faţa creşterii pericolelor hitlerist şi revisionist (1934–1937)." *File din istoria militară a poporului român* 8 (1980): 107–42.

―――. *Diplomaţie şi apărare: coordonate ale politicii externe româneşti, 1933–1939*. Bucharest: Editură ştiinţifică şi enciclopedică, 1988.

Taylor, Telford. *Munich: The Price of Peace*. New York: Vintage, 1980.

Teske, Hermann. *General Ernst Köstring: der militärische Mittler zwischen dem deutschen Reich und der Sowjetunion 1921–1941*. Frankfurt am Main: Mittler, 1965.

Walters, Francis P. *A History of the League of Nations*. London: Oxford University Press, 1952. 2 vols.

Wandycz, Piotr S. *The Twilight of French Eastern Alliances, 1926–1936*. Princeton, NJ: Princeton University Press, 1988.

Watt, Donald Cameron. *How War Came: The Immediate Origins of the Second World War*. New York: Pantheon, 1989.

Watts, Larry L. "Romania as a Military Ally (Part 1): Czechoslovakia in 1938." *Romanian Civilization* 7 (1998): 21–54.

Weber, Eugen. *The Hollow Years: France in the 1930s*. New York: Norton, 1994.

Weinberg, Gerhard L. *The Foreign Policy of Hitler's Germany: Starting World War II, 1937–1939*. Chicago: University of Chicago Press, 1980.

Werth, Alexander. *The Twilight of France, 1933–1940*. New York: Howard Fertig, 1966.

Westwood, J. N. *A History of Russian Railways*. London: Allen and Unwin, 1964.

Wheeler-Bennett, John. *Munich: Prologue to Tragedy*. New York: Viking, 1964.

Young, Robert J. *In Command of France: French Foreign Policy and Military Planning, 1933–1940*. Cambridge, MA: Harvard University Press, 1978.

Żarnowski, Janusz, ed. *Przyjaźnie i antagonizmy: stosunki polski z państwami sąsiednimi w latach 1918–1939*. Warsaw: Polish Academy of Sciences, 1977.

Zeman, Z. A. B. and Antonín Klimek. *The Life of Eduard Beneš, 1884–1948: Czechoslovakia in Peace and War*. Oxford, England: Clarendon, 1997.

Zgórniak, Marian. *Europa w przededniu wojny: sytuacja militarna w latach 1938–1939*. Krakow: Księgarnia akademicka, 1993.

―――. *Wojskowe aspekty krysysu czechosłowackiego 1938 roku*. Krakow: Krakow University Press, 1966.

Zorach, Jonathan. "Czechoslovakia's Fortifications: Their Development and Role in the 1938 Munich Crisis," *Militärgeschichtliche Mitteilungen* 2 (1976): 82.

Index